Performing Gods in Classical Antiquity and the Age of Shakespeare

Bloomsbury Studies in Classical Reception

Bloomsbury Studies in Classical Reception presents scholarly monographs offering new and innovative research and debate to students and scholars in the reception of Classical Studies. Each volume will explore the appropriation, reconceptualization and recontextualization of various aspects of the Graeco-Roman world and its culture, looking at the impact of the ancient world on modernity. Research will also cover reception within antiquity, the theory and practice of translation, and reception theory.

Also available in the Series:

Alexander the Great in the Early Christian Tradition: Classical Reception and Patristic Literature, Christian Thrue Djurslev

Ancient Magic and the Supernatural in the Modern Visual and Performing Arts, edited by Filippo Carlà and Irene Berti

Ancient Greek Myth in World Fiction since 1989, edited by Justine McConnell and Edith Hall

Antipodean Antiquities, edited by Marguerite Johnson

Classics in Extremis, edited by Edmund Richardson

Faulkner's Reception of Apuleius' The Golden Ass in The Reivers, by Vernon L. Provencal

Frankenstein and its Classics, edited by Jesse Weiner, Benjamin Eldon Stevens and Brett M. Rogers

Greek and Roman Classics in the British Struggle for Social Reform, edited by Henry Stead and Edith Hall

Greeks and Romans on the Latin American Stage, edited by Rosa Andújar and Konstantinos P. Nikoloutsos

Homer's Iliad and the Trojan War: Dialogues on Tradition, Jan Haywood and Naoíse Mac Sweeney

Imagining Xerxes, Emma Bridges

Julius Caesar's Self-Created Image and Its Dramatic Afterlife, Miryana Dimitrova

Kinaesthesia and Classical Antiquity 1750–1820: Moved by Stone, Helen Slaney

Once and Future Antiquities in Science Fiction and Fantasy, edited by Brett M. Rogers and Benjamin Eldon Stevens

Ovid's Myth of Pygmalion on Screen, Paula James

Reading Poetry, Writing Genre, edited by Silvio Bär and Emily Hauser

Sex, Symbolists and the Greek Body, Richard Warren

The Classics in Modernist Translation, edited by Miranda Hickman and Lynn Kozak
The Classics in South America: Five Case Studies, by Germán Campos Muñoz
The Codex Fori Mussolini, Han Lamers and Bettina Reitz-Joosse
The Gentle, Jealous God, Simon Perris
The Thucydidean Turn: (Re)Interpreting Thucydides' Political Thought Before, During and After the Great War, Benjamin Earley
Translations of Greek Tragedy in the Work of Ezra Pound, Peter Liebregts
Victorian Classical Burlesques, Laura Monrós-Gaspar
Victorian Epic Burlesques, Rachel Bryant Davies
Virgil's Map: Geography, Empire, and the Georgics, Charlie Kerrigan

Performing Gods in Classical Antiquity and the Age of Shakespeare

Dustin W. Dixon and John S. Garrison

BLOOMSBURY ACADEMIC
LONDON • NEW YORK • OXFORD • NEW DELHI • SYDNEY

BLOOMSBURY ACADEMIC
Bloomsbury Publishing Plc
50 Bedford Square, London, WC1B 3DP, UK
1385 Broadway, New York, NY 10018, USA
29 Earlsfort Terrace, Dublin 2, Ireland

BLOOMSBURY, BLOOMSBURY ACADEMIC and the Diana logo are trademarks
of Bloomsbury Publishing Plc

First published in Great Britain 2021
This paperback edition published 2023

Copyright © Dustin W. Dixon and John S. Garrison 2021

Dustin W. Dixon and John S. Garrison have asserted their right under the Copyright, Designs and Patents Act, 1988, to be identified as Authors of this work.

For legal purposes the Acknowledgements on p. ix constitute an extension of this copyright page.

Cover design: Terry Woodley
Cover image © Masanobu Katsumura as Jupiter and Hiroshi Abe as Posthumus with artists of the company in the Ninagawa Company's production of William Shakespeare's Cymbeline directed by Yukio Ninagawa at the Barbican in London. Photo by robbie jack/Corbis via Getty Images.

All rights reserved. No part of this publication may be reproduced or transmitted in any form or by any means, electronic or mechanical, including photocopying, recording, or any information storage or retrieval system, without prior permission in writing from the publishers.

Bloomsbury Publishing Plc does not have any control over, or responsibility for, any third-party websites referred to or in this book. All internet addresses given in this book were correct at the time of going to press. The author and publisher regret any inconvenience caused if addresses have changed or sites have ceased to exist, but can accept no responsibility for any such changes.

A catalogue record for this book is available from the British Library.

Library of Congress Cataloging-in-Publication Data

Names: Dixon, Dustin W., author. | Garrison, John S., 1970-author.
Title: Performing gods in classical antiquity and the age of Shakespeare / Dustin W. Dixon, John S. Garrison.
Description: London: New York: Bloomsbury Academic, 2021. | Series: Bloomsbury studies in classical reception | Includes bibliographical references and index.
Identifiers: LCCN 2021004143 (print) | LCCN 2021004144 (ebook) | ISBN 9781350098145 (hardback) | ISBN 9781350098152 (ePDF) | ISBN 9781350098169 (eBook)
Subjects: LCSH: Theater–Greece–History–To 500. | Theater–Rome–History–To 500. | Gods in literature. | Classical drama–History and criticism. | Theater–Great Britain–History–16th century. | Theater–Great Britain–History–17th century. | English drama–Early modern and Elizabethan, 1500-1600–History and criticism. | English drama–17th century–History and criticism. | Renaissance–England. | Mythology, Classical, in literature.
Classification: LCC PA3203 .D59 2021 (print) | LCC PA3203 (ebook) | DDC 792.0938–dc23
LC record available at https://lccn.loc.gov/2021004143
LC ebook record available at https://lccn.loc.gov/2021004144

ISBN: HB: 978-1-3500-9814-5
PB: 978-1-3502-3943-2
ePDF: 978-1-3500-9815-2
eBook: 978-1-3500-9816-9

Series: Bloomsbury Studies in Classical Reception

Typeset by RefineCatch Limited, Bungay, Suffolk

To find out more about our authors and books visit
www.bloomsbury.com and sign up for our newsletters

Contents

List of Illustrations — viii
Acknowledgments — ix
A Note on the Text — x

Introduction: The Gods Take Stage — 1

1 Approaching Divinity — 19

2 Under the Actor's Spell: Audiences in Euripides' *Helen* and Marlowe's *Doctor Faustus* — 47

3 An Actor Ascends: Status and Identity in Plautus' *Amphitruo* and the Court Masque — 67

4 Authoring Gods in Aeschylus' *Oresteia* and Shakespeare's *Hamlet* — 93

5 To Die Is Human, To Act Is Divine — 117

Afterword: Entertaining Gods in Zimmerman's *Metamorphoses* — 139

Notes — 149
Bibliography — 177
Index — 195

Illustrations

1. *As You Like It*. Reproduced by permission of The Metropolitan Museum of Art, New York — 41
2. Attic skyphos, *c.* 490 BCE. Boston. 13.186. Museum of Fine Arts — 51
3. Red-figure oenochoe, *c.* 430–420 BCE. Vatican. 16535. Museo Gregoriano Etrusco — 51
4. The Phanagoria Chous, *c.* 400 BCE. St. Petersburg. Fa. 1869–47. The State Hermitage Museum. Photograph © The State Hermitage Museum. Photo by Natalia Antonova, Inna Regentova — 88
5. "Hamlet, Horatio, Marcellus, and the Ghost," Robert Thew (Engraver), after Henry Fuseli (1796). Reproduced by permission of The Metropolitan Museum of Art, New York — 104
6. *Cleopatra*. Dir. Mankiewicz, Twentieth Century-Fox Film Corporation (1963) — 129
7. "Nymph of Immortality, Attended by the Loves, Crowning Shakespeare," Francesco Bartolozzi (1784). Reproduced by permission of The Metropolitan Museum of Art, New York — 135
8. *Jupiter and Mercury in the House of Baucis and Philemon*, Hyacinthe Collin de Vermont (eighteenth century). Reproduced by permission of The Metropolitan Museum of Art, New York — 141

Acknowledgments

We are grateful to many individuals who made this book possible. Conversation with members of our seminar on "Shakespeare's Greek" at the Shakespeare Association of America Conference added a new dimension to our thinking about classical reception in early modern England. We wish to thank those scholars: Tom Bishop, Larry Bonds, John Hugh Cameron, David Currell, Lynn Enterline, Andrew Fleck, Erich Freiberger, Jason Gleckman, Jonathan Goossen, Michael Anthony Ingham, Robert Miola, Su Fang Ng, Curtis Perry, and Jane Raisch. Over the years, there have been key interlocutors both about the book's theme and about classical receptions more broadly. These include Leah Allen, Emily Austin, Chris Bates, Catherine Chou, Joe Cummins, Monessa Cummins, Ruben Espinosa, Margaret Ferguson, Jeff Fisher, Laura Garofalo, Stephen Guy-Bray, Jeff Henderson, Jess Lamont, Jerry Lalonde, Angelo Mercado, Marissa Nicosia, Colin Pang, Kyle Pivetti, Vanessa Rapatz, John Rundin, Saiham Sharif, Niall Slater, Alex Sorosa, Goran Stanivukovic, Rex Stem, and David Angus Traill. Jason Inskeep, Ryan Bailey, Chris Cinereski, and Jon Muller kept our spirits up. Katherine Kopp lent content knowledge and close attention to detail in the final copy-editing and formatting. Diana Chege and Cole Polglaze assisted with images.

Several research centers and organizations inspired and supported this project. These include the American School of Classical Studies at Athens, Folger Shakespeare Library, Harry Ransom Center at U.T. Austin, Department of English at Grinnell College, and Department of Classics at Grinnell College.

At Bloomsbury Academic, key people challenged us to make this book as excellent as possible and supported that effort. These individuals include our editors, Alice Wright and Georgina Leighton, as well as Lily MacMahon, our expert guide through the production process. We also wish to thank the anonymous readers at Bloomsbury, who helped bring deeper nuance to the study.

Chapter 2 appears in a slightly different form as "The Spectacle of Helen in Euripides' *Helen* and Marlowe's *Doctor Faustus*" in the *Classical Receptions Journal*.

A Note on the Text

Unless stated otherwise, all translations of the Greek and Latin texts are original. The texts follow the most recent *Oxford Classical Text*, with the following exceptions: we follow Martin West's Teubner editions of Homer; Diels-Kranz (D-K) for the text of Gorgias and Xenophanes; the tragic fragments follow *Tragicorum Graecorum Fragmenta* (*TrGF*); the comic fragments follow *Poetae Comici Graeci* (*PCG* or K-A).

All quotations from Shakespeare in this book, unless otherwise noted, are drawn from William Shakespeare, *The Complete Works: Modern Critical Edition*, ed. G. Taylor, J. Jowett, T. Bourus, and G. Egan (New York: Oxford University Press, 2016).

We have modernized the spelling and punctuation for all of the early modern texts. The use of i, j, u, v, and w has been regularized to conform to modern usage, and we have expanded contractions where appropriate to increase readability.

All references to English word origins and definitions in this book draw from the *Oxford English Dictionary Online*, www.oed.com.

Introduction: The Gods Take Stage

The gods have much to tell us about performance. Breathing life into these deities onstage, dramatists of classical antiquity and early modern England did not hide from their audiences' sight the divine machinery driving the lives of the characters who occupied their stages, but instead Aeschylus, Sophocles, Euripides, Aristophanes, Plautus, Shakespeare, and Marlowe—the poets who attract most of our attention in this book—attempted to embody the gods in human actors. What we find through these poets' varied attempts to stage the gods of the Greek and Roman pantheon is a persistent awe. Awe at the manifestation of divinity. Awe at their powers. Awe at their limitations, so often those shared with mortals. When depicting the gods onstage, the dramatists were limited not by their imagination but by the bodies of their actors and by the limited special effects available to them. Nevertheless, whatever a god may look like, the ancient and early modern playwrights sought to convey the sublime nature of divinity.

Inspect, for a moment, this book's cover, an image from the production of Shakespeare's *Cymbeline* directed by Yukio Ninagawa at the Barbican Theatre during London's 2012 World Shakespeare Festival.[1] The play was performed in Japanese with English subtitles. In any language or even in the absence of language, who could not find startling this appearance of the god Jupiter, played by Masanobu Katsumura, flying above a sleeping Posthumus, played by Hiroshi Abe. The scene functions in a variety of dimensions to capture the traditional hierarchies of gods and mortals.[2] Jupiter, perched above the human characters, is bathed in light. Posthumus, who will receive a life-changing prophecy from the god, sleeps unaware of this divine presence and unaware of the supernatural presence, too, of the ghosts of his ancestors who watch over him. The scene's stunning visuals thus symbolize, for those spectators with and without the fluency of Japanese, both the haunting presence of the past as well as, our focus here, the arresting power of the divine.

As powerful as the staging may be, further scrutiny of this image reveals how Ninagawa's production showcases its own artificiality. The giant eagle upon which Jupiter rides is an inanimate cutout in profile, driven around stage by a visible crane. The bright light, though shining from the space above the stage which the early moderns termed "heaven," seems more harshly electric than ethereal. As for the supreme divinity of the Roman pantheon himself, he, alone of the characters onstage, wears a stylized, obviously artificial mask reminiscent of those worn in the ancient theater. He appears amidst thunder to deliver a softly chanted speech in "an archaic register that suggests a religious text."[3] Some reviewers found that the unexpected mode of delivery made it the most striking speech of the play. Others found it "disappointing."[4]

Yet the very impossibility of rendering Jupiter in all his divine splendor in a truly convincing way lies at the intersection of divine power and the power of the theater. The actor Masanobu Katsumura is not Jupiter. His presence onstage is not a divine epiphany. But the audience, as much as the actors themselves, must invest in the idea that Katsumura is Jupiter lest the illusion of the theatrical spectacle fail. Here, we can recall Jean-Paul Sartre's statement that, "It is not that the character is *realized* in the actor, but that the actor is *irrealized* in the character."[5] In the case of Ninagawa's *Cymbeline*, the existence of an actor named Katsumara is made unreal by the character of Jupiter, by his stylized mask, by his artificial eagle, by his archaic diction. The actor's claim to temporary godhood has much to say about the art that makes the claim plausible.

Indeed, it is the very impossibility of such transformations that dramatists used as starting points for rumination not only on these transformations but on the nature of the theater, in particular theatrical illusion and performance within their own plays. As Ismene Lada-Richards has noted of Greek tragedy, "Although they are not theoretical documents, the tragic texts themselves explore acting and actors in manifold and subtle ways, rivaling in their complexity that high-water mark of artistic self-consciousness, the drama of the English Renaissance."[6] While nearly any character in a theatrical production requires the impossible transformation of an actor into another person and would, therefore, allow for the kind of self-conscious exploration that Lada-Richards describes, the gods are especially interesting characters to explore because actors playing gods must transcend both identity and mortal ontology. Actors on classical and early modern stages become not just Mycenaean heroes and Danish princes but the Greek goddess of the hunt and the Roman god of war.

What interests us in the chapters that follow are those passages of texts and those moments of staging in which the gods draw our attention to theatrical artifice. It is these metatheatrical, meaning-laden moments that inspire playgoers to feel as if they are in the presence of "great reckonings in little rooms." This phrase, which Bert O. States draws from Shakespeare's Touchstone in order to title his monumental study of theatrical phenomenology, speaks well to those engagements with the artifice of the theater that we trace in our own study. Our book's thread of continuity, the metatheatricality of divine figures across theatrical traditions, may be surprising given the vastly different religious and cultic contexts in which these divine metaphors are deployed. Yet the gods of antiquity—their protean natures, and the public, spirited debates about their divinity—allowed the dramatists of Greece and Rome to depict the gods as evocative metaphors for theatrical power, while the same license to embody the Christian God, the God of the state, onstage was not widespread among the dramatists' early English theaters.

For the Greeks and Romans, as Hegel remarks, "the gods are formed by human imagination, and they originate in a finite fashion, being produced by the poet, by the muse."[7] And Denis Feeney's wonderful survey of ancient theological debates reveals how poets from Homer onward played a crucial part in public discourse that shaped and challenged contemporary audiences' understanding about the nature of the divine.[8] Indeed, even before the invention of theater, the seeds of the gods' theatricality appear already in the epics of Homer, where deities often disguise themselves in mortal flesh during their encounters with human beings. In the climactic battle between Achilles and Hector in the *Iliad*, the goddess Athena likens her appearance and voice to those of the Trojan prince Deiphobus (Δηιφόβῳ εἰκυῖα δέμας καὶ ἀτειρέα φωνήν, 22.227) in order to give vain courage to Hector before his confrontation with Achilles. After encouraging him, Athena disappears from the battle, and Hector laments the deception of the goddess: "Athena deceived me" (ἐμὲ δ' ἐξαπάτησεν Ἀθήνη, 22.299). In the *Odyssey*, a common device of Homeric storytelling is the use of divine mist to protect or hide the identity of someone or something from another mortal. Such a moment occurs, for example, when Odysseus enters the city of the Phaeacians, and Athena likens her appearance to a young maiden (παρθενικῇ εἰκυῖα νεήνιδι, 7.20) while she guides him to the palace. The goddess also veils him in a thick mist (πολλὴν ἠέρα, 7.15), later called a divine fog (ἀχλὺν / θεσπεσίην, 7.41–42), so that the locals do not ask his identity before he reaches his destination.

As we will see in Chapter 1, Homer's anthropomorphizing the gods, both in form and in morality, was controversial, particularly among philosophers. However, the gods' inscrutability and their propensity for deception proved useful starting points for dramatists' exploration of the mysterious spectacle of their own theatrical art. Like Athena, the space of the theater produces a divine fog of distortion. In order for the theatrical spectacle to be effective, audiences of classical Athens must see not (only) the stage of the theater of Dionysus but (also) a palace of bronze-age Thebes or a temple at which heroes of the distance past worshipped Apollo in Delphi. But, in the theater of Dionysus, rather than a god taking on mortal flesh to trick Hector or Odysseus, mortal actors attempt to transform their bodies and their voices into convincing imitations of the powerful gods of the pantheon.

Reception and Theatricality

So, too, did Shakespeare and his contemporaries see the potential of using the ancient gods for metatheatrical purposes, just one thread of continuity from antiquity forward or just one mode of engagement with classical literature in the early modern period.

Our study builds upon and complicates work by scholars who have investigated the influence of classical myth on Renaissance humanism.[9] The classical gods' appearance onstage may not be surprising in a period that embraced classical ideals and saw its own culture as a hybrid of ancient knowledge and Christian ideologies. The introduction of classical elements into early modern culture brought with it new ways of knowing and relating. Gods onstage embody that wonderful phrase that Edgar Wind uses to describe the presence of the Graces in Renaissance art and literature: "perilous alchemy."[10] In a broad sense, this phrase speaks to the dangerous richness of the cultural elements received from classical antiquity. For Renaissance audiences and readers, "Greece was an enigma [as] the original and idealized pinnacle of Western philosophy, tragedy, democracy, heroic human endeavour and, at the same time, an example of decadence: a fallen state, currently under Ottoman control, and therefore an exotic, dangerous 'other' in the most disturbing sense of the word."[11] A variety of historians and literary scholars have demonstrated how pagan deities provided not only a host of shared symbols for early modern writers but also a trope of *metamorphosis* that helped these writers conceptualize their historical period's relationship to the classical past. Leonard Barkan, for instance, characterizes the early modern period as one where classical elements are changed to fit the later contexts in which they are absorbed while culture is simultaneously shaped by the classical elements it inherits; thus "*metamorphosis* becomes a ruling conceit of *Renaissance.*"[12] While our book brings new perspectives, both in its specific focus and its integration of concerns from performance studies and studies in genre, we build upon previous studies that have traced the myriad influences of classical mythology on early modern culture.

Yet for all of the classical world's strangeness to the early modern world, certainly one offered a compelling mirror for the other. Don Cameron Allen notes the "patent similarities between the pagan and Christian systems."[13]

We will see classical gods (in both antiquity and the early modern world) engaging in divine intervention, ranging from providing redemption, performing miracles, and delivering needed retribution. For the purposes of our study, we argue that interpolating classical gods into stage action in the early modern theater at once alerts the audience to the profound influence of classical culture on their own and signals the performance itself as artifice. Eric Auerbach has remarked, "The way in which we view human life and society is the same whether we are concerned with things of the past or things of the present."[14] This claim invites us to see how these dramas use the past to speak of present concerns, whether the Greek and Roman playwrights are staging myths of the heroic past or their early modern counterparts are bringing ancient gods into the present. By adding a new dimension to the study of both how Roman culture inherited that of the Greeks and how the Renaissance inherited classical figures, our book complements the study of how cultures relate to their pasts and draw upon the pasts of others.[15] But to those readers familiar with Ben Jonson's quip that William Shakespeare had "small Latin and less Greek," it may come as a surprise to hear that the presentation of the gods in Greek literature, rather than Greek literature mediated through Latin literature, had any influence on the period's most well-known English playwright.[16] In the elegy introducing the First Folio of Shakespeare's *Comedies, Histories and Tragedies* in 1623, Jonson says:

> For, if I thought my judgement were of years
>   I should commit thee surely with thy peers,
> And tell, how far thou didst our Lyly outshine,
>   Or sporting Kyd, or Marlowe's mighty line.
> And, though thou hadst small Latin, and less Greek,
>   From thence to honour thee, I would not seek
> For names; but call forth thund'ring Aeschylus,
>   Euripides, and Sophocles to us,
> Paccuvius, Accius, him of Cordova dead
>   To life again, to hear thy buskin tread,
> And shake a Stage: Or, when thy socks were on,
>   Leave thee alone, for the comparison
> Of all that insolent Greece, or haughty Rome
>   Sent forth, or since did from their ashes come.
>
>   27–40

One interpretation of "small Latin and less Greek" holds that Shakespeare may have been able to read Latin, as we can infer from the influence of Roman comedy and of Senecan tragedy as well as from the number of Shakespearean coinages derived from the language of Rome, but the Greek language itself has few perceptible vestiges in Shakespeare's poetic feet.[17] What is Ἑκάβη to him? Michael Silk, to name just one scholar, denied traditional modes of reception of Greek drama by Shakespeare, despite their "real affinity."[18]

Colin Burrow's reinterpretation of the quip's context, however, has invigorated recent approaches to the influence of the classical canon on Shakespeare. Burrow proposes that we read the clause "though thou hadst small Latin and less Greek" counterfactually: as if, "even supposing thou hadst small Latin and less Greek."[19] Jonson's judgment of Shakespeare, as Burrow notes, was double-edged as he subtly underscores how far his own classical training outstripped that of Shakespeare. Jonson emerged from a university education with advanced humanist training. Nonetheless, both Jonson's and Shakespeare's plays are steeped in references to ancient history and culture, and Shakespeare, even with only a grammar school education, would have been immersed in classical literature and mythology.[20] Micha Lazarus has helped to unsettle the traditional consensus further, having shown that training in ancient Greek was more widespread in early modern English schools than scholars had known.[21] Regardless of Shakespeare's own facility for reading Greek, his contemporaries, some of whom are also considered in this study, were adept readers of the language of Aeschylus, Sophocles, Euripides, and Aristophanes, and several of their Athenian dramas would have been available to Shakespeare, either in the original Greek or in a Latin translation.

In the spirit of considering questions of reception from new, not strictly philological, perspectives, we draw attention to the few lines that follow "small Latin and less Greek."[22] After those five words that have attracted so much scholarly attention, Jonson underscores how Shakespearean performance rivals even that of the ancients, both Greek (Aeschylus, Euripides, Sophocles) and Roman (Paccuvius and Accius, whose works survive only in fragments, as well as Seneca the Younger). These major tragic dramatists of antiquity are "dead" and "ash," but Jonson imagines summoning them to life to spectate a drama of Shakespeare, whose own performances are not only watched by the ancient canonical dramatists but are also described in ancient terms. The "buskin" denotes the boot that Greek tragic actors wore in performance. Thus, Jonson imagines that the playwright both rivals and revivifies the ancient stages, a claim that also would apply to Shakespeare's contemporary rivals of the stage.

Though Ovid's pervasive influence on Renaissance literature has occupied many recent studies, invited by Jonson, we turn once again to drama.[23] While we will at times suggest the direct influence of a classical author on an early modern text, we are more interested in tracing broader patterns of thought that carried forward from and across antiquity and into the Renaissance.

In addition to the thoroughly explored reception of classical mythology in the early modern period, one striking thread of continuity across these majors theatrical traditions is the dramatists' intense interest in unmasking the artifice of their art within their own dramas. Thus, the language of both traditions also enriches study of the poets' understanding of performance and performativity. As Oliver Taplin says at the beginning of his important work on the performances of Greek drama, "Behind the words of Greek tragedy there is action."[24] The baldness of the claim is a harbinger to the boldness of his study. Because ancient and early modern scripts largely lack any stage directions, we must rely on the words of the text to reconstruct the visual aspect of drama, a matter to which, Taplin contends, the dramatists paid significant attention. Their words also reflect, as much recent work has shown, their thinking on the nature of imitation, the powers of performance, and the craft of dramaturgy.[25] Behind the words and actions of onstage gods, there is introspection.

Divinity and Performativity

The fundamental interests of performance studies appeal to us as an innovative lens through which to explore the function that gods play onstage. Richard Schechner, in an oft-cited phrase, calls acting "restored behavior."[26] Attention to staged gods complicates our understanding of Schechner's phrase. That is, acting in a realist fashion surely mirrors actions and reactions in the social sphere. Famously, Hamlet instructs a visiting group of actors that "the purpose of playing [. . .] was and is, to hold, as 'twere, the / mirror up to nature" (3.2.16–18).[27] The behavior of a god onstage does not necessarily re-enact behavior witnessed among humans outside the theater, except in the sense that gods are sometimes portrayed as having similar foibles to humans. A way to extend the implications of Schechner's phrase is to consider the staged god as a metatheatrical element, a dramatic component meant to restore or reenact the experience of making, performing, or witnessing the theater itself.

This perspective allows us to incorporate further some of the other early and influential hypotheses put forth by those theorizing performance. Sociologist Erving Goffman was one of the first modern scholars to use theatrical language to describe the behavior of people in day-to-day culture.[28] One of his foundational claims applies as much to dramatic actors as it does to the rational actors in society:

> When an individual plays a part, he implicitly requests his observers to take seriously the impression that is fostered before them. They are asked to believe that the character they see actually possesses the attributes he appears to possess, that the task he performs will have the consequences that are implicitly claimed for it, and that, in general, matters are what they appear to be.[29]

It should be immediately apparent that this claim does not track explicitly to situations involving staged gods, as there is an additional step of suspension-of-disbelief to buy into the divine presence onstage. Of course, within the context of the theatrical narrative, the god would have supernatural power. What observers "take seriously," we will argue in this book, are the fundamental ways that classical gods are inherently theatrical. That is, audience members will believe that a person can become someone else. They will believe that someone's actions might be scripted at another entity's commands. They will believe that a spectacle can stun those who look upon it. The very experience of the play they are watching demands as much.

Even early articulations in what would later become the field of performance studies key us into the vital purchase that the staged behavior of gods has on understanding human behavior. "There is no performance without pre-formance," John MacAloon has remarked.[30] Obviously, the "pre-formance" familiar to playwrights, actors, and audience members will not be the experience of having lived as a god. Instead, it will be the experience of having been part of the world of theatre. The drama on the stage is doing emotional and mental work on the audience. In turn, each audience member will carry these after-effects to subsequent productions and into the world beyond the theater. Further, in scenes where the audience will recognize themselves onstage, we find "the audience as a partner in the production of meaning on the [. . .] stage."[31] That is, the emotions of playgoers can rarely be disaggregated from the emotions experienced by their counterparts before them.

References to ancient gods abound throughout the extant texts from antiquity and the early modern period, and these references constitute key evidence for the study of the reception of figures and ideas from the past. As Virginia Mason Vaughan remarks in her recent book-length study of the appearance of gods in Shakespeare's work, "he looked back to Greece and Rome, and we look back to him."[32] Her study focuses largely on tracing allusions and on recovering those "discursive resources that recounted the classical gods' nature and activities and were available to early modern readers."[33] Our focus on performance differentiates our study from others such as that of Vaughn. We are not so interested in allusion so much as illusion.

A recent study by Lisa Maurice has argued that depictions of deities in twentieth- and twenty-first-century television and film "reveal an almost traumatized relationship with the divine," evincing cinema's "deep fascination with the idea of divinity, even as it rather uncomfortably denounces its very existence."[34] We similarly find that the appearance of the gods in classical and early modern drama can instigate a rupture in the narrative, though such divine interjections do not consistently constitute sites of "trauma." Performed gods were not "denounced" in the periods upon which we dwell, even if the figures were overtly represented as fictions. Instead, these gods of the theater often act to suture the real-world experience of the audience, actors, or the playwright with the fictive space, time, and narrative of the action onstage. To put it another way, dramatists use divine epiphanies in the theater to explore the seemingly seamless intrusion of a mimetic fiction in the reality of all who experience the theatrical. What does it mean for a dramatist and an actor to transcend, at least momentarily, their mortality when the former composes divine utterances for a god and the latter becomes one? What does it mean for the audience to witness, and to accept, an actor as an embodied epiphany of a god in the theater as well as the words composed by a poet as the words of a divinity? These questions have motivated this study.

Experiences of the divine in the theater are, of course, complicated by the varying beliefs in the gods, as ancient audiences performed sacrifices to them and early moderns would tend to see them as cultural inheritances. Questions concerning belief are, naturally, fiercely debated by critics of both theatrical traditions. Some have argued that gods onstage are convenient fictions of the dramatists' imagination—irrespective of, possibly even hostile to, contemporary religious practice. Jon Mikalson, for example, has said that "the gods of poetry are [...] the products of literary fantasy and genius, not of the Greek religious spirit."[35] Our view is that the gods of the stage were, for the original Athenian audience, the gods of cult. When the gods of tragedy and of comedy are presented onstage, they are, to be sure, portrayed according to the conventions of those genres. The gods, played by human actors, must be anthropomorphized. So, we follow those scholars who have argued that dramatists used gods to explore the mysterious nature of divinity.

The ancient imagination allowed for the anthropomorphizing of gods not only in literature but in cult as well. In an important study of religion and the theater, Christiane Sourvinou-Inwood explicitly rejects Mikalson's attempts to disentangle the "fantastic" gods of the theater from the "real" gods of cult. She has underscored similarities of theatrical and cultic practice in the depiction of the gods, noting that as part of sacred acts, for instance, the gods were often impersonated by, frequently masked, priests or priestesses.[36] Thus, to see a human embodying a god was an event customary to both the theater and the sanctuary.

We have also found compelling her hypothesis, articulated in an earlier essay, that deities in classical drama reflect the audience's "notion of the ultimate unknowability of the transcendental," an idea also explored in Mary Lefkowitz's stimulating study of Euripides.[37] As both Sourvinou-Inwood and Lefkowitz argue, a character who expresses doubt about the existence or power of the gods does not reflect the poet's impiety or even atheism but rather his—and his audience's—abiding curiosity about divinities, their place in the cosmos, their relationship to the mythological heroes of the past, and their relationship to human beings of the present. The ancient religious tradition not only tolerated but even welcomed such provocative theological discourse in public spheres, in which the voices of poets played a traditionally prominent role. Fundamental to our analysis is the tendency in the plays to scrutinize both the inscrutability of the divine and the inexplicable power of the theater. In this way, we follow an intriguing essay by Pat Easterling, who finds that the gods onstage serve, "to invite awareness on the part of the audience of the creative power of the dramatic experience and to explore, in action and experimentally, dilemmas and contradictions that are hard to grasp conceptually."[38] Both the embodied performative aspects of cult and the epistemologies of ancient religion were productive launching pads for the ancient, and early modern, dramatists' traveling into and puzzling over the power of the theater.

While these studies focus primarily on the gods of tragedy, our study includes much discussion of comedy, a genre whose humorous treatment of the gods may strike some modern spectators and readers as irreverent. Our modern sensibilities, however, are not those of the ancients. Recent work has challenged the notion that ancient audiences' understanding of the divine was not influenced by comic productions. Robert Parker argues that the gods of tragedy and of comedy were part of the Athenian religious experience, that the Dionysus of Euripides' tragedy *Bacchae* and Aristophanes' comedy *Frogs*, for example, "was part of an Athenian's experience of Dionysus no less than was the Dionysus of the *Anthesteria*," a religious festival in the god's honor.[39] In a more robust treatment of comedy and religion than Parker's illuminating but brief comments, Sarah Miles bridges the comic and tragic perspectives on gods, noting the similarities between Attic festival processions of divine figures and the introduction of divine characters into the fictional Athens created by Aristophanes onstage.⁴⁰ Roman comedies were also performed at a religious festival, and, as Anna Clark suggests, "the gods of comedy and their portrayal were themselves part of and contributed to the complex amalgam of ideas about the divine in Rome."⁴¹

Therefore, our own study treats comedy as an earnest participant in public religious discourse. In fact, comedy's sweeping and sophisticated engagement with the nature of theatrical illusion through metatheatricality makes several comedies compelling case studies of gods onstage.

Though Christian writers in early modern England cast pagan religion in a negative light, what we see as ancient debates about the theater conducted simultaneously with religious discourses influenced the literature and culture of Renaissance England. In fact, early modern dramatists regularly incorporate references to and even present gods of this pagan past onstage. Those gods of the English stage are startlingly out of time. The dramatists transport the deities from an earlier epoch into fictional times and places that did not believe in or sacrifice to the gods of Greece and of Rome. Though the ancient dramatists sometimes blur the lines between the Bronze Age mythological setting of the plays by introducing problems that obviously concern their contemporary audiences, the treatment of gods on English stages is, in this sense, radically different.

Early modern writers embraced a variety of strategies to overcome the problem of depicting pagan deities as powerful and immortal for Protestant playgoers and readers. Christian apologists portrayed the tales as allegories or early iterations of Biblical stories. In doing so, they aimed to frame this pantheon as "idolatry long since extinct" in order to suggest that "their existence had been reduced to mere a literary convention."⁴² Mythographers, in their popular dictionaries and encyclopedias of ancient myth, positioned tales of ancient deities as fables with deeper meanings and described gods as personifications. These compilers of ancient myths contributed to the Renaissance-as-renaissance given how "the mythographer [...] confronts a dead past, indeed the death of the gods, and imaginatively revives them."⁴³ Most importantly for our project, Renaissance playwrights located stories about these gods in often only nominally ancient settings.

Intriguingly, literary representations occasionally embraced the freedom to violate the notion of a linear progress of historical time—one that locates early modern individuals and their religious system as superseding those of classical antiquity—by depicting Greco-Roman deities as present in scenes taking place in Renaissance cultural contexts. We explore what new insights might be generated by considering alternatives to the paradigm of a temporal progression that involves supersession of new ideas onto old ones. Such an approach offers opportunities to frame the early modern present as a hybrid and re-evaluate the implications of Frances Yates' claim that "the great forward movements of the Renaissance all derive their vigor, their emotional impulse, from looking backwards."[44]

Although we look at case studies across the early modern period, we do pay particular attention to the work of Shakespeare, as his plays may be most familiar to our readers and because of his particularly intriguing embodiment of classical deities. David Scott Kastan remarks, "what is everywhere evident is Shakespeare's awareness of the inescapability of religion in his England."[45] When we accept this premise, we are able to examine the classical gods for their role in embodying the performativity of drama itself, rather than functioning as an analogue for—or serving to throw into belief—Christian figures and ideas.[46] Because Shakespeare's plays "clearly assume a world in which God is immanent, even if that immanence is not their subject," we can ask questions about what other kinds of forces these gods represent onstage.[47] Throughout this book, we pursue these questions in the work of playwrights beyond Shakespeare. At the same time, we acknowledge that his work is often the central case study in studies of the interplay between affective expression and personal belief in early modern theater.

A focus on the gods as metatheatrical devices is not, of course, an argument that this represents their sole purpose onstage.[48] Daryl Kaytor, for example, argues that by depicting deities "outside the boundaries of systemised theology, Shakespeare illuminates the political necessity of a new spiritual destiny for the English-speaking world."[49] For Kaytor, the gods stand in for a desired political reform that links Shakespeare's thinking to Plato's. Whether or not the audacity of Kaytor's claim rings true for us, it is undeniable that the spectacles presented on the early modern stage were designed to move playgoers, both in terms of the affective dimension of emotion transmitted from actors to audience and in terms of being transported to new worlds that might model new ways of being and thinking. Steven Mullaney aptly captures the productive complexity of this aspect of staged drama:

> Like any performative mode of production, early modern drama was a distributed phenomenon in an affective as well as cognitive sense. It extended beyond the acting space or scaffold to take place in and with the audience, its necessary participant and dramaturgical collaborator.[50]

The claim of course holds true for classical (and modern) drama.

The gods onstage must have tested the limits of that trans-affective operation that Mullaney describes as so crucial to the success of a theatrical production. These deities opened the audience's eyes, as they open our eyes now, to what Rebecca Schneider calls the "curious inadequacies of the copy."[51] An authentic portrayal of an immortal, nearly omnipotent figure is impossible. Divinity makes even a convincing portrayal improbable. An actor playing Zeus will be inadequate. But we know that audiences in antiquity and in the early modern period were invested in these performances. Some did believe, at least momentarily, that supernatural beings shared their space.

The Scope of This Study

As we hope is clear by now, this book will assess a range of receptions across the classical and the early modern periods. In some cases, we consider how a classical figure or narrative was received in the early modern period. Chapter 2, for instance, dwells on the figure of Helen of Troy. We evaluate, though, both how she was diversely received by ancient authors as well as how later narratives dealt with her. In Chapter 4, we consider how the *Oresteia* resonates within *Hamlet*, and in Chapter 3 how the theme of metamorphosis is put to varied uses by ancient and early modern playwrights.

This is a book for classicists, for early modernists, and for general readers. Therefore, we modernize English spellings, and we also include the original Greek and Latin. Some readers may note that we use the terms "Renaissance" and "early modern" interchangeably in the volume. For English literary scholars, both typically denote the same time period. It begins around 1485, when Henry VII attains the throne to begin the Tudor line and when William Caxton publishes Sir Thomas Malory's tales of Arthurian adventure and lament for a bygone era of chivalry in England: *Le Morte D'Arthur*. These events typically signal the end of the medieval era. The Renaissance or early modern period is then typically thought to end in 1700. Any effort to divide history into periods is fraught and so is any effort to name those periods. "Renaissance" is typically understood to celebrate the *rebirth* of classical learning and literature in the fifteenth century. "Early modern" is typically understood to signal the ways that many of our contemporaneous ideas found embryonic expression in the age of Shakespeare. Both ideas are over-simplifications. We use these terms all the while that we are aware of their limitations.

Limitations also apply to the nomenclature and periodization of the ancient Greek and Roman worlds. Classical antiquity is a capacious term that spans even beyond the periods under consideration in this book, including the archaic (roughly the eighth through sixth centuries BCE), classical (roughly the fifth and fourth centuries BCE), and Hellenistic periods (323–331 BCE) of Greece as well as the late Roman republic (first century BCE to 31 BCE) and the early imperial period (31 BCE through the early first century CE). The periods are usually anchored around significant historical events (for example, the death of Alexander the Great in 323 BCE and the defeat of Mark Antony by Octavian at the Battle of Actium in 31 BCE). It is debated whether the application of these terms is usefully applied to the study of literature and art.[52] Though we use "classical antiquity" and "Greek and Roman antiquity" to cover this chronological scope, readers will also note that the terms "classical Athens" and "classical Greece" refer particularly to the fifth and fourth centuries BCE.

We have sought to balance both canonical works and non-canonical works as case studies, and we include references to scholarship that we feel will be most helpful to a broad readership. For antiquity, we are restricted by those handful of plays that do survive by only a few poets, but we have included references to some fragmentary plays by these same poets and other dramatists where appropriate. In terms of early modern plays, we discuss non-Shakespearean case studies throughout this book, including depictions by authors such as Francis Beaumont, Samuel Daniel, Thomas Heywood, Ben Jonson, John Lyly, Christopher Marlowe, John Milton, and others. We use Shakespeare's work as a frequent touchstone because in many cases readers may have familiarity with his work. We "take Shakespeare as an instrument of inquiry into the nature of stage performance," as the author of a recent volume on the significance of Shakespearean performance nicely puts it.[53] We acknowledge that the focusing on this playwright because his work is so widely known ultimately reaffirms his place at the center of the canon.

We have noted scholarship that might be helpful to readers, especially to those either looking for an introduction to ideas raised in the book or to students looking to pursue particular lines of inquiry. Where possible, we keep discussions of extant scholarship to the notes, and we favor studies that will be accessible to the novice in the study of at least one of our time periods. However, because we hope this book will appeal to a wide audience, we do not always exhaustively cite scholarship on a particular topic.

Overview of the chapters

Each of the chapters in this book explores case studies of gods onstage in classical antiquity and in the early modern period. Because this book seeks to illustrate how a focus on these deities can open up new readings of texts, we take a variety of approaches across the chapters. As described below, some chapters focus on the reception of a single figure among a small handful of texts, while others trace a strand of thought across an array of texts. What is shared across these diverse approaches is a singular line of inquiry: what can staged gods tell us about the nature of theatrical presentation and practice?

The first chapter argues, in quick brushstrokes, for the vitality of considering gods as focal points for exploring metatheatricality. We put forth a series of guiding contentions, each functioning as a miniature polemic, that will find fruition throughout the book. Our main contention here is that scholars have certainly discussed the gods who appear onstage—sometimes as central to their arguments about a play and other times dismissively—but rarely have these figures been considered for their force as commenting on the nature of performance. Our inventory of polemics both argues for the insight to be gained from studying staged gods and provides starting points for such study.

Chapter 2 then traces a line of thought through post-Homeric receptions of Helen, taking as its primary case studies Euripides' *Helen* and Christopher Marlowe's *Doctor Faustus*. Both plays feature Helen as a figure for articulating the phenomenological challenges that audiences face when viewing mimetic art on the stage. Examining an array of classical and early modern texts that trace the lines of reception that inform subsequent depictions of Helen, we find writers continually returning to the performative nature of her divinely-rooted beauty. In turn, a focus on this character has much to say about the performative nature of theatrical speech and action.[54] The chapter argues that these profoundly metatheatrical plays use scenes of characters' seeing the impossibly beautiful Helen to explore the power of theatrical spectacle.

The third chapter pivots to explore the theme of change, or metamorphosis, that both dominated the worldviews of our two cultures under consideration and speaks directly to the work of drama. For our early modern case studies, we examine two lesser-studied dramas. Much scholarship has shown that "it would be difficult to overestimate Ovid's importance to Shakespeare's imaginary," but we pursue directions beyond Shakespeare and beyond simply tracing allusions to Ovid in this chapter's discussion.[55] Rather than considering Shakespeare at his most Ovidian in *A Midsummer Night's Dream*, we turn our attention to two court masques that deploy the theme of change in courtly contexts. We explore the aims of Samuel Daniel's *The Vision of the Twelve Goddesses* (1604) as it transforms the noblewomen of the English court (including the queen) into ancient goddesses. We then consider the implications of Francis Beaumont's *The Masque of the Inner Temple and Gray's Inn* (1613) turning statues into noblemen. The fact that the second play features the first instance in English of the phrase "artificial life" points to how the classical gods can be depicted to imbue vitality into dramatic performance and imbue this vitality in such a way as to reify social status and hierarchies that sustain cultural power. A similar dynamic is explored in Plautus' Roman comedy *Amphitruo*, a play in which the gods Jupiter and Mercury transform into doubles of Amphitruo and his slave Sosia. This play, which ties the performance to divine powers, implies that an actor might transcend his social status as a slave when he assumes the persona of the character he plays.

In the fourth chapter, we investigate situations where the gods direct action of the plot. Whereas Chapter 2 focuses on the reception of a single figure across an array of texts, here we explore how a shared narrative structure plays out differently in a classical context and an early modern one. We discuss two dramas that seem quite similar on the surface: Aeschylus' *Oresteia* and Shakespeare's *Hamlet*. We draw attention to the subtle metatheatricality of Aeschylus' trilogy of plays, and we argue that the human characters' contested interpretations of divine will in the first play cast doubt on the divine dictates of the final play. In *Hamlet*, the prince, of course, is not influenced by the gods directly. However, the play itself is notable here for the way it intermingles a pagan setting with intermixed Protestant and Catholic ideologies. For this play, we contemplate the ghost of Hamlet's father as a supernatural force that directs action in the play and we trace references to classical gods throughout the play. These works of Aeschylus and of Shakespeare remind us that, even when the characters are driven by gods or supernatural forces, humans produce the stories.

Chapter 5 turns to humans. We begin by addressing the absence of gods in ancient and early modern plays, highlighting passages from *King Lear*, *Hamlet*, and *Antigone* in which humans lament the lack of gods or define the human condition *vis-à-vis* the gods. We then associate this strand of thought with passages that link immortality with performance. For example, Shakespeare's Cleopatra expresses disappointment in her mortal status in the same breath with which she objects to the way that actors will portray her after her death. Finally, we find that anecdotes about performances in both periods reveal the power of reperformance to bring dramatists and actors back from the dead. Drawing on Greek and Roman tragedy and comedy, dramas by Shakespeare and his contemporaries, and dedicatory and sepulchral poems about the playwrights, this chapter suggests that ancients and early moderns considered the immortality of performance.

Our book closes in the present. An Afterword meditates on the role of the gods-as-humans and humans-as-gods in Mary Zimmerman's *Metamorphoses*.

This play allows us to think about two models for the theater: the stage as a mirror and the stage as a space of hospitality. Our particular case study is the play's re-telling of the myth of Baucis and Philemon, a tale with intriguing purchase on questions of metatheatricality.

1

Approaching Divinity

When we think about gods onstage, perhaps the first notion that comes to many of our minds is the *deus ex machina*, literally "a god from the machine."[1] In classical antiquity and often later, stage machinery, the *mechane*, was used to transport a god onto the theater in miraculous fashion to join the human characters, who are usually positioned on the stage below, as in Ninagawa's production of *Cymbeline* that is featured on the cover.[2] The moment can make for a startling effect. As we noted in the discussion of Ninagawa's depiction of Jupiter, the *deus ex machina* conjures the power of divine beings even as its artificiality is laid bare to playgoers. The device—both literary and mechanical—thus perfectly instantiates Victor Turner's conception of performance as "a dialectic of 'flow,' that is, spontaneous movement in which action and awareness are one, and 'reflexivity,' in which the central meanings, values and goals of a culture are seen 'in action,' as they shape and explain behavior."[3] The *deus ex machina* was often used to resolve conflicts or complexities that had just moments before seemed irresolvable during the drama's brief traffic on the stage. Because of this tendency, the phrase "deus ex machina" has become more commonly used as a critical shorthand for any narrative ending that is too pat, that resolves conflict too quickly, or that resolves several crises at once too easily. Even in antiquity, the plot device was not received uncritically. The fourth-century comic poet Antiphanes criticizes tragedians for using the *mechane*, after they have exhausted their creative powers, in a form of surrender (fr. 189.13–16), and Aristotle warns against uses of the *mechane* that lack credibility or are illogical (*Poetics* 1454a–b).

Yet to fixate on this well-known trope obfuscates the range of roles that gods played in early theater. Only a handful of plays in antiquity ended with a *deus ex machina*. None of the seven extant plays attributed to Aeschylus includes this device, only one of Sophocles' seven, and ten of Euripides' nineteen.[4] Several plays, such as Aeschylus' *Eumenides*, which will be discussed in Chapter 4, feature sustained interaction between gods and mortals within the main action of the narrative. Gods are featured in the prologues of several plays, such as Sophocles' *Ajax* and Euripides' *Bacchae*. Still, gods do not appear at all in many others, though their presence is nearly always felt, as with Sophocles' *Oedipus the King*. Whether in the presence of mortals onstage or merely on their minds, as we will see in the coming chapters, gods play a variety of roles throughout ancient and early modern dramatic plots—sometimes resolving conflict and other times causing it.

Our focus throughout the book is not on the role of gods within the narrative *per se*, a topic that has been the object of scholarly discussion and debate even in fifth-century criticism. Instead, we focus on what the appearances of gods onstage have to say about theatrical performance itself. Even the *deus ex machina*, for example, demands the audience's perceptual investment in the possibility that a human actor can transcend mortality and become a god. This possibility is spotlighted when, at the end of dramas such as Sophocles' *Oedipus at Colonus* and Euripides' *Helen*, the apotheosis of a human character is implied or foreshadowed. For these denouements to be convincing, let alone effective, the audience must accept the mutability of the figures of the mythological past—heroes and heroines becoming divine—and so the very stories of classical tragedies, which were comprised primarily of myths, suggest the possibility that the actors charged with playing such powerful roles could themselves temporarily transform into divine figures.

In this chapter, we consider a handful of examples that demonstrate the diversity of expression and the complexity of this dynamic, and we have organized these examples into the following eight *contentions* that have inspired lines of inquiry throughout the book. Not all of these contentions are explored equally or even explicitly throughout the book, but they serve as a useful prologue for our study of how performing gods can illuminate the very nature of playgoing, as well as the work of playwrights and actors who make the drama come to life.

We contend . . .

1. Gods Create (Dis)order Through Speech

The gods via *deus ex machina* typically reorder, albeit often provocatively, the chaos that reigned onstage into harmony. However, when speaking the prologue, that section of the drama when a character has the audience alone before the arrival of the chorus, the gods are themselves typically agents of chaos, framing the action of the play through the creation of conflict. A god speaks the prologue in one play of Sophocles, his *Ajax*, and in five plays of Euripides: his *Alcestis*, *Hippolytus*, *Trojan Women*, *Ion*, and *Bacchae*. In these and other plays, the gods' words alone have power. While the performative turn in scholarship over the recent decades reminds us that it is essential to consider the action of the stage, the gods often create order and disorder rarely by action and most often simply by speaking.

Though Dionysus of Euripides' *Bacchae* may come to mind first as the god who creates the disorder that drives the drama, we begin instead with Euripides' *Hippolytus*, in which the goddess Aphrodite is angry at the young man Hippolytus for his shunning of sex. The goddess herself speaks the prologue and teases the destruction that will befall the play's hero. She opens:

πολλὴ μὲν ἐν βροτοῖσι κοὐκ ἀνώνυμος
θεὰ κέκλημαι Κύπρις οὐρανοῦ τ' ἔσω·

Great among mortals and in the heavens, I, not nameless, am called the goddess Cypris.

1–2

While the staging of the scene cannot be overlooked, as the actor's costume would mark him as Aphrodite, the words forge the identity. The actor becomes the god simply by stating her name. She goes on not to describe her powers as the goddess of love but rather speaks in divine generalities that would not be out of place from the mouth of any god, noting that she honors mortals who revere her, that she trips up those who are too proud to do so, that all gods enjoy being honored by mortals. She then pledges to "reveal soon the truth of these words" (δείξω δὲ μύθων τῶνδ' ἀλήθειαν τάχα, 9). Because "words," *mythoi*, can also mean story, plot, or myth, her statement creates an evocative ambiguity in the Greek. In addition to expressing confidently her divine power, how much guiding of the plot will Aphrodite do?

The demonstration of her divine prerogative is not simply conveyed in the ensuing description of Hippolytus' eschewing Aphrodite and love in favor of Artemis and hunting. Any mortal character could provide this background information of the *mythos* that is necessary for the audience to understand the plot—a typical function of the prologue. Because "I will reveal," however, is spoken by the god, the speech possesses the force to propel the action of the entire play and presages the destruction of the mortal Hippolytus. Thus, this line is an important transition from the divine powers of Aphrodite to the narrative of the play and charges the *mythoi*—the actor's words and the instigation of the plot—with the powers of the goddess. Later in the prologue speech, Aphrodite moves from the past and the present once again to the future ("I will avenge," τιμωρήσομαι, 21) and through her use of the future tense, what we might call the prophetic future, she would be imbued with clairvoyance by the audience. Her plan has long been in the works, since she made Hippolytus' stepmother fall in love with him, and now her plans for the future become more explicit as she once again promises that she will reveal (δείξω, 42) to Theseus his stepmother's passion. Aphrodite sketches his downfall at the hands of his father, who will curse him in prayers to Poseidon. It has often been noted that the gods stand in for the dramatist himself, seemingly crafting the plot of a play and putting it into action, and we certainly see Aphrodite serving such a function in this prologue. The goddess does not act. She speaks, and through speaking both introduces and promises the completion of the conflict that will drive the play.

This prologue's implicit metatheatricality, based primarily on the ambiguity of *mythoi*, is made more explicit in other plays. In Euripides' *Bacchae*, for example, the disorder is grounded in an illusion created by the god Dionysus, thus reinforcing the connection between divine power and the theater. The god of theater himself, who is the speaker of this prologue, shows up in human form— in a costume—promising to deceive and to punish the mortals for not believing in his divinity. Not only has Dionysus, as he says, "changed from a god to a mortal form" (μορφὴν δ' ἀμείψας ἐκ θεοῦ βροτησίαν, 4). "I have," he says later in the prologue, "stung the women with madness" (ᾤστρησ' ἐγὼ / μανίαις, 32–33) and "have forced them to bear the accoutrements of my rites" (σκευήν τ' ἔχειν ἠνάγκασ' ὀργίων ἐμῶν, 34). This prologue, indeed the entire play, abounds with vocabulary that invites a metatheatrical reading. Dionysus adopts an outward appearance meant to deceive those who see him, and to "bear the accoutrements" of the god of drama suggests theatrical performance itself, a reading reinforced by the word accoutrements (*skeuē*), which can mean both religious garb and the trappings of tragedy.

Those readers familiar with Shakespeare will find here the roots of Hamlet's feigned madness in Dionysus' implication that performance is a kind of god-inspired mania. The notion is found also in the prologue of Sophocles' *Ajax*.[5] The prologue of this play, though more subtly than the *Bacchae*, also invites consideration of the nature of the theatrical experience, all of whose aspects— dramaturgy, acting, and spectating—are controlled by the goddess Athena. In the stunning opening of this play that depicts Ajax's fury and his suicide after losing the arms of Achilles to Odysseus, Athena manipulates the vision of both

Odysseus (her interlocutor in this conversational prologue) and Ajax. She says that she cast mistaken forms before Ajax's eyes (51–52) and afflicted him with a "mad sickness" (μανιάσιν νόσοις, 59) so that he thought that he was slaughtering the soldiers of the Greek army for their overlooking his claim to Achilles' possessions. She speaks first, introducing the theme of spectatorship when she claims always to watch (cf. δέδορκα, 1) and now to see (cf. ὁρῶ, 3) Odysseus, who responds that he can hear her voice but she remains "invisible" (ἄποπτος, 15) to him.[6] In the ensuing conversation, Athena reveals to Odysseus that Ajax has slaughtered the Greeks' flocks, and she "will reveal his sickness" (δείξω ... νόσον) to Odysseus, all the while concealing her favorite mortal from Ajax's view (66–70). Odysseus is frightened, but Athena assures him: "I will blind his eyes, even though they see" (ἐγὼ σκοτώσω βλέφαρα καὶ δεδορκότα, 85). Odysseus retorts that anything may happen if a god devises it (γένοιτο μέντἂν πᾶν θεοῦ τεχνωμένου, 86). Athena then orders Odysseus to stand in silence as Ajax enters the stage.

The emphasis on sight and on voices is striking, and it gestures in many ways to the act of theater itself. The prologue clearly marks Athena as a producer of this play-with-a-play, and as Pat Easterling has noted, also engages ideas of spectatorship:

> [T]here is a strong stress on the extreme fragility of the "reality" seen or constructed by human beings, brought out by the insistent play on what is seen by the different characters and by the audience. In a context where madness and sanity, seeing and not seeing, are so much at issue, this little "play" put on by Athena for Odysseus' benefit illustrates the function of theatre to create models for us to try out.[7]

While all prologues function to bridge the boundary between the worlds of the audience and that of the characters, a framing delivered by the gods draws attention to the temporary, fictional world wrought for audiences by playwrights. Some of the suspense must hinge on whether the audience is skeptical of Athena's assurances that Odysseus will be safe or if her confident use of the prophetic future tense suffices for the audience. Reactions likely differed. But the immediate vindication of her promise associates the goddess and her powers with the power of theatrical illusion. Like the dramatist who has already finished the last line of the play before an actor speaks the first line in front of an audience, Athena can be confident that her plan and the chaos planned for the mortals will be executed.

While this notion of the "god as *didaskalos*" (producer)—to borrow Easterling's formulation—is pervasive on the Athenian stage, the notion that the god's speech generates disorder and drives the plot of the play also finds ample expression in early modern drama. At times, it fuels the disorder that constitutes the narrative conflict and in turn must be re-ordered to deliver narrative resolution. Take, for example, Robert Wilson's *The Cobbler's Prophesy*. Mercury sends a prophecy to Mars. He entrusts the message to a human named Raph and curses the man's wife, Zelota, with madness. After encountering various muses, Echo, and Charon (the ferryman of the underworld), Raph thwarts the assassination of a Duke and finally delivers his prophecy to Mars. The prophecy reveals that the god of war is being cuckolded by his lover Venus, who is pregnant with her lover's child. In the end, Raph is rewarded by the Duke for his courage, and Mercury cures Zelota. Were it not for Mercury entrusting these divine words to a human (and were it not for these words causing romantic strife among the gods), the subsequent drama of the play would not ensue.

Prophecy also creates both order and disorder in Shakespeare's *The Winter's Tale*. Midway through the play, a pronouncement from Apollo seems as if it will settle the human conflict. It announces that the queen is innocent of adultery and that her child is, in fact, the king's.[8] The prophecy itself sounds like the conclusion to a narrative plot:

> Hermione is chaste, Polixenes
> blameless, Camillo a true subject, Leontes a jealous tyrant, his innocent
> babe truly begotten
>
> 3.2.130–32

Yet this divine proclamation only sends the royal husband into a deeper jealous rage as he rejects the prophecy, condemns his wife, and exiles his newborn child. In fact, the final two lines of the prophecy predict this conflict even as they warn against it: "and the King shall live without an heir if that which / is lost be not found" (3.2.132–33). It will be up to humans to clear characters' names and reunite the family. Mortals must resolve this state of profound disorder where the speech of a god only further fractures family members and friends.

These classical and early modern examples underscore for us that edicts and prophecies from the gods, whether obeyed or disobeyed, not only drive plots but also make plain how words have power and constitute actions in and of themselves. As J. L. Austin famously remarked, "To *say* something is to *do* something."[9] This statement aptly describes the performative power of discourse within the lived social sphere and nicely captures the world of the theater where dialogue and action are difficult to disaggregate. When gods speak, the amplified power of their words drive the heightened action of drama.

2. Gods Feed Human Fantasies of Control

Though the natural hierarchy of humans and gods in the ancient imagination may suggest that the former would be consistently depicted as puppets of the latter, the relationship between gods and humans onstage is by no means so simple and universal. If we follow Jaques' famous statement in *As You Like It* that "all the world's a stage," humans, to put it in theatrical terms, would naturally seem to be manipulated actors in the theater of the world scripted and directed by the gods. Yet, as we will see throughout this book, it is often the gods who are put to human characters' uses on the stage.

In the early modern canon, Shakespeare's *The Tempest* offers a useful case study for tracing the dynamics through which humans put gods to use (even just at the level of theatrical impersonation) in their efforts to control the world. *The Tempest* is often regarded as one of Shakespeare's most metatheatrical plays. The wizard Prospero manipulates the emotions and movements of a variety of characters stranded on his island. His shape-changing servant Ariel can be seen as an analogue for an actor as he takes on many roles and guises in order to affect Prospero's captive audience. The prevailing idea that *The Tempest* particularly meditates on the nature of the theater draws, in part, from this play's status as the last one that Shakespeare seems to have written on his own and from its final speech that can be read as his farewell to the theater. There is even the alluring myth that Shakespeare himself played Prospero on the stage.[10]

No gods actually visit the island upon which *The Tempest* takes place, but magic abounds. Supernatural creatures are among the characters, some of whom worship the Patagonian god Setebos, and there is even mention of the devil being one character's father. Toward the end of the play, Prospero demands a dramatic performance at the wedding of his daughter Miranda to the stranded Prince Ferdinand. He calls upon his servant Ariel to direct a masque, one of those elaborate courtly performances involving music. Ariel commands his fellow spirits to take the roles of Iris (a Greek goddess and divine messenger), Ceres (Roman goddess of the harvest), and Juno (Roman queen of the gods and goddess of marriage).[11]

The performance opens with Iris inviting Ceres to "come and sport" and "to entertain" on "this grass-plot" (4.1.73–75). The term "sport" functioned as a synonym for "entertain" in the early modern period, and the invitation thereby doubly emphasizes that this theatrical performance is meant for the benefit of its audience. The scene thus has an external and an internal audience. The internal audience members being celebrated here are a prince and a young woman who has just realized that she is the daughter of a duke. The audience in the theater proper is simultaneously watching a masque and watching those watching the masque.[12] Playgoers see themselves mirrored in the performance and are welcomed to imagine that this royal masque might also be for them. Such a mise-en-abyme (or play-within-a-play) demands that the theater audience become active participants in the meaning of the drama and spectatorship. Alison Hopgood puts this idea nicely, as she invites us to begin "imagining [playgoers] not as disciplined receivers of dramatic passions but rather as potent and productive co-creators of the drama they attended."[13] The presence of the performing gods in *The Tempest* ignites the possibility for metatheatricality. We not only have multiple layers of audience (as the audience in the theater watches the audience in the play) but we have multiple layers of directing and acting (beyond Shakespeare's direction of the play, Prospero commands Ariel to command spirits to play gods).

There is yet one more layer here, as Ceres makes clear that her own summoning by Iris is at the behest of the queen of the gods:

> Hail, many-coloured messenger, that ne'er
> Dost disobey the wife of Jupiter;
> Who with thy saffron wings upon my flowers
> Diffusest honey-drops, refreshing showers;
> And with each end of thy blue bow dost crown
> My bosky acres and my unshrubbed down,
> Rich scarf to my proud earth: why hath thy queen
> Summoned me hither to this short-grassed green?
>
> 4.1.76–83

The masque thus eagerly anticipates the arrival of Juno, and after more banter between Iris and Ceres, she arrives. When she does, Ceres remarks, "Great Juno, comes; I know her by her gait" (4.1.102). The fact that one god recognizes the other based on how she moves underscores the performative element of being a god. To be Juno is to be someone with a particular way of walking, and this kind of movement can be mimicked by an actor determined to convince us that he is god-like. Ceres' statement simultaneously functions as an embedded stage direction and as an interpretation of the meaning of the action to come as the minds of spectators are now primed to perceive the actor playing Juno as regal and godly.

Prince Ferdinand, although he has just witnessed a group of mystical beings refer to each other as classical gods, sees through the illusion of theater, and Prospero affirms his suspicions. The prince says to Prospero,

> This is a most majestic vision, and
> Harmonious charmingly. May I be bold
> To think these spirits?
>
> 4.1.118–20

Ferdinand recognizes the performance both as an affirmation of Prospero's power and as a theatrical presentation of gods but not the appearance of actual gods. His use of the term "majestic" nods to the wizard's elevated position of authority, both as someone who rules the island and as someone who can command actors to put on a stunning performance. His question of whether he has beheld spirits is an intriguing one, as it both reveals that he does not actually believe that he saw ancient gods before him and still emphasizes that he saw magic in the performance. Prospero replies,

> Spirits, which by mine art
> I have from their confines called to enact
> My present fancies.
>
> 4.1.120–22

By describing the performance as "mine art," Prospero seizes upon a multivalent term in the early modern period. While "art" today likely brings to mind creative works, the term in Shakespeare's time was a capacious one, closer to the Latin *ars*, that could denote the creation of machinery, experiments in the physical sciences, or indeed theatrical production. As Elizabeth Spiller puts it, "Prospero's 'Art' expresses the remarkable power of [the] model of art as a knowledge practice."[14] Before the "modern science of facts," the term "art" captured a range of desirable modes of knowledge linked to the practice of creation, in the most creative and most mechanical of senses.[15] So Prospero here is a kind of divine avatar, an individual with supernatural powers who has mastered the machinery of magic, of actors, and of staging. Prospero is sure to note that these actors "enact" his imagination, his "fancies."

Prospero ends the performance abruptly, remembering other business to which he needs to tend. He proclaims,

> Our revels now are ended. These our actors,
> As I foretold you, were all spirits, and
> Are melted into air, into thin air;
> And, like the baseless fabric of this vision,
> The cloud-capped towers, the gorgeous palaces,
> The solemn temples, the great globe itself,
> Yea, all which it inherit, shall dissolve,

And, like this insubstantial pageant faded,
Leave not a rack behind. We are such stuff
As dreams are made on, and our little life
Is rounded with a sleep.

4.1.148–58

Here we have one of Shakespeare's most famous speeches. Importantly, Prospero reveals to us that Ceres, Iris, and Juno were simply "actors." He nods to Shakespeare's own Globe Theatre when he narrates how the scenes and backdrops in "the great globe itself" now fade.[16] when he tells us that "We are such stuff / As dreams are made on," he tells us both that theater is the source of dreams and that humans can be creators themselves. As Sarah Beckwith notes, the play presents us with "images of spectatorship and participation that themselves compose metatheatrical spectacles of gazing" that culminate in a moment where Prospero even "theatricalizes himself."[17] Yet, for all his boasting about his power to re-create the world as spectacle, he nonetheless admits the limitations of such stage magic. He admits that the revels must at some point end and that its "thin air" and "baseless fabric" could not be sustained outside the momentary reality effects of dramatic representation.

In the Epilogue, Prospero will stand alone onstage and ask for the audience's applause to set him free from his island prison:

Now I want
Spirits to enforce, art to enchant;
And my ending is despair
Unless I be relieved by prayer,
Which pierces so, that it assaults
Mercy itself, and frees all faults.
As you from crimes would pardoned be,
Let your indulgence set me free.

Epilogue 12–19

Lacking actors or any other means for making, Prospero will engineer the closure in this play by soliciting applause. The audience becomes the god in and out of the machine. They allow the actor, who has played the author of the drama, to exit the stage and for the narrative to come to a close.[18]

Shakespeare's great distance from the pagan past affords him flexibility not expressed in the theaters of classical antiquity, and so it is perhaps not surprising that no ancient dramatists so explicitly depict human control over divinities in the way Prospero's masque depicts. Yet ancient comedians, who indulge in human fantasies of control far more than their tragic counterparts, sometimes depict human beings cleverly and skillfully and absurdly circumventing the gods.

While Aristophanes' *Frogs* offers a memorable depiction of the god Dionysus in his comic mode, it is the *Birds* that so clearly dramatizes humans usurping the powers of the divine. In this comedy, two disgruntled Athenian citizens, Peisetaerus and Euelpides, colonize the sky to cut the gods off from sacrifices made to them by mortals, and, to do so, the vainglorious pair must rally the birds to support their cause. They plan to supplant the gods of Olympus.

In order to support the new divine regime's claims to cosmic authority over the Olympians, the new avian accomplices revise traditional accounts of the origins of the cosmos and the gods. Though, as with all Greek and Roman myths, there is no dogmatic version of creation—indeed, it is this mythic license that permits the avian revision—the account likely most familiar to the audience would have been Hesiod's account of creation in his *Theogony*. Hesiod's version begins with four primordial entities, Chaos, Earth, Tartaros, and Eros, who are followed by Darkness and Night, both born from Chaos (*Theogony* 116–25). The new theogony in *Birds*, addressed to the audience in a metatheatrical speech, finds inspiration in Hesiod's version, but the differences are clear:

Χάος ἦν καὶ Νὺξ Ἔρεβός τε μέλαν πρῶτον καὶ Τάρταρος εὐρύς·
Γῆ δ' οὐδ' Ἀὴρ οὐδ' Οὐρανὸς ἦν· Ἐρέβους δ' ἐν ἀπείροσι κόλποις
τίκτει πρώτιστον ὑπηνέμιον Νὺξ ἡ μελανόπτερος ᾠόν,
ἐξ οὗ περιτελλομέναις ὥραις ἔβλαστεν Ἔρως ὁ ποθεινός,
στίλβων νῶτον πτερύγοιν χρυσαῖν, εἰκὼς ἀνεμώκεσι δίναις.
οὗτος δὲ Χάει πτερόεντι μιγεὶς νύχιος κατὰ Τάρταρον εὐρὺν
ἐνεόττευσεν γένος ἡμέτερον, καὶ πρῶτον ἀνήγαγεν εἰς φῶς.
...
                    ὧδε μέν ἐσμεν
πολὺ πρεσβύτατοι πάντων μακάρων ἡμεῖς.

There was first Chaos, Night, dark Erebus, and broad Tartarus. There was no Earth, nor Air, nor Sky. In the boundless bosom of Erebus, black-winged Night bore first of all a wind egg, from which Eros, full of desire, was born when the seasons rotated. His back gleamed with golden wings, and he seemed like a swiftly whirling wind. He mingled with winged Chaos at night in broad Tartarus and hatched our race, and he brought us into the light first. . . . Thus, we are by far the oldest of all the blessed gods.

693–703

This new myth about the origins of the cosmos gives priority to the birds over the gods in support of the physical blockade of Mt. Olympus that will allow the birds to intercept sacrifices made to the gods, robbing them of their source of strength.

The birds plead with the audience to worship them as gods and promise to bestow wonderful gifts in return, including "But we here will give to you yourselves, your children, and your children's children wealthy health, livelihood, peace, youth, laughter, choruses, dances, and the milk of birds" (ἀλλὰ παρόντες δώσομεν ὑμῖν / αὐτοῖς, παισίν, παίδων παισίν, / πλουθυγίειαν, βίον, εἰρήνην, / νεότητα, γέλωτα, χορούς, θαλίας / γάλα τ' ὀρνίθων, 729–33). All of this is obviously supposed to be funny. But it speaks not only to the ambition of the birds and the mortals to force their will on the traditional Olympians but also the ease with which they suspect this will be possible.

Their plot is wildly successful. Despite attempted interventions by gods, including Poseidon and Heracles, Zeus, who does not appear onstage himself, surrenders the true source of his power, a divinely personified Kingship (*Basileia*). The protagonist Peisetaerus weds Kingship to herald his ascension to the cosmic throne (*Birds* 1712–65). In a famous essay on this play, William Arrowsmith notes that "in the dazzling hypnotic pride of his flight, the godlike hero has no eyes to see his own absurdity or the fate which awaits him, like [Icarus], in the sea (or earth, as the case may be) below."[19] The comedy's metatheatricality, particularly the birds' recruitment of the audience into their agenda, suggests, maybe with a touch of irony, the hilarious ease with which usurpation of divine power would be for them, too.

3. Gods Offer Humans the Fantasy of Control, Only to Take It Away

Yet the gods are not always so amenable to surrender their power to human beings. In the absence of divine voices, mortals often attempt to claim divine mandate for their actions, but the lack of clarity of gods' true wishes reveal mortal beings' tenuous grasp on understanding the gods. Sophocles is a master of creating plays in which, though gods pull the levers, the mortal characters cite the gods as justifications for their actions, for the origins of their conflict with one another. The poet's *Antigone* is a well-known example, featuring Antigone and Creon's clash over the will of the gods, and though no gods appear onstage to effect their will, the divine proxy Tiresias, with emphatic encouragement from his son Haemon and the Chorus, eventually persuades Creon of Antigone's position. Creon's autonomy is short-lived and severely punished as his actions lead to the suicides of his son and his wife.

Sophocles' *Philoctetes* features a similar momentary thrill of mortal autonomy only to have the illusion of their own desires be snatched away by a *deus ex machina*. The drama tells the story of Philoctetes, who is ill and isolated and angry at the Greeks who had left him abandoned on an island before the start of the Trojan War. The troops at Troy, however, receive a prophecy that the city will fall only with the help of Philoctetes. The Greeks, therefore, try to win him over, sending Odysseus and Neoptolemus to persuade the scorned hero back into the Greek fold. The play is perhaps Sophocles' most metatheatrical, featuring a clever mise-en-abyme as Odysseus orders Neoptolemus to feign hatred of Odysseus himself to win Philoctetes over. Odysseus directs. Neoptolemus acts. When Odysseus and his plot are revealed to Philoctetes, the two dispute whether Odysseus' actions are divinely sanctioned:

ΟΔΥΣΣΕΥΣ   Ζεύς ἐσθ᾽, ἵν᾽ εἰδῇς, Ζεύς, ὁ τῆσδε γῆς κρατῶν,
Ζεύς, ᾧ δέδοκται ταῦθ᾽· ὑπηρετῶ δ᾽ ἐγώ.

ΦΙΛΟΚΤΗΤΗΣ   ὦ μῖσος, οἷα κἀξανευρίσκεις λέγειν·
θεοὺς προτείνων τοὺς θεοὺς ψευδεῖς τίθης.

ΟΔΥΣΣΕΥΣ   οὔκ, ἀλλ᾽ ἀληθεῖς. ἡ δ᾽ ὁδὸς πορευτέα.

Odysseus   It is Zeus, so that you know, Zeus who rules this land, Zeus to whom this seemed best. I myself serve him.

Philoctetes   Oh hateful man, what discoveries of words you make. Offering the gods as pretext, you make the gods liars.

Odysseus   No, but truth tellers. The road must be traveled.

989–93

Without the direct intervention of a god, the will of Zeus would remain contested, but Neoptolemus' decision to abandon the plan to take Philoctetes back to Troy—a shocking reversal of the mythological tradition—requires the intervention of the son of Zeus Heracles *ex machina*. The god, claiming to set forth the plan of Zeus (τὰ Διός ... βουλεύματά, 1415), bids Neoptolemus and Philoctetes to leave the island to return to Troy. After Heracles dispenses orders to the humans who were about to deviate from Zeus' will, he reminds them how inconsequential they are in the scope of cosmic time. "For piety does not die along with mortals. Whether they live or die, it is not lost" (οὐ γὰρ ηὐσέβεια συνθνῄσκει βροτοῖς· / κἂν ζῶσι κἂν θάνωσιν, οὐκ ἀπόλλυται, 1443–44). Even Philoctetes immediately gives in.

For an intriguing early modern example, we need look no further than George Peele's *The Arraignment of Paris* (1584). The play was performed by a company of boy actors at court. It follows the ancient myth of the Judgment of Paris insofar as a shepherd-prince is asked to judge the three goddesses who enter themselves into this contest. However, in this version, he is deemed to be partial and the goddess Diana steps in to deliver the judgment. She chooses a nymph named Eliza as the most beautiful (exceeding the appeal of even Venus). While the play wrests the decision-making power from the human and places it in immortal hands, it ultimately reinforces political hierarchies. Diana, as the goddess of chastity, was often an analogue for Queen Elizabeth, and the nymph's name points to the queen as well. The play, then, has it both ways. The gods claim control, only to allow the real-world human ruler to be both the ultimate arbiter of the beautiful and to be the paradigm of that same quality.

4. Gods Are Both Force and Counterforce

The polytheistic pantheon of antiquity featured, by definition, a number of different gods with various domains and prerogatives. Yet each god or goddess can also be thought of as a polytheistic system in himself or herself, as all gods have a range of attributes that can be activated in different cultic settings. Gods can be worshipped as a divine manifestation of a power as well as the opposite of that power, such as Apollo who at times heals and at other times plagues. The gods of ancient and early modern drama are no different in this regard. They are force and counterforce.

Shakespeare's *Timon of Athens* takes place in ancient Athens, and the opening finds Timon throwing an extravagant party for Athenian noblemen. The festivities are interrupted by a servant who informs him that "there are certain ladies most desirous of / admittance" (1.2.102–3). The lord enjoins the servant to let the women in. The first person to enter is someone dressed as Cupid. The individual is clearly intended to be not the little love god but rather an actor hired by Timon. The entertainment thus positions the gods as able to be impersonated by humans and moreover positions Cupid as a symbol for not only the romantic energies within the performance but also the emotion flowing through the party itself. The visitor enters and makes the following pronouncement:

> Hail to thee, worthy Timon, and to all that of his bounties taste!
> The five best senses acknowledge thee their patron, and come freely to gratulate
>   thy plenteous bosom.

> There taste, touch, all, pleased from thy table rise.
> They only now come but to feast thine eyes.
>
> 1.2.108–12

On one level, the boy-god is simply praising the party. It is a feast for the senses, he proclaims. But he also points to the emotional tensions that the theatrical audience will come to see as brimming over in this play.

This first moment, now presided over by Cupid, may seem to the theatrical audience and to Timon himself to be a gathering of loving friends. However, the people at the party are just there to feast on Timon's "bounties" and to "gratulate" his "plenteous bosom." That is, they are just here to use their friend and to tell him what he wants to hear in exchange for favors. By extension, the Cupid presented on the stage is not the mischievous love-god of antiquity. This Cupid is the embodiment of "cupidity," an early modern term that denoted "ardent desire, inordinate longing or lust; covetousness" and "inordinate desire to appropriate wealth or possessions; greed of gain." He signifies the denigrated side of the binarism between *caritas* and *cupiditas*. These terms emerged in the medieval period to describe loving charity and generosity on the one side and greedy, voracious desire on the other.[20]

Cupid thus appears in this play to reveal the motivations behind the partygoers' overt praise of Timon and to reveal Timon's own limitations in being unable to see his guests for the false friends that they are. Timon lacks the wisdom embodied in commonplace advice on friendship from Shakespeare's era. Consider, for example, these comments by the early modern editor and translator of Plutarch's essays. He frames the ancient author's "How a Man May Discern a Flatterer from a Friend" with this headnote:

> often times, that we esteem them to be our perfect friends, so skillful are they in counterfeiting; and withall, when they find us disposed to entertain such company, our own indiscretion deprive us of that true insight and view, which our soul ought to have in discerning a false friend from a true.[21]

The translator here draws our attention to the flatterer's skill in "counterfeiting," a term we might well apply to acting, and the headnote's use of "entertain" further underscores that we must beware the flatterer's skill at acting like a true friend. When the First Lord remarks upon Cupid's performance, "You see, my lord, how ample you're beloved," one cannot help but hear that this love is conditional, material, and most importantly performative (1.2.115). In his essay on discerning friends from flatterers, Plutarch warns that flatterers are like the shape-changing god Proteus, whose abilities to change surface-level characteristics throw into relief true friendship as they "strive to assimilate character and feelings and conversations and pursuits and dispositions" (αἱ δὲ φιλίαι τὰ ἤθη ζητοῦσι συνεξομοιοῦν καὶ τὰ πάθη καὶ τοὺς λόγους καὶ τὰ ἐπιτηδεύματα καὶ τὰς διαθέσεις, *On Having Many Friends* 9). As we will see in Chapter 3, Proteus' changeability linked him to acting and to the theater in the early modern period.

As Timon's party continues, Cupid leaves briefly and re-enters with ladies costumed as Amazons. Another lord remarks, "Hey-day, / what a sweep of vanity comes this way!" (1.2.116–17). The lord, who has been an audience member for the performance that Timon has just witnessed, announces what we already know. Then men dance with the ladies, "with much adoring of Timon" (s.d. 1.2.130). Jane Kingsley-Smith has traced a resurgence of interest in Cupid in the early modern period, identifying a paradox wherein Cupid at once stood for a "multiplicity" of desires but also "was deployed to 'police' desire."[22] The little love god in this play is here, then, to throw into relief the protagonist's flaws. Such a performance would have a place in at least one strand of early modern thinking about the theater. Thomas Heywood's *The Apology for Actors* (1612) defends the portrayal of those "who have been dishonourable, unjust, false, gluttonous, sacrilegious, bloody-minded, and brochure of dissension."[23] The "fates and ruins" of such characters help honorable players stay committed to their positive virtues.[24]

The god who we see in the machine is here to help us see the humans in the machine. We will see this pattern both reinforced and interrupted in the chapters that follow, especially in early modern drama. Kathryn Schwarz observes that Cupid's "masque takes Timon both as author and as object."[25] The masque itself, then, is a mockery of the role of love in the play. Adulation is performative, gestural but it is not real love. These false friends only pretend to adore Timon now while he gives them many gifts. They will abandon him when he needs them. Love in this play, like the cupid and amazons who appear in this party promenade, is a fiction.

5. Gods Claim Their Realness by Demanding Disbelief

When Aeschylus' Chorus of Furies entered the orchestra of the Theater of Dionysus at the premiere of his *Oresteia* in 458, they shocked (ἐκπλῆξαι) the audience so much that children fainted (ἐκψῦξαι) and pregnant women miscarried (*Life of Aeschylus* 9).[26] Though the exact cause of the bedlam has been debated since antiquity, the anecdote draws attention to a phenomenological issue of theatrical performance. The visceral reaction of the audience suggests that they were so enraptured by the theatrical illusion that the fiction in the orchestra and on the stage had consequences in reality. The audience did not perceive the Chorus members as they truly were—masked Athenian citizen men, but as they pretended to be—frightening chthonic deities.

Similarly, audiences attending Christopher Marlowe's *Doctor Faustus* are reported to have believed, as we will see in the next chapter, that they did not just see a demon character on the stage but that demons in fact joined the human actors in the theater. The presence of these creatures in the playhouse exemplifies the curious boundary-breaking that gods onstage make possible. Audiences need to suspend belief enough to perceive a human actor as a supernatural being. To do so opens the possibility that supernatural beings might actually enter the playhouse. In an early modern attack on the theater, Stephen Gosson claimed that plays were the "doctrines and inventions of the devil" because of their origins in celebrations of pagan gods.[27] At the heart of Gosson's concern is the capability of plays to depict "such things as never were."[28] In the plays we will encounter in this study, such gods are celebrated. Yet they are not celebrated as pagan heresy but rather as emblems of the magic of the theater.

These experiences of spectators recall what Stephen Halliwell describes as ecstasy, literally the state of being outside oneself: a state of "intense psychological absorption and transformation ... as experienced in direct encounter with song or poetry."[29] These spectators accepted or sought a supernatural explanation for what they saw in the theater. After all, audience members are taken out of themselves not only emotionally but also temporally. The theater or playhouse is, after all, a space of heterochrony.[30] That is, it is a place where one finds oneself in two time periods at one: that of the time of the production and that of the time of the story. The story often takes place in the past or takes place in a period of time that exceeds the actual duration of the play. In order to believe in the reality of the play being witnessed, one must disbelieve one's own time and place.

6. Gods Embody the Challenges of Dramatic Mimesis

Depicting the divine is problematic. The criticism of depictions of the Greek and Roman gods is nearly as old as their first extant portrayal in literature. Xenophanes, one of the preeminent philosophers of the archaic age, criticized Homer and Hesiod not only for attributing human follies and foibles to gods (see DK B11) but also for the way gods' bodies are considered in epic poetry:

ἀλλ' οἱ βροτοὶ δοκέουσι γεννᾶσθαι θεούς,
τὴν σφετέρην δ' ἐσθῆτα ἔχειν φωνήν τε δέμας τε.

But mortals suppose that gods are born and that they have their own clothes, voice, and form.

DK B14

In another fragment:

ἀλλ' εἰ χεῖρας ἔχον βόες <ἵπποι τ'> ἠὲ λέοντες
ἢ γράψαι χείρεσσι καὶ ἔργα τελεῖν ἅπερ ἄνδρες,
ἵπποι μέν θ' ἵπποισι βόες δέ τε βουσὶν ὁμοίας
καί <κε> θεῶν ἰδέας ἔγραφον καὶ σώματ' ἐποίουν
τοιαῦθ' οἷόν περ καὐτοὶ δέμας εἶχον ἕκαστοι.

But if cattle and horses and lions had hands, or could draw with hands and do the same things that men do, then horses would draw the forms of gods similar to horses, cattle similar to cattle, and they would make the bodies of gods just like their own forms.

DK B15

As in fragment B14 above, Xenophanes here focuses on the body, suggesting the folly of assuming that divine beings have the same physical features as human beings.

Xenophanes is critical of the epic poets' limited imagination about the forms of gods, but the dramatists confronted this and other obstacles. Not only are the classical tragedians and comedians a part of the intellectual milieu that followed philosophers such as Xenophanes, but also the range of special effects, or lack thereof, impeded the craft of spectacle that is an inherent part of theater. Dramatists could, of course, have constructed narratives that avoid depicting gods themselves onstage. We can imagine plays similar to Sophocles' *Antigone*, in which the human characters in the absence of gods onstage wage debates, with intermediary signs such as omens and auguries as evidence, over the conflicting, often inscrutable will of divine beings. After all, as Mary Zimmerman has remarked, the world of myth is characterized by "the irrational and the ambiguous."[31] Intriguing, though, the dramatists did choose to represent their gods onstage in the bodies of actors. This ongoing choice, lasting through the fifth and into the fourth century BCE, is even more striking given that Plato assumes the mantle of Xenophanes by criticizing the poets, especially the dramatists, for their representations of the gods.[32]

As we saw in the Introduction, scholars of classical antiquity have debated whether or not gods onstage are literary, artistic devices only or are thought to be embodiments of the gods of cult. Our own work builds upon those scholars who argue that the gods of the theater represent those of cult, even though they serve as useful metaphors for theatrical and literary difficulties. But it is precisely the difficulty in determining and depicting the nature of the gods that allows them to serve as vessels for the deep thinking of Aeschylus, Sophocles, Euripides, Aristophanes, and the other dramatists on the nature of their art and the problems of writing lines for gods and of playing their parts. We point to the famous Hymn to Zeus, whose beginning "Zeus, whoever he is" (Ζεὺς ὅστις ποτ' ἐστίν, *Agamemnon* 160) articulates how difficult it is to understand not only Zeus' will but also his nature. Yet within the same trilogy, Athena and Apollo claim to represent Zeus and his will onstage, though they are, we must remember, human actors speaking lines written by a man.

Euripides' plays are likewise, and infamously, full of doubt about the nature of the divine. One of the most explicit speeches casting doubt on the nature of divinity is found in Euripides' *Heracles*. Heracles, having just been deluded by Hera to kill his own wife and children, says:

> ἐγὼ δὲ τοὺς θεοὺς οὔτε λέκτρ᾽ ἃ μὴ θέμις
> στέργειν νομίζω δεσμά τ᾽ ἐξάπτειν χεροῖν
> οὔτ᾽ ἠξίωσα πώποτ᾽ οὔτε πείσομαι
> οὐδ᾽ ἄλλον ἄλλου δεσπότην πεφυκέναι.
> δεῖται γὰρ ὁ θεός, εἴπερ ἔστ᾽ ὀρθῶς θεός,
> οὐδενός· ἀοιδῶν οἵδε δύστηνοι λόγοι.

> I do not believe that the gods desire affairs irreverently and bind each other with their hands. Neither do I think, nor will I ever be persuaded, that any god is born master of another. For the god, if he is rightly a god, needs nothing. These are the wretched stories of poets.
>
> 1341–46

Passages such as this one helped create the tradition, dating back to antiquity itself, that Euripides was an atheist. As Mary Lefkowitz has shown, however, Euripides' works wrestle with the nature of divinity itself.[33] Skepticism is not atheism. Indeed, beyond the fallacy of attributing Heracles' sentiments to the poet, Heracles himself does not dispute the existence of the gods, only their nature. The poets have misunderstood the nature of the gods. A true god, according to Heracles, needs nothing. His peculiar reference to the gods' hands (χεροῖν, 1342), which recalls Xenophanes' criticism of Homer and Hesiod (cf. χεῖρας in DK B15), draws attention to and perhaps complicates the notion of divine bodies. Earlier in the play, however, gods do appear as Iris and the personified goddess Madness (*Lyssa*) drive Heracles to the mad state in which he slaughters his wife and children.

Though Euripides is aware of the problems of divine embodiment, he puts gods onstage nonetheless and challenges spectators to recognize these problems as implicit and explicit drivers of narrative conflict. Most famously, he does so in the metatheatrical tour de force *Bacchae*. When Pentheus questions Dionysus, whom the Theban king believes to be only a priest of a false god, on the god's appearance, Dionysus replies that he appeared as he wished (ὁποῖος ἤθελ᾽, 478). Pentheus then wonders about whether the god himself will appear to help his followers: "And where is he? He is not evident to my eyes" (καὶ ποῦ 'στιν; οὐ γὰρ φανερὸς ὄμμασίν γ᾽ ἐμοῖς, 501). Dionysus rebuts, "Beside me: and you, because you are impious yourself, do not see him" (παρ᾽ ἐμοί· σὺ δ᾽ ἀσεβὴς αὐτὸς ὢν οὐκ εἰσορᾷς, 502). After the god miraculously escapes from prison, Pentheus confronts him and continues to deny the divinity of Dionysus, but Dionysus enchants him into wanting to see the bacchants worshipping the god on the mountainside. Pentheus claims that he now sees Dionysus as a bull, and Dionysus replies "Now you see what you ought to see" (νῦν δ᾽ ὁρᾷς ἃ χρή σ᾽ ὁρᾶν, 924). Pentheus now is the only person in the theater who can see Dionysus in what seems to be his true form, though he still does not understand that the person before him is not a priest of the god but the god himself. Pentheus' difficulty, even refusal, to perceive Dionysus as Dionysus is the problem of theatrical mimesis writ large. Just as the gods claim their realness by demanding disbelief, so Euripides insists that audience members embrace the Dionysian nature of attending one of his plays. Their genuine experience of joy relies upon overlooking the disingenuous presentation that fuels that ecstasy of spectatorship.

While gods onstage demonstrate the work of mimesis, they also sometimes render visible how the challenges of mimetic performance are overcome, especially as a collaboration between performers and perceivers, between actors and audiences. Briefly consider, for example, how Christopher Marlowe's *Dido, Queen of Carthage* opens with the stage directions of "Jupiter dandling Ganymede upon his knee."[34] The play shows us the cooing and physical flirtation of these divine same-sex lovers before Venus bursts in to remind them of the plight of Aeneas. After what might seem like an unorthodox framing device, the plot shifts to the plight of human characters and of one of history's most famous pairs of heterosexual lovers. The two might seem worlds apart: immortal male lovers on Olympus, doomed heterosexual lovers in the Mediterranean. Yet attention to theatrical mimesis helps us see the kinship between the framing device and the main plot.

Suspension of disbelief allows us to see the human actors as gods, certainly. However, it is also such suspension that allows us to see Aeneas and Dido as a man and a woman in love. When the early modern playgoers watch the main action of the play, they both recall and forget that Aeneas and Dido are played by an adult man and a boy, displaying the very same erotic dynamic that we have seen the gods display. The convention of young men playing women on the Renaissance stage demanded a double-awareness: when heterosexual couples were portrayed, playgoers would see both a male/female pairing and also a male/male pairing. The presence of the gods here in Marlowe's play reminds playgoers of that double-work of mimetic representation of gender on the early modern stage. Seeing two male characters flirting with each other showcases the fact that the male/female couple on stage also presents two men flirting with each other. For us today, Marlowe's framing device also reminds us of the differing perceptions of gender between the earlier period and our own. As Stephen Orgel has shown, "the homosexual, and the particularly pederastic component of the Elizabethan erotic imagination is explicit and for the most part surprisingly unproblematic."[35] Marlowe pulls back the curtain, as it were, to show playgoers both the fluidity of gender on the stage and the fluidity of desire that the stage dramatized.

7. Gods Reveal the Humans Behind the Supernatural Effects

Though belief in the gods can stand in for the audience's requisite investment in the supernatural aura of the theater, the gods are sometimes used to draw attention to the human players who work to create the special effects that accompany dramatic presentation. As we have already seen, the *mechane*, the machine used to fly the gods onto the ancient stage, allows for a stunning visual effect, and its use is primarily reserved for the *deus ex machina*. Yet mortal characters do sometimes seize the stage device for themselves. In a twist of the traditional *ex machina* at the end of Euripides' *Medea*, the heroine reappears in a flying chariot over the other characters onstage, a visual that underscores Medea's association with her divine grandfather, Helios, and her own supernatural prowess in mixing potions. Human capture of this divine device could have the opposite effect, that is to underscore human frailty. In Euripides' *Bellerophon*, a play now only preserved in fragments, the hero flies off to the heavens on Pegasus before being bucked off after Zeus sends a horsefly to bite his winged steed. This mortal deployment of the *mechane* for Bellerophon's flight would have demonstrated his recklessness and the inherent folly in his mission.[36]

Though in the *Medea* and the *Bellerophon*, the mortals' use of the *mechane* are subtle reminders that human actors always substitute for gods in the theater, Aristophanes explicitly reminds us, also, that humans pull the levers of the *mechane* to render visually the gods' awesome power. In a memorable episode of a mortal seizing control of the *mechane* for himself, the protagonist of Aristophanes' *Peace*, Trygaeus, rides a dung-beetle to the heavens to confront Zeus. This comic flight explicitly parodies, in fact, the scene from Euripides' *Bellerophon*, with a less noble mount substituted for Pegasus. In a moment of metatheater reminiscent of the visible crane in Ninagawa's production of *Cymbeline*, which we discussed at the opening of our study, Trygaeus asks the machine operator (μηχανοποιέ, 174) to pay attention so that he has a smooth ride. This moment reveals that human beings operate the machine that produces the most impressive tableaux of divinity in drama.

Even when an actual god from antiquity appears at the end of the play, Shakespeare toys with our expectations that the deity might be needed to resolve a complicated plot. Hymen, the ancient Greek god of marriage ceremonies, appears onstage to perform four simultaneous marriages that bring closure to the comedy *As You Like It*. Yet while the god will deliver the rites of matrimony, it is a human character who devises the machinations that allow these marriages to occur. Rosalind, disguised as the youth Ganymede (and taking the name of one of Zeus' male consorts) has brought all of the lovers (including herself and her beloved Orlando) together and in turn has untwisted the plot strings to make this comedy end happily. Hymen seems to admit as much, when he states,

> Then is there mirth in heaven
> When earthly things made even
> Atone together.
>
> 5.4.90–92

Heaven seems but an audience to the mortal drama that has occurred in this play, which will reunite family members, mend relations between rival siblings, and align lovers into married couples. Even when Hymen suggests that he has brought Rosalind from heaven to reunite with her father and marry Orlando, the audience knows that this occurs because of a human-orchestrated plan.

Hymen even asks the Duke to join his daughter's hand to her beloved, suggesting there is no need for a divine entity to preside over this wedding:

> Good Duke, receive thy daughter;
> Hymen from Heaven brought her,
> Yea, brought her hither,
> That thou mightst join [her] hand with his
> Whose heart within his bosom is.
>
> 5.4.93–97

Hymen has come "from heaven," suggesting his status as a divine entity and also pointing to his status as part of the stage machinery (Fig. 1). Recall that, in Shakespeare's time, "heaven" referred to the scaffolds above the stage and "hell" referred to the area below the stage. In this moment, the god himself nods to the fact that he has been lowered by stage hands and that the stage crew is behind the scenes and able to observe the play. We know that Rosalind herself is the architect of this play's ending, bringing herself to this spot that she has chosen for the wedding.

Fig. 1 Ancient Hymen stands out among courtly humans who can solve their own problems in *As You Like It*. William Francis, "*As You Like It*: Hymen, Rosalind, Orlando, &c., Act V, Scene IV" (nineteenth century). Reproduced by permission of The Metropolitan Museum of Art, New York

If the plot complications have already been resolved by human characters, why has Hymen arrived at the very end of this play?[37]

Hymen, we suggest, is there for another purpose, then. Not to resolve the plot but to render visible the metatheatricality of the scene. A broad-strokes gloss of the play would seem to suggest a comedy dedicated to the power of marriage and a final scene honoring Hymen's ability to solemnize such unions. In Stephen Gosson's 1582 attack on the theater, he asserts, "Stage plays [...] were consecrated to the honour of heathen gods, therefore consecrated to idolatry."[38] We might easily dismiss Gosson's accusation by countering that to present a classical god onstage does not necessarily lead to the worship of pagan gods. However, the controversy casts light on the dynamics of the stage. Kendall L. Watson remarks that, "imaginings are made more vivid by the *presence* of the actors."[39] So to show a classical god is to do more than simply allude to one. A viewer of a play where a deity is staged may not believe in that deity, but certainly the viewer becomes more aware of their imagination being at work.

The five lines quoted just above contain a common change or *emendation* made by modern editors of Shakespeare's play. Consider how the lines appear in the first printed collection of Shakespeare's work:

> Good Duke receive thy daughter,
> Hymen from Heaven brought her,
> Yea brought her hither,
> That thou mightst join *his* hand with his,
> Whose heart within his bosom is.
>
> 5.4.101–5[40]

As the italics emphasize above, the original text reads "his hand with his." Noting that the folio text is almost universally emended to render the line "her hand in his," Jeffrey Masten urges readers not to "exclude too quickly the possibility of two male hands joined in the last scene of a play that repeatedly directs attention to the boy actor playing Rosalind, has emphasized the choice of the homoerotically charged name 'Ganymede,' [and] has that character invoke Jove/Jupiter several times in the course of the play."[41] For Masten, this detail in the original text highlights what has been occurring throughout the play. The audience has been invited to simultaneously see two men courting each other onstage, both as the youth Ganymede teaches Orlando about love and as two male actors woo each other onstage. To add yet a third level, the audience has witnessed Rosalind and Orlando, a woman and a man, courting each other onstage. Hymen arrives at the end of the play not only to resolve a complex plot in fact already resolved by the humans. He also, through the gendered language in the original text, pronounces for the audience the male-male pairing they have already seen within the heterosexual romance at the very center of this plot. Hymen appears elsewhere on the Renaissance stage, notably in Ben Jonson's *Hymenaei* (1606). The god appears onstage to join together eight male masquers and eight female masquers, who at one point form the initials of the bride and groom being honored with the performance of the masque. We will see this dynamic of intermingled solemnization in the discussion of masques in Chapter 3.[42]

8. Gods Embody the Potential for the Immortality of Art

Within the drama, the divine characters have the quality that distinguished gods from mortals in ancient thought: immortality. In their art, the poets often think of reputation as a substitute for immortality and poetry as a vessel for creating immortality, not only for the subject of the poetry but the poet himself or herself. Sappho's "someone else, I say, will remember us" (μνάσεσθαί τινά φαιμι † καὶ ἕτερον † ἀμμέων, fr. 147) implicitly reminds us that her poetry is the only reason that the "us" of the poem will be remembered in the future. Horace makes the sentiment more explicit in the final poem of his third book of odes. He boasts, "I have completed a monument more lasting than bronze" (*exegi monumentum aere perennius*, 3.30.1), contrasting the materiality of a bronze statue with the written word. His poetic achievement, he thinks—rightly, so far—will lead to his own quasi-immortality: "I will not die entirely" (*non omnis moriar*, 3.30.6).

Yet the performance context of both ancient drama and early modern drama contains a tension between the immortality of the divine characters and the ephemerality of production. In antiquity, as far as we can tell, plays were composed primarily for a single production in a single location, but the plays often have their eyes on the future, even the distant future, via the gods. In Aeschylus' *Eumenides*, the final play of his *Oresteia*, as we shall see in Chapter 4, Athena urges a continuity of legal practices from the play's setting (bronze age Athens) into the future. Such statements are common in the *deus ex machina* at the end of the play. In Euripides' *Ion*, for example, Athena, *ex machina*, resolves the tension of identity that has built throughout the narrative and also looks beyond the temporal limitations of the play. She tells Ion's mother Creusa to take him to Athens and place him on the throne of the goddess's city (1571–74). "He will be famous," Athena says, "throughout Greece" (ἔσται δ' ἀν' Ἑλλάδ' εὐκλεής, 1575). She even predicts the rise of Athenian hegemony throughout the Aegean on islands and the coasts throughout Europe and Asia. This temporal disruption—the bronze age past of the characters and the audience's own present—lends legitimacy to Athena's claims. In Euripides' *Hippolytus*, the link between mortal immortality via memory is explicitly tied to poetry. On the cusp of death, the goddess Artemis tells Hippolytus that she will establish the greatest honor (τιμὰς μεγίστας, 1424) to Hippolytus in the form of a ritual in which unwed girls will offer their shorn hair to Hippolytus, and he will be the subject of their song (ἀεὶ δὲ μουσοποιὸς ἐς σὲ παρθένων / ἔσται μέριμνα, 1428–29). Despite the play produced ostensibly for a particular moment, the dramatists, via their gods, ponder the potential perpetuity afforded by poetry.

Some of the appearances detailed in this chapter may look like straightforward *deus ex machina*, but they often underscore the capability of humans to be poets and to be makers. In what might seem like a *deus ex machina*, Diana—to whom characters have been appealing throughout the play—appears in a vision to the titular character of Shakespeare's *Pericles*. Before she vanishes, she declares,

> My temple stands in Ephesus. Hie thee thither,
> And do upon mine altar sacrifice.
> There, when my maiden priests are met together
> [...
> ...] before the people all,
> Reveal how thou at sea didst lose thy wife.
> To mourn thy crosses, with thy daughter's, call
> And give them repetition to the life.
> Perform my bidding, or thou liv'st in woe;
> Do't, and be happy, by my silver bow.
> Awake, and tell thy dream.
>
> 5.1.227–37

Pericles inherits from this god what Walter Benjamin describes as "the incomparable aura about the storyteller."[43] The gift of resurrection is inherently tied to the theater here as Pericles' wife, missing and presumed dead, will be reunited with him here at the altar of Diana. The promised scenes, with its actors ("maiden priests are met together") and audience, speaks to the power of the theater and the instigation of the drama relies on Pericles' re-telling of his vision. Richard McCoy observes that "Even with *deus ex machina* descents in *Pericles* and *Cymbeline*, the happy ending depends less on gifts from gods than on merely human virtues of fidelity, forgiveness, and good fortune."[44] Just as in the case of Rosalind in *As You Like It* above, it feels as if mortal humans have seized the power of art-making from the gods. We will encounter such a situation in much more detail with *Hamlet* in Chapter 4. As we will see, the arrival of these gods at the end of the play will have strong resonances for an analysis of metatheatricality.

We offer these contentions as starting points, as hypotheses, and as models. Not all operate in all case studies. Some work in tandem. Some oppose each other. Sometimes those that oppose each other work in tandem. These contentions have begun to model how we have come to think about gods onstage in classical antiquity and in the early modern period. As the book progresses, we will see these come to life as the theater welcomes its divine guests.

2

Under the Actor's Spell: Audiences in Euripides' *Helen* and Marlowe's *Doctor Faustus*

In the now-classic 1971 ballad "If," written by David Gates of Bread, the singer pines, "If a picture paints a thousand words, then why can't I paint you? / [...] / If a face could launch a thousand ships, then where am I to go?"[1] In its casual reference to the Greek armada's pursuit of Helen, the song not only adapts a haunting description of Helen that can be traced back to Lucian (*Dialogues of the Dead* 5.2) but also engages an expansive tradition regarding the disorienting effect of her beauty. The song finds another curious antecedent in classical antiquity, albeit one unlikely to be known by Gates. According to Cicero (*De Inventione* 2.1), when the renowned figural painter Zeuxis sought to include Helen among a set of paintings commissioned by the citizens of Croton about 410 BCE, he combined the attributes of the five most beautiful maidens of the city (*ex istis virginibus formosissimas*), believing that no single body had all the qualities he sought for his representation of beauty (*ad venustatem*). Aelian (*Historical Miscellany* 14.47) records the reaction of Zeuxis' younger colleague Nicomachus, whom this masterpiece rendered stunned (ἐξεπλήττετο) and astonished (τεθηπώς).[2] Together, these two anecdotes reveal the dynamics of rendering Helen's beauty visually as well as the effect that supernatural beauty has on those who see her. Indeed, it is the disbelief generated by gazing upon her that secures her nonpareil status. This chapter explores those dynamics of Helen's appearance which, since antiquity, has challenged poets, dramatists, and artists as well as those who witness even an approximation of her appearance.

Embodying Helen's beauty is an especially acute challenge onstage, as the mere presence of Helen in the theater attenuates claims about her unrivaled appearance. How can any single actor convincingly portray a woman whose stunning appearance is tantamount to no other. Taking as its primary case studies Euripides' *Helen* and Marlowe's *Doctor Faustus*, this chapter argues that both plays use Helen's incredible beauty as a focal point for exploring theater's power to render the impossible possible.[3] Both *Helen* and *Doctor Faustus* draw attention to theater's power over audiences when Helen's appearance, despite its uniqueness, does not suffice as confirmation of her identity even within the dramatic fiction. The profound metatheatricality of both plays then invites their audiences to understand the phenomenological challenge of theatrical mimesis *vis-à-vis* the characters seeing Helen onstage. In other words, Euripides and Marlowe use Helen to explore the power of theatrical mimesis writ large: why does the audience accept the facade of an actor embodying another person?

Though some scholars have explained audiences' perceptual investment in the dramatic illusion with reference to the deceptive skills of actors or the inexperience of spectators, this chapter argues that these two dramatists, through the figure of Helen, equate the power of drama with the supernatural.[4] We shall first examine Helen's association with mimesis and divinity in Homer, and after tracing the reception of this association in several works of archaic and early classical literature and art, we explore its manifestation in Euripides' *Helen*. Throughout this play, Euripides links the titular heroine's beauty with divinity, and other characters' reactions to her appearance provide various models of spectatorship, the success of which depends on accepting Helen, despite the sheer implausibility, as Helen. We then turn to Helen on the stage in early modern England. Marlowe's *Doctor Faustus* introduces its Helen as a demonic figure that engenders doubt but also promises a singular experience of represented desirability. The argument builds upon Pat Easterling's interpretation of the roles of gods onstage, whose presence invited "awareness on the part of the audience of the creative power of the dramatic medium."[5] This chapter argues that in these two dramatists' exploration of mimetic effect, actors hold an inscrutable power over spectators akin to witnessing the supernatural.

Before we begin, a caveat. Some readers will raise reasonable objections to the inclusion of the mortal Helen in a book on gods. Though Helen is not a goddess in either of these plays, as we will see, Euripides does associate her form with divine creation, and he nods to her divinity in the play's concluding *deus ex machina*, performed by her divine brother Castor, who says that after her death she "will be called a goddess" (θεὸς κεκλήσῃ, 1667). What our dramatists seem to find so wonderfully useful about her persona is precisely her intersecting supernatural characteristics (her immaculate beauty from her divine lineage) and mortal identity. The figure of Heracles, with his mortal and divine qualities, offers a mythological parallel. Michael Silk has described Heracles as a figure who "lies on the margins between human and divine; he occupies the no-man's-land that is also no-god's-land; he is a marginal, transitional or, better, *interstitial* figure."[6] The same could be said of Helen. Euripides and Marlowe bring Helen's interstices to the fore to underscore the creative power of drama, the product of mortals, to stun and to astonish audiences in ways typical of divine epiphany.[7]

Helen, Mimesis, and Divinity in Archaic and Early Classical Imaginations

In her first appearance in extant literature, Helen weaves a robe, depicting in its fabric the contests of the Trojan War, the very war of which she is the ostensible cause (*Il.* 3.121–28). This tableau, the subject of the *Iliad* itself, prefigures her depiction as a metapoetic figure aware of her own place in the mythological tradition.[8] The *Odyssey* depicts her as a performer. When Telemachus visits Menelaus and Helen in Sparta, Menelaus tells the story of his wife's attempted betrayal of the Greeks hiding in the Trojan horse (*Od.* 4.235–89). Helen, Menelaus says, "mimicked the voices [of the infiltrators'] wives" (φωνὴν ἴσκουσ' ἀλόχοισιν, 4.279), and her virtuoso performance so moved the Greeks that they would have cried out and thus foiled the ruse of the Trojan horse had Odysseus not restrained them. Although typically it is Helen's appearance that proves so dangerous to irrational men, in this moment it is via her voice that her destructive allure penetrates the wooden frame of the horse. Yet, unlike her appearance, Helen's voice *per se* does not move the Greek men; rather, the manipulation or the modulation of her voice to mimic the sound of other women, an act which a scholiast describes as mimesis (ἡ τῶν φωνῶν μίμησις), endangers them.[9]

Despite this potential danger, the power of Helen's voice to stir her audience and to evoke poignant memories nods towards the mimetic representations of speech in epic poetry. Because the success of the bard's own performance depends on the audience's accepting his voice as that of Menelaus, Telemachus, Helen herself, and all the other characters who speak in his poems, this episode charges verbal mimesis with Helen's own erotic charm. As Froma Zeitlin has noted, "Helen is the figure who [...] links *eros* and poetics together under the rubric of mimesis."[10] Helen's performance stirred in the men such a powerful desire to be reunited with their wives left in Greece that they do not consider the sheer impossibility of their wives' presence in Troy. Thus by linking *eros* with Helen's mimetic powers, the scene also nods to the irrational requisite of accepting mimesis as reality lest mimesis have no effect. Without the audience's imaginative investment in the impossible, mimesis loses its power.

While Helen's efficaciousness depends on seduction, the episode also links her verbal performance to divine inspiration. Menelaus supposes that Helen "must have come under the compulsion of some 'divine spirit' (δαίμων), wishing to grant glory to the Trojans" (*Od.* 4.274–75), and Pallas Athena intervened to drive her away (4.289). Helen's divinely-inspired (or compelled) performance recalls not only the numerous times throughout the epics and Greek literature in general that gods change their appearances to deceive mortals but also, once again, Homer's own divinely-inspired song with its polyphony of voices. Thus through the figure of Helen, whose ability to drive men to an irrational acceptance of the impossible, Homer gestures toward but does not completely resolve the mysterious power of mimesis.[11]

This web of associations—Helen, beauty, persuasion, irrationality, divinity—inspired subsequent artists exploring the power of their own media. In Sappho's poem on beauty and the power of *eros* (fr. 16), Helen is no longer a potentially dangerous figure and instead becomes a positive exemplum of love's effect on mortals, and a number of metapoetic readings of this poem, among others in her corpus, have enriched understandings of Sapphic poesis.[12] Gorgias also seizes upon Helen as a figure for explaining the power of persuasion in his *Encomium of Helen*. This rhetorical tour de force parries arguments that were undoubtedly used against Helen and wields them in her defense. Though ostensibly his speech exculpates Helen of blame for the Trojan War, Gorgias' primary interest is persuasion. He uses Helen, whose "beauty rivals the gods" (τὸ ἰσόθεον κάλλος, 4), as a focal point for his theorization of the power of speech (*logos*) and sight (*opsis*) on the soul, both of which are associated with irrationality and divine enchantment.[13]

Particularly germane to our discussion of seeing Helen onstage is a series of vases depicting the recovery of Helen from Troy by Menelaus. One example (Fig. 2) depicts Menelaus, on the right, intending to kill his wife, just to his left, but he fumbles his sword upon seeing her. Aphrodite, standing behind Helen, symbolizes the disarming effect of his wife's appearance. The composition of the scene throws into stark relief a significant change that the second vase-painter has made in the iconography of the reunion. This other vase (Fig. 3) represents seeing Helen's beauty as supernatural by depicting Aphrodite standing between husband and wife. In depicting the reunion of her and Menelaus after the Trojan War, the vase-painter has captured the striking power of Helen's appearance on her husband. Menelaus, intending to stab his wife, charges in her direction, but his sword has slipped from his grasp. This scene is popular in visual art, and the iconography of the scene is standard across several vases: Menelaus, mid-stride, drops his sword before he can stop his charge.[14] Menelaus' momentum conveys the sudden and unexpected effect that Helen has on one who sees her. The

Fig. 2 Attic skyphos, *c.* 490 BCE. Boston. 13.186. Museum of Fine Arts.

Fig. 3 Red-figure oenochoe, *c.* 430–420 BCE. Vatican. 16535. Museo Gregoriano Etrusco.

presence of Aphrodite between the couple on the vase cleverly signifies the sensuality of Helen, the couple's erotic bond, and the husband's fond memories of his wife that overcome him even after ten years of war on her behalf—the power of which is all personified by Aphrodite. By framing the scene so that as Menelaus looks upon Helen, he also sees the goddess Aphrodite, the painter has rendered Helen's beauty as supernatural and has equated the effect of seeing her beauty to witnessing the epiphany of a god.

Supernatural Spectacle in Euripides' *Helen*

These evocative associations that are found in archaic and classical literature and art had a natural appeal to Euripides, whose penchant for exploring the nature of mimesis and theatrical illusion in his dramas has been notorious since antiquity and well-studied.[15] Unlike the depiction of Helen in *Trojan Women*, however, *Helen* draws attention to the titular heroine's associations with mimesis and poetics as part of the play's engagement with questions of theatrical illusion and the epistemological challenges presented by a mythological tradition that is, by definition, protean.

Skepticism—about the gods, appearances, and reality itself—pervades the play and is a conspicuous feature of the Euripidean corpus, which, as Donald Mastronarde notes, has the tendency to "dramatize crises of interpretation, faith, and intelligibility."[16] Froma Zeitlin reminds us that "The emphasis in theater must inevitably fall upon the body,"[17] and in the *Helen*, Helen's appearance and skepticism about her identity draw attention to the fine veneer of theatrical illusion. Euripides has drawn on the long tradition of Helen as an enigmatic and metapoetic figure but has repurposed this tradition to explore dramatic illusion and his audience's perceptual investment in it. For theater to be effective, spectators must willingly accept the implausible and allow appearances to drive them from rational thought. Spectatorship in the *Helen* is compared to witnessing the supernatural.[18]

Even at the most fundamental level of the plot, Euripides' *Helen* engages traditional representations of Helen by depicting an alternative version of her character. While in the most common, Homeric version of the myth, Helen is taken to Troy by Paris, Euripides reimagines the origins of the Trojan War and claims that Helen spent the war in Egypt while a copy, an eidolon, of her goes to Troy in her stead. The eidolon, however, still affects Helen's reputation, as she must confront from afar slander against her on account of the eidolon. Though Euripides was not the inventor of this plot device, he cleverly deploys the artificial Helen to draw attention to the artificiality of myth.[19]

Yet our focus here is not so much the well-explored plasticity of mythology but on Helen and her eidolon as embodiments of the artificial doubling and duplicitousness that theatrical mimesis requires. The prologue introduces a number of concepts that will occupy Euripides' attention throughout the play, including, as Eric Downing has shown, the dimensions of deception that are central to the crafting of fictional drama.[20] Helen delivers a prologue that disorients the audience spatially and mythologically. Her very first word "Nile"

(Νείλου), which will serve to localize the play to Egypt, focuses the audience's attention on a location not commonly associated with the titular heroine. Before even hinting at her identity in the sixteenth line of the prologue, she first describes the setting of Egypt and the lineage of its ruling family. She does presently reveal her own identity and lineage, with an abrupt and emphatic shift to herself ("as for me," ἡμῖν, 16), and the bizarre circumstances of Helen's birth establish her as an apt figure for exploring the deception that is a quintessential aspect of the theater:

> ἔστιν δὲ δὴ
> λόγος τις ὡς Ζεὺς μητέρ' ἔπτατ' εἰς ἐμὴν
> Λήδαν κύκνου μορφώματ' ὄρνιθος λαβών,
> ὃς δόλιον εὐνὴν ἐξέπραξ' ὑπ' αἰετοῦ
> δίωγμα φεύγων, εἰ σαφὴς οὗτος λόγος·
> Ἑλένη δ' ἐκλήθην.
>
> There is some story that Zeus, taking the form of a swan, flew after my mother, and he, fleeing the pursuit of an eagle, achieved a deceitful bedding, if this story is accurate. My name is Helen.
>
> *Helen* 17–22

She doles out information piecemeal and tarries momentarily on her parentage before finally revealing her name. And just as the prologue establishes major themes of the drama, so Helen's mythological beginnings reveal her to be an appropriate persona for exploring the nature of dramatic mimesis. In particular, her origins in Zeus' metamorphosis (μορφώματα) and tricking (δόλιον) of Leda introduce the themes of deception and disguise that will underlie Euripides' exploration of theater's artifice through the figure of Helen.[21] She is a child of Zeus' protean nature.

Helen's skepticism about her origins only draws attention to and magnifies the inherent challenge of theatrical mimesis, which, like Helen herself, is the product of deception. Her dismissal of traditional mythological accounts as "some story" (λόγος τις) of questionable authenticity—"if this story is true" (εἰ σαφὴς οὗτος λόγος), she says—contributes to the prologue's whirl of disorientation and obfuscates the truth from the audience. Her criticism of the myth of her birth is founded upon notions of realism that are absent from the accounts, and she will again criticize accounts of her birth from an egg as unrealistic when she reminds the Chorus that "neither Greek nor foreign women produce a white vessel for chicks" (γυνὴ γὰρ οὔθ' Ἑλληνὶς οὔτε βάρβαρος / τεῦχος νεοσσῶν λευκὸν ἐκλοχεύεται, 257–58).[22] Though, despite her protests, this myth is never discredited in the play, her mythological skepticism is projected onto herself and the present production when she hesitantly claims not to be Helen, only to be called Helen (Ἑλένη δ' ἐκλήθην, 22). With Helen's hedging language, she focuses questions of reputation as well as the problem of ontology on herself.

The ontological issues of the play and the artificiality of this Helen are underscored by the eidolon, which, like Helen herself, is a product of divine machinations. Friedrich Solmsen's important study of the play reveals Euripides' interest in perception and cognition at the textual level, and Karen Bassi has considered how the eidolon reproduces the perceptual challenges of theatrical production itself.[23] Coined from *eidos* (appearance), the word "eidolon" signifies the visual deception of the phantom, who is a kind of actor, assuming the appearance of Helen, pretending to be her, and fooling all of the Greeks and the Trojans.

Yet, as in the Homeric episode of Helen at the Trojan horse, mimesis is once again associated with divinity. Made by Hera "from the heavens" (οὐρανοῦ, 34),[24] the eidolon is also the product of a divine trick. The gods' interventions in human affairs continue as Hermes took Helen—the real Helen—from Sparta, and he placed her "in the folds of the aether" (ἐν πτυχαῖσιν αἰθέρος, 44) and enveloped her in a "cloud" (νεφέλῃ, 45).[25] This description of Helen's abduction echoes that of the eidolon's creation from the heavens (cf. οὐρανοῦ, 34; αἰθήρ, ὅθεν σὺ θεοπόνητ' ἔχεις λέχη, 584).

By associating Helen and the eidolon in this way, Euripides uses the prologue both to introduce illusion as a significant theme of his drama and, importantly for our present purposes, to reveal the role of divinities in the successful fruition of illusion. The deception in the mythological narrative and the theatrical illusion are collapsed when Helen says that Paris "thinks he holds me, a hollow belief, though he does not" (καὶ δοκεῖ μ' ἔχειν, / κενὴν δόκησιν, οὐκ ἔχων, 35–36). The grammar of the sentence presents a ruse of its own to equate the eidolon's artifice with Helen herself. In the accusative case, κενὴν δόκησιν ("hollow belief") must be an internal accusative; as Allan says, "imagining the 'empty' result of Paris' imagining (δοκεῖ)."[26] But the accusative could also stand in apposition to the accusative με, and so Helen herself becomes, although only momentarily, a "hollow belief."

In these ways, the prologue gestures towards Euripides' interest in exploring the audience's investment in the dramatic illusion, a requisite of the theatrical experience.[27] Even the real Helen is manifestly not the most beautiful woman standing alongside the Nile but a male actor wearing a mask in the Theater of Dionysus in Athens. Crucial for Euripides' engagement with the nature of theatrical illusion are two scenes, the first featuring Teucer's failure to recognize

Helen and the second the successful recognition of Helen and Menelaus. In this first scene, Teucer contributes to the sympathetic portrayal of Helen as it underscores the suffering that she and her family and all of the Greeks have endured because of the eidolon. The scene also prefigures the recognition scene between Helen and Menelaus. Teucer seems to recognize Helen by her appearance, but because he believes that Helen was at Troy and not in Egypt, he does not accept her as Helen (71–77).

The later scene with Menelaus, in which the king sees the real Helen for the first time, models a theory of spectatorship as, like the audience, Menelaus is presented with a novel Helen whose unrivaled beauty has apparently been replicated. When Menelaus washes up on the shores of Egypt and first encounters his wife, neither recognizes the other. Helen, believing that this man will abduct her, seeks refuge from him at the tomb of the former Egyptian king. Her flight and his pursuit restage the myth seen on the vase-paintings noted above that depict their reunion, a myth that serves as a palimpsest for Euripides' new variant. As in the traditional reunion, Menelaus is struck by her appearance: "You revealed your appearance, and how you render me stunned and speechless!" (ὡς δέμας δείξασα σὸν / ἔκπληξιν ἡμῖν ἀφασίαν τε προστίθης, 548–49). Echoing the stunning effect of Zeuxis' Helen on Nicomachus (cf. ἐξεπλήττετο, Aelian *Historical Miscellany* 14.47), Menelaus' language reveals the startling impact (ἔκπληξιν) both of Helen's beauty and of recognition.[28] Yet despite this initial twinge of recognition, Menelaus notes only the resemblance of her appearance (ὄψιν σήν, 557) to that of his wife: "I have never seen a form more similar" (οὐπώποτ' εἶδον προσφερέστερον δέμας, 559). Even the language of the scene produces an ironic doubling of Helen's identity. When Menelaus says, "I see that you are very similar indeed to Helen, woman" (Ἑλένῃ σ' ὁμοίαν δὴ μάλιστ' εἶδον, γύναι, 563), because the Greek word *gyne* has two common meanings, he addresses her not only as "woman" but also as "wife." For her part, though Helen initially echoes his skepticism (ἐγὼ δὲ Μενέλεῳ γε σ'·, 564), she presently accepts the man as her husband (566).

Menelaus' skepticism and ultimate recognition draw new attention to the fallibility of human experience to discern reality from fiction. Because Menelaus has left the eidolon of Helen at the site of his shipwreck, he refuses to accept Helen as his wife. Instead, Menelaus believes that he may be seeing a ghost (φάσμα, cf. 569) sent by the goddess Hekate or that his eyes are sick (cf. νοσεῖ, 575; νοσοῦμεν, 581). Menelaus' stunned reaction to the seemingly impossible presence of his wife dramatizes the vase-painting's rendering of Helen's beauty through the symbolic epiphany of Aphrodite. Menelaus speaks of Helen's presence as if it were the epiphany of a chthonic demon or an illness, but Helen insists that her appearance alone should satisfy her husband's skepticism: "Look at me. What clearer proof do you need?" (σκέψαι· τί σοι δεῖ πίστεως σαφεστέρας, 578). Menelaus protests that his experiences at Troy are the most reliable witness to the truth, and while Helen is technically correct, one cannot overlook the irony that Helen, whose reputation has been shattered by a doppelgänger, urges her husband to rely exclusively on his sense of sight.

The lengthy and difficult resolution of this epistemological impasse indicates how the supernatural troubles recognition. At the beginning of the scene, Helen explicitly ties the gods to recognition: "Oh gods—it is divine also to recognize loved ones" (ὦ θεοί· θεὸς γὰρ καὶ τὸ γιγνώσκειν φίλους, 560). The act of recognition itself is a divinity while simultaneously linked to what it means to be human. Though Helen yields, Menelaus does not. The gods, then, intervene with the miraculous disappearance of the eidolon, which a messenger arrives to report, and thereby bring to a close the unresolvable tension between Menelaus' experiential epistemology and Helen's position, ultimately untenable given the circumstances, that the senses are the ultimate arbiter of reality. The messenger reports that the eidolon has vanished into the heavens and that, while departing, she reveals herself to be a false Helen crafted by Hera. The messenger, so exasperated by the events, has yet to notice Helen until he finishes his report of the eidolon's disappearance, and he says:

ὦ χαῖρε, Λήδας θύγατερ, ἐνθάδ᾽ ἦσθ᾽ ἄρα.
ἐγὼ δέ σ᾽ ἄστρων ὡς βεβηκυῖαν μυχοὺς
ἤγγελλον εἰδὼς οὐδὲν ὡς ὑπόπτερον
δέμας φοροίης

Greetings, daughter of Leda. So there you are. I was announcing that you had entered the recesses of the stars, and did not know that you have a winged body.
616–19

The humor of the messenger's words resolves the tension that had crescendoed throughout the scene. The ease with which he accepts Helen as Helen, even in this wildly impossible scenario, contrasts starkly with Menelaus' belabored questioning and extreme skepticism.

Afterwards, however, Menelaus accepts the messenger's report as confirmation of Helen's story and immediately recognizes her as his wife, and Menelaus' immediate acceptance of the messenger's report and sudden change of heart speaks to those conditions necessary for drama's mimetic effect to persuade.

Suspension of disbelief relies not only on appearance and character but also on a co-spectator whose own acceptance of the illusion lulls one into accepting it for oneself (mutually reinforcing the acceptance of one's neighbor in the theater). The messenger, in fact, recedes into the background of the action for nearly 80 lines and watches from onstage the reunion of husband and wife. When he finally re-enters the conversation, Menelaus readily admits that they all were deceived by the gods (πρὸς θεῶν δ' ἦμεν ἠπατημένοι, 704).

The *Helen* thus speaks to the gods' power to manipulate reality and fabricate it, so to speak. The senses of human beings are impotent tools for seeing through the gods' machinations. Yet *Helen* has repurposed the figure of Helen, the powerful and bewildering emotions she stirs, and her association with mimesis, poetics, art, and deception so that she, not the gods, serves as the focal point for exploring theatrical audiences' willingness to be persuaded by dramatic illusion. Menelaus is wary of Helen's identity, but the ease with which he first denies and then accepts Helen's true identity highlights that the dramatic illusion is fragile yet requires spectators' ready belief. The illusion cannot be created or maintained through rational processes but is akin to witnessing the inscrutable powers of the divine.[29] Helen thus prefigures in subtle ways the Dionysus of Euripides' *Bacchae*, a play in which, as Dobrov has argued, Dionysus-inspired delusions of madness provide a "broad foundation for Euripides' metadramatic construction."[30] Even the role of *eros* in mimesis resurfaces in Dionysus' enchanting Pentheus to desire to spectate the Bacchic revelries of the women on the mountain.[31] Helen provides an especially compelling figure for the Euripidean conception of drama because her mortality coupled with supernatural beauty proves a productive bridge between accepting the epiphany of gods in the theater and actors playing mortal roles.[32]

Helen on the Renaissance Stage

Helen proved a powerful figure for poets and playwrights of the English Renaissance, and they appear to wrestle with similar complexities involved in considering how to portray her as well as the nature of her status as a human who has been doubled as a divinely wrought eidolon.[33] In some ways, the early modern English theater involved similar dynamics of suspension-of-disbelief to what we find in theaters of antiquity. Helen would have been played by a male actor, and her status as a universally desired woman would have required projection of these qualities upon the actor. Yet the early modern theater presented significant differences. For example, actors rarely wore masks. Further, Helen's paradigmatic beauty derived from her ties through parentage to a god in whom the English Protestant audience did not believe. The reception of her figure in Christopher Marlowe's sixteenth-century play *Doctor Faustus* offers a rich case study for exploring early modern notions about Helen's particular ability to compel audiences both because the figure plays a memorable role in the narrative and because the narrative itself stages a series of spectacles for its titular character.

In Marlowe's drama, Faustus summons the demon Mephistopheles and demands that he perform a series of magical spells during a twenty-four-year period in exchange for the University of Wittenberg scholar's soul. One of these spells seems to summon Helen from the past. Immediately upon seeing her, though, Faustus declares, "Was this the face that launched a thousand ships / And burnt the topless towers of Ilium?" (5.1.90–91).[34] This often-quoted line is simultaneously an expression of wonder and also a question that any viewer of Helen onstage might ask. It not only expresses disbelief as Faustus wonders if the magic has succeeded, but it also might voice a kind of disappointment when he beholds the legendary beauty. In this instance, Faustus asks the question that audiences ask of all characters onstage when, as Bert O. States puts it, "the actor invites the audience to look through him at someone else."[35] As shown above, Helen offers a particularly charged case study for the problem of whether a figure onstage should be considered *real*. The operations in the early modern play parallel those discussed above in Euripides' *Helen*, where "Helen and her *eidolon* are the twin signifiers of the disavowal of the absent body as a necessary condition of dramatic performance."[36] That is, Marlowe presents Doctor Faustus with a Helen who might be a demon or might be the actual woman. This point in the drama invites exploration of the function of audience reception in generating suspension of disbelief.

Faustus' question above seems to suggest that as soon as he encounters the figure—staged before him by a deceptive Mephistopheles and representing a kind of Platonic ideal of beauty—he doubts, as does Euripides' Menelaus, what he perceives. Yet the reaction suggests that he is preparing to accept the impossible as fact. The notion that Troy possessed "topless towers" suggests the city itself was unimaginable and thus to be stunned by the impossible might be proof of the reality of the spectacle encountered. One might argue that any encounter with an actor playing a historical figure commences with disbelief, and Marlowe's play dramatizes this when the early modern Faustus looks upon the supposedly classical Helen. Indeed, the inability to confirm Helen upon sight points to a dilemma faced by adaptors and directors of the play. Modern stage performances have used a variety of strategies to portray Helen's beauty—ranging from shrouding the actress in a black veil to allow the audience to project its fantasies upon her or presenting an actor in a demon's mask to suggest Faustus' own gullibility.[37] He suspends disbelief, as the audience does, yet for him to not see Helen as leading him towards damnation has much more grave consequences.

Writers contemporaneous to Marlowe also asserted that believing in Helen's status as extremely beautiful relied on suspension of disbelief. John Lyly's *Euphues* (1578) describes Helen as having a scar on her chin.[38] The detail suggests that her extreme beauty is simply a fantasy of the spectator who gazes upon her. However, Lyly suggests that acknowledging such a disconnect between appearance and the notion of Helen is necessary for her desirability. A perfect appearance would simply not drive the same levels of attraction as the imperfect one. The poet explains that "in all perfect shapes, a blemish brings rather a liking every way to the eyes, than a loathing any way to the mind."[39] Within the calculus of Lyly's formulation, perhaps we can imagine how an actor who is clearly not Helen would be the most accurate. Arthur Golding's 1567 translation of Ovid's *Metamorphoses* has her weeping "when she saw her aged wrinkles in / A glass".[40] That is, even Helen realizes that she is not the "Helen" of epic. Or, put another way, any notion of a perfect Helen from antiquity may carry a sense of being inadequate.[41]

Renaissance writers embraced diverse strategies to make sense of how they might depict the classical past in poetry and drama. Religious discourses of classical antiquity—which Christian writers in early modern England framed as myths derived from pagan society—influenced the literature and culture of Renaissance England. Myths frequently were translated or adapted by Renaissance writers, who seized upon them as powerful source material and as a shared conceptual language among readers. As we observed in the introduction, these early modern writers embraced a variety of strategies to overcome the problem of depicting the pagan supernatural for Christian readers and audiences. Christian apologists portrayed the tales as allegories or early iterations of Biblical stories; mythographers positioned them as fables with deeper meanings and described gods as personifications; and, most importantly for the present chapter, poets and playwrights most commonly located stories about these gods in ancient settings. Circumscribing pagan gods within the ancient world reinforced an absolute temporal divide between the culture that believed in their divinity and the culture that revived their stories to instruct and to entertain. This allows for a play such as Shakespeare's *The Winter's Tale,* for example, to depict Apollo as divine and to stage a scene in which a statue comes to life in a nod to the stories of both *Alcestis* and *Pygmalion*. The magic in *The Winter's Tale* doubles for the magic of theater as the audience remains unsure if the statue truly comes to life. Marlowe's *Doctor Faustus* follows some of the same logic in its contemplation of metatheatricality—the audience is not as sure as Faustus that Helen (like the statue in Shakespeare's play) is a result of magic—yet is perhaps more radical in the sense that the conjuration of Helen places her in an early modern temporal setting.

Marlowe's Faustus seems to already sense that an encounter with Helen is an encounter with something not the actual element beloved by a previous spectator. When he describes her as "spoils" that Paris brings to Troy (5.1.23), we understand her both as something to be treasured and as something perhaps already past its prime.[42] Marvin Carlson reminds us that "even when an actor strives to vary his roles, he is, especially as his reputation grows, entrapped by the memories of his public, so that each new appearance requires a renegotiation of those memories."[43] So to see an actor playing Helen is to remember his previous roles before playing her. The dynamic works in the obverse as well. Bert O. States observes that "there is also an unintentional, and far more interesting, sense in which the actor remains in character—to put it a better way, the character remains in the actor, like a ghost. It is not at all a clean metamorphosis." In the next chapter, we will see how the theme of metamorphosis speaks profoundly to the operations of both classical and early modern acting.[44] For the present discussion, consider the notion that to encounter Helen—whether in the body of an actor or in the body of a Helen who has aged—is always to imagine an earlier Helen.

The Stage as a Space of Conjuration

On more than one occasion, early modern audiences seemed to have claimed that actual devils showed up at a performance of the play. During a production of the play in Exeter,

> as certain number of Devils kept everyone his circle there, and as Faustus was busy in his magical invocations, [...] there was one devil too many amongst them; and so after a little pause desired the people to pardon them, they could go no further with this matter; the people also understanding the thing as it was, every man hastened to be first out of doors. The players (as I heard it) contrary to their custom spending the night in reading and prayer got them out of town the next morning.[45]

So the invocation of devils in the form of actors makes for good theater. Just as an actor in costume conjures the idea of a devil, portraying a devil onstage now appears to be so transgressive that it actually summons the real thing. That is, the fact that audience members imagine that a real devil appears onstage implies the function of the spectator's mind to stop seeing actors and to see only characters. A similar episode where devils appears during a performance of Marlowe's play is recounted in William Prynne's *Histriomastix* (1633):

> the visible apparition of the devil on the Stage at the Bel-savage Playhouse in Queen Elizabeth's days (to the great amazement both of the Actors and Spectators) whiles they were there profanely playing the History of Faustus (the truth of which I have heard from many now alive, who well remember it) there being some distracted with that fearful sight.[46]

It would seem that performing the supernatural has consequences. Here it is "*the* devil" (our emphasis) who comes to be an actor and a spectator—those same roles that are conflated in the scene described by Prynne. The author's parenthetical remark that "many now alive [...] well remember it" emphasizes that the event had similar impression-making effects as theatrical performance.

Helen's appearance in this scene may suggest that beauty such as hers is only something to be imitated or gestured toward when represented on the stage. It can exist as a paradigm or archetype—as an actor does—but cannot be translated into the social sphere. Earlier in the play, Mephistopheles delivers a wife for Faustus. The stage directions make clear that the demon enters "with a devil dressed like a woman, with fireworks" (s.d. at 2.1.149). The human dismisses her as a "hot whore" but does not seem to recognize her as non-human (2.1.151). When Mephistopheles presents Helen to an audience of Faustus and several of his fellow scholars at the University of Wittenberg, the stage directions read "Music sounds and Helen [led in by Mephistopheles] passeth over the stage" (s.d. at 5.1.24).[47] Juxtaposed to one another, the two stage directions introduce a productive ambiguity. The Renaissance reader cannot believe this is actually a figure transported across time by a devil. Such a feat would directly counter Reformation beliefs and the typical reading of the play where the devil's tricks are not magic but simply those of the theater. Functioning much like the messenger in *Helen* who reports that the eidolon has vanished, these three scholars play a witnessing role that gives the protagonist permission to believe that the present Helen is the actual woman.[48]

Thus, the scene leaves interestingly ambiguous whether the play lampoons scholars or theater audiences (or both).[49] That is, the play could be playfully nodding to Marlowe's own background as a Cambridge University graduate or as a participant in the theater industry. He gains profit from people believing in the value of the university of education or of live performance. Or is this play more genuinely explaining the compelling effects of theater itself? When Faustus kisses Helen, he declares: "Here will I dwell, for heaven be in these lips, / And all is dross that is not Helena" (5.1.95–96). It is a crucial moment in the play. If we read, as some have done, Helen as a disguised demon, we could see a scene of the man's soul being stolen by an entity similar to a succubus.[50] Further, it is the scene of a man so in love with the past (like those students at Cambridge studying the classics) or so in love with an idol (like Catholics so frequently lambasted by English protestants) that he cannot see the truth. Such an interpretation of this play would align the text with the tenets of anti-theatrical discourses in the period. *Playes Confuted in Five Actions* (1582) by Stephen Gosson (a former actor), for example, argues that theater's pagan origins make plays the "doctrines and inventions of the Devil."[51] Because within them "things are feigned as never were," plays for Gosson are the work of the father of lies.[52] However, the theater's audience members might be prone to forgive Faustus for believing the illusion. After all, they too are choosing to be moved by a performed spectacle. In this more nuanced reading of the scene, especially in the context of Helen herself as a master of mimesis, we see this as the experience of a playgoer encountering an actor. It is surely an illusion in any circumstance but is no less fulfilling.

Faustus' demand of Helen, "make me immortal with a kiss" (5.1.92), speaks to the desire of an audience member to be transported when witnessing a compelling actor or to experience something larger than life. But the play goes even further than this. Faustus seems not just to wish he could be in the presence of supernatural beauty but to wish that he could be like a fictional character himself. Thinking that he can will himself into a literary narrative, Faustus inserts himself into the action of the *Iliad* and then transfers the events of the Trojan War to his own contemporaneity:

> I will be Paris, and for love of thee
> Instead of Troy shall Wittenberg be sacked,
> And I will combat with weak Menelaus,
> And wear thy colours on my plumèd crest.
> Yea, I will wound Achilles in the heel
> And then return to Helen for a kiss.
>
> 5.1.97–102

Faustus now finds himself wishing to play new parts. He is no longer a university scholar. He is a mythical warrior and a lover. In his fantasy, he "will be Paris" as if he is an actor playing a role. Garrett Sullivan comments that "the kissing of the succubus Helen marks the culmination of Faustus' self-forgetting."[53] We see this idea dramatized here as he forgets his status in life and imagines that he can briefly be someone else, just as an actor becomes a character.[54] Michael Keefer reads the encounter between Faustus and Helen as an instance of "sexual commerce between corporeal and disembodied beings."[55] Keefer sees Faustus as a mortal man inhabiting a physical body and Helen as an illusion. Yet the famous kiss between these characters implies that, even if the woman is an illusion, Faustus believes her to be real.

Faustus imagines that an encounter with Helen makes him not just an actor—in the sense that he imagines himself able to play the role of Paris, but also a playgoer—in the sense that he thrills at spectacle and believes it to be reality. Even as early as the second act, Faustus refuses to repent for his congress with the devil and focuses instead on how "sweet pleasure conquered deep despair" because he "made blind Homer sing to me" (2.3.25–26). Even before what he perceives to be a physical encounter with Helen's body, he imagines himself being entertained by ancient performers. The use of "sing" here emphasizes that this is fantasized to be a live (or revivified) performance. Tanya Pollard has argued that "Greek tragic women on early modern stages represent not only the affective transmission of the theater, but also complex processes of literary transmission."[56] Although Pollard does not mention Helen in her study, which includes Alcestis and Hecuba, we can extend her claim to include Marlowe's depiction of the paradigmatic beauty. Helen's ability to convince Faustus of the veracity of what he sees can function as an apt metaphor for the operations of theater.

The startling nature of Marlowe's Helen seems closely tied to her ability to generate fantasies as a performed figure rather than a real-world one. M.L. Stapleton has argued that Faustus' plea for a kiss "emphasizes [...] his lack of normal interaction with women and his ignorance of matters generally associated with the female sex. His Helen is unreal, delusory."[57] Jan Frans van Dijkhuizen similarly suggests that, although Faustus sees and eventually kisses this woman onstage, "Helen of Troy remains a distant fantasy for John Faustus."[58] That is, his encounter with Helen physically in his room may only reinforce for him that she cannot be the real Helen, and thus *Doctor Faustus* enters the tradition that accepts that Helen was replaced by an eidolon. As noted above, ancient authors, including Stesichorus, Herodotus, and Euripides, take up the notion that Helen does not accompany Paris to Troy. Instead, she patiently and chastely awaits Menelaus' return while what goes along with the Trojans is a simulacrum of Helen created by Hera. In the context of Euripides' metatheatrical *Helen*, the eidolon is often interpreted as a vessel for commentary on acting, and, similarly, we can understand a demonic replica of Helen to signify an actor. Marlowe's character at first longs to have been a figure in the battle at Troy and then wishes that he could have re-staged the battle in Wittenberg of his day. George Peele's depiction of Helen reinforces such a reading of the ancient figure. In "The Tale of Troy" (a long poem published in the same year in as Marlowe's play), she seems to double herself when

> her heart was from her body hent,
> To Troy this Helen with her Lover went
> Thinking perdie a part contrary kind
> Her heart so wrought, her self to stay behind.[59]

The desiring heart is seized upon, or "hent," in the moment and leaves the hesitant body behind, thus creating a double of the self. Part of Helen stays behind to lament her place in history while a phantasmatic, desiring self goes with Paris.

A long genealogy of writers have seized upon the idea that Helen might be split into multiple selves, one a spectral double of the other. There is an intriguing echo of this notion in George Seferis's poem "Helen":

> At Troy, nothing: just a phantom image.
> That's how the gods wanted it.
> And Paris, Paris lay with a shadow as though it were a solid being;
> and for ten whole years we slaughtered ourselves for Helen.[60]

And then it also appears in the film *Troy* (Dir. Petersen, 2004), when Helen tells Paris, "before you came to Sparta I was a ghost. I walked and I ate and I swam in the sea, but I was a ghost." The claim reminds us that the role of Helen is very much what Marvin Carlson has termed a "ghosted role," one for which any actor playing a given character always invokes earlier actors who have played the role.[61] We can add to this notion that seeing an actor as a character also invokes other characters that actor has played and thus places even more demand upon a spectator to look past the evidence presented to the senses in order to believe in the fiction of the character's veracity.

Helen, from Euripides to Marlowe via Lucian

The study of classical receptions, particularly in the Renaissance, often requires a leap of faith that an author or artist is familiar with the classical text posited as a source. In the specific case of Marlowe and Euripides, despite Marlowe's training in Greek and the well-established place of Greek literature in the Cambridge curriculum when Marlowe began his studies in 1580, conclusive evidence for Marlowe's direct engagement with tragedy in the original Greek remains elusive. Nevertheless, as Neil Rhodes has noted, prose authors, including Xenophon, Demosthenes, Isocrates, Plutarch, and Lucian, attracted more attention than poetry among the sixteenth-century English writers, who read a number of prose authors either in the Greek original or with a Latin trot.[62] We can, therefore, trace Marlowe's engagement with sources of Helen indirectly to Euripides via Lucian, who also exploits Helen's reputation for unparalleled beauty to explore the ineluctable challenges of mimesis.[63] If Marlowe did not adapt his famous line "Was this the face that launched a thousand ships / And burnt the topless towers of Ilium" (5.1.90–91) directly from Lucian's Greek, "And therefore on account of this [i.e., Helen's skull] were the thousand ships filled from all of Greece and so many fell, Greeks as well as foreigners, and so many cities were overturned?" (εἶτα διὰ τοῦτο αἱ χίλιαι νῆες ἐπληρώθησαν ἐξ ἁπάσης τῆς Ἑλλάδος καὶ τοσοῦτοι ἔπεσον Ἕλληνές τε καὶ βάρβαροι καὶ τοσαῦται πόλεις ἀνάστατοι γεγόνασιν; *Dialogues of the Dead* 5.2), then he found it in Erasmus' Latin edition of the original (*et hui scilicet ossis gratia, mille naves universa Grecia acto delectu sunt impletae: tantaque tum grecorum tum barbarorum multitudo conflixit: tot urbes sunt eversae*).[64] Lucian himself was steeped in fifth-century drama and thus serves as a bridge between Euripides' erroneously slandered heroine and Marlowe's devilishly beautiful Helen.[65]

Lucian offers Marlowe not only a provocative question but also the ontological and the epistemological challenges of seeing Helen's beauty that the question encapsulates. Like Doctor Faustus' Helen, Lucian's Helen is not a goddess, but she resides in the underworld. Led on a tour of the underworld by Hermes, Menippus is keen to see the beautiful people, but now these are nothing but skulls (ὀστᾶ μόνα ὁρῶ καὶ κρανία τῶν σαρκῶν γυμνά, ὅμοια τὰ πολλά, 5.1). Here, Lucian creates a macabre pun on γυμνά, meaning both bare and nude, and so Menippus, seeing the bones of ancient beauties, including Helen, stripped of flesh, fulfills the fantasy of seeing Helen nude.[66] Death and time, however, have rendered her nudity equal to that of everyone else, and thus the beauty for which she continues to be known is merely ephemeral, a moralizing precept about the pleasures and vanity of the flesh that haunts Doctor Faustus. Menippus, therefore, cannot identify Helen's bones, and Hermes picks up a skull and asserts, "This very one is Helen" (τουτὶ τὸ κρανίον ἡ Ἑλένη ἐστίν, 5.1). Hermes' confidence seems, at first, unfounded. How can he know? But his bald claim succinctly recapitulates the issues at the core of recognizing Helen. Hermes claims not that the skull is Helen's but rather is Helen herself. The impossible beauty of Helen does not exist and resides only in the imagination of her beholder. Her skull, like a mask of the ancient theater, is a blank canvas on which spectators project their own desires, making Helen's appearance paradoxically unparalleled and replicable, intrinsic and unrecognizable. A spectator's *eros* for this beauty of his own creation brings Helen to life, even from the dead. Her beauty, like drama, can only be a product of the imagination.

3

An Actor Ascends: Status and Identity in Plautus' *Amphitruo* and the Court Masque

It should come as no surprise to say that change is at the heart of acting and central to the notion that a human actor might convincingly portray a supernatural being. Although a recognizably famous actor might overwhelm a character with their celebrity, it can also be the case that to remark that an actor was unrecognizable in a role can be the highest compliment.[1] We can imagine that such adulation might be especially elevating when the actor plays someone at the level of a god. Understanding unrecognizability as an achievement in acting complicates the notion that "the history of fame is really about the cultural role of the individual" as the actor becomes famous for the ability to fully become another person or persons.[2] As we saw in the discussion of Helen in the previous chapter, it is not simply that an actor becomes the character through changes related to donning a mask, make-up, or costume. Rather, our own experience of the figure changes as we, the audience members, choose to believe in *who* or *what* the narratives tell us these characters are.

While changeability lies at the heart of acting in both earlier epochs and today, the notion that mutability was the inherent nature of all things was integral to wide-ranging belief systems circulating in classical and Renaissance cultures. Even better to say: mutability was, for many in classical antiquity and in the early modern period, at the foundation of their conceptions of their worlds. Early articulations of the mutability of the cosmos can be found in the Greek philosophers of the archaic period, such as Heraclitus, who reportedly compares the fundamental mutability of existence to the flow of a river (Plato, *Cratylus* 402a). For the early modern period, two Roman epics, Lucretius' *De Rerum Natura* (*On the Nature of Things*) and Ovid's *Metamorphoses*, however, have played an important, enduring role in literary and scientific spheres. In Lucretius' poem, he seeks to broaden the appeal of Epicureanism for his Roman audience by proffering a philosophy of self-sufficiency and tranquility accomplished through the study of natural science. Such study will not only reveal that all earthly and cosmic bodies are constantly in motion, in flux, in the midst of creation, change, disintegration but also will expunge bodily desires and the fear of death and of the gods. Thus, Lucretius' didactic poem evinces a theoretical unity for myth, human experience, and physics, a unity grounded in change. Ovid's epic poem *Metamorphoses*, largely regarded as the great classical work on the theme of change, was a crucial source for those medieval and early modern mythographers who presented the ancient stories to a wide readership. The numerous tales of gods and mortals changing forms occupy Ovid's epic poem, as the proem reveals:

> in nova fert animus mutatas dicere formas
> corpora; di, coeptis (nam vos mutastis et illas)
> adspirate meis primaque ab origine mundi
> ad mea perpetuum deducite tempora carmen!
>
> My mind carries me to speak of beings changed into new bodies. Gods, inspire my beginnings (for you have changed them, too) and from the primordial origins of the world draw out a continuous song to my own times!
>
> Met. 1.1–4

The epic work thus begins by introducing its dominant theme—the transformation of bodies—and ties that theme to the poet's inspiration for his poem. Further, this chain of transformed bodies is what links primordial times to his own, as Ovidian time is unified by a series of gods disguising themselves as humans or animals, humans becoming plants or animals, and even humans becoming immortal.

Renaissance literature is rife with influence from these ancient strands of thought about mutability being at the heart of existence. Texts reflecting a fascination with such ancient ideas range from Arthur Golding's popular translation of *Metamorphoses* to John Donne's reflections on atomism in *The First Anniversary* to Shakespeare's depiction of the transformed body of Bottom in *A Midsummer Night's Dream*. We will not rehearse the long history of the influence of Ovid's and Lucretius' work here, as many excellent scholars have done so.[3] Suffice it to say that mutability offered a compelling explanatory system for early moderns seeking to make sense of the world and their place in it. As Edmund Spenser puts it in the "Mutabilitie cantos" that open his epic poem *The Faerie Queene* (1609):

> What man that sees the ever-whirling wheel
> Of *Change*, the which all mortal things doth sway,
> But that thereby doth find, & plainly feel,

How *MUTABILITY* in them doth play
Her cruel sports, to many men's decay?

1–5[4]

Spenser posits that change is the world's constant and that all people both experience this constant and also see how it brings us closer to death. The brief passage here captures the thrill ("play") of this state and the morose ("cruel") side of this state. The theater, as a form of play and also a site that presents a mirror of the world, offered both an expression of such mutability of the world and also an opportunity for writers to meditate upon it.

The present chapter concerns the way that mutability informs understandings of how actors become characters. Particularly, we find intriguing how ancient gods provided a working vocabulary to describe the ascension to convincing acting and how the ability to play a god signaled a type of apotheosis, both on and off the stage. Indeed, early modern commentators would frequently use figures of classical antiquity to describe the work of actors. Thomas Heywood, for example, describes the renowned actor Edward Alleyn—who had portrayed the lead roles in Christopher Marlowe's *Doctor Faustus*, *The Jew of Malta*, and *Tamburlaine*—as a "*Proteus* for shapes, and *Roscius* for a tongue, / So could he speak, so vary."[5] Heywood compares Alleyn not only to the Roman actor Roscius, who was famous in the first century BCE, but also the god Proteus. This god, famous for his ability to change shape, certainly speaks to this actor and other actors' ability to take on new identities.[6] On another level, the extent to which this affinity might be extended can be surprising. We argue here that actors' bodies seem to change as they take on new roles. The mask does not simply cover the face but rather becomes the face. The actor steps into the role and steps into a new body, one that blends an actor's own persona and the character or characters he plays.

We open our discussion here with two lesser-known works from the Renaissance period, both dramas performed in intimate settings. The first is Samuel Daniel's *The Vision of the Twelve Goddesses* (1604), which was staged at the Great Hall in Hampton Court Palace. The drama transforms the noblewomen of the English court (including the queen) into ancient goddesses. The second is Francis Beaumont's *The Masque of the Inner Temple and Gray's Inn* (1613), a play performed at a royal wedding. It features Zeus and Mercury turning statues into men and features the first instance in English of the phrase "artificial life."[7] We then turn to the performance of gods in Plautus' Roman comedy *Amphitruo* (early first century BCE), the only extant comedy from classical antiquity to feature gods and heroes in a mythological plot. As we shall see, Plautus is interested in the status of his actors, typically slaves, and how the roles that they play onstage may have effects in the real world. Perhaps no greater transformation can occur than a slave playing the part of the supreme divinity of the cosmos. We end the chapter by turning briefly to depictions of Zeus in Greek drama and to Shakespeare's *Cymbeline*, examples which signify in different ways the power of an actor's transformation. Taken together, these unusual case studies point to the ways in which bodies of characters are considered different bodies than those of the actors and how this metamorphosis has purchase on political and social hierarchies when this transformation involves the gods.

As will see, such transformations speak directly to issues of power. In the case of the early modern examples, the playwrights and performers seize the power to re-deploy pagan gods and inspiration and to showcase nobles as god-like individuals. Plautus' *Amphitruo* showcases the ability of a dramatic performance to raise the status of any individual actor, even a slave. Those individuals acting in the dramas find their bodies transformed as they are explicitly presented as elevated beings yet implicitly shown to need the fiction of celebrity and pageantry to shore up that elevated status.

Becoming a Goddess

The genre of Renaissance performance called the "masque" involved elaborate performance, typically at court, and relied primarily on spectacle. Productions involved rich sets, props, tapestries, and costumes while song was favored over dialogue. Though Francis Bacon dismisses them as "toys" in his *Essays*, the performances played a role in demonstrating the power of the crown and the nobility.[8] Martin Butler describes the masque genre as:

> the seventeenth-century cultural form par excellence in which systems of aesthetic representation were co-opted into the service of kingship, the outstanding symbolic instances of the necessary and disenabling involvements of cultural production in the economies of power.[9]

Given the way they make explicit the connections between performance and power, masques make a particularly apt case study for an examination of acting as a kind of ascension or apotheosis. Given their focus on spectacle as a means to affect audiences, a discussion of the masque seems a natural segue from our discussion of the staging of Helen of Troy in the previous chapter.

Samuel Daniel's *The Vision of the Twelve Goddesses* is paradigmatic of the masque genre. In this case, a courtly audience encountered a rich visual display of the pantheon of ancient female gods. It was performed in the Great Hall at Hampton Court on the night of Sunday, January 8, 1604.[10] Iris, playing her traditional role from classical literature as a messenger of Juno, informs the audience that a group of goddesses will appear in the Temple of Peace as entertainment. As the performance opens, the goddesses (played by female actors) emerge and dance among the audience members present in the hall. Their promenade is accompanied by songs. Juno, the queen of the gods, takes her throne while each goddess brings her a gift. All the while, actors playing the three Graces sing lyrics that begin with and then repeat the words "Desert," "Reward," and "Gratitude" and thus imply the transferred wealth and economic network that subtends the courtly community that both performs and witnesses the masque.[11]

The drama of this performance hinges on a scene of transformation. During these initial dances, the women are announced to be ancient goddesses. It is not simply that the actors, who are in fact the queen herself and her ladies-in-waiting, have been transformed into goddesses by pronouncement of their characters' names. The dynamic between actors and audience makes manifest a relationship we see dramatized throughout the case studies in this book. To have the actors be members of the court takes to a new level the notion that, as Amanda Bailey and Mario DiGangi put it, early modern playgoers experienced a play as "an event that immersed them in experience of the transmissibility and translatability of affect between and among players and audience members."[12] In this case, the playgoers are as much part of the play as they are part of the courtly group that watches the play. Audience members recognize the actors as members of their social circle, and they are told that these women are also deities. After dancing among the audience, these goddesses are called by Iris to return to the Temple from which they emerged. The audience is told that the goddesses—unseen to the audience—encounter Queen Anne and her ladies in waiting in the space of the temple (which is, essentially, the back-stage of the court-turned-theater). The goddesses, we are told, are so enamored of these women, that they take the mortal women's forms and return to the stage (thereby unmasking to reveal themselves as the actors).[13] So, the audience ends the masque by seeing once more the women familiar to them, only to be told that they are actually seeing goddesses playing the roles of the noblewomen.

The full title of the masque tells us that the goddesses are "*personated* by the Queen's Most Excellent Majesty, attended by eleven ladies of honour" (our emphasis). While the word "personated" might seem to be a cognate functioning in the same way as our modern-day term "impersonate," the word had a range of meanings in the seventeenth century, some of which are now rare and others have become obsolete. In the early modern period, "personate" carried the now-obsolete meaning of "to act or play the part of (a character in a play, etc.)" and thus did function like our term "impersonate," though the early modern word referred especially to the theater. With this connotation, the title makes clear that the queen and her noblewomen are actors. Yet two other seventeenth-century meanings complicate our understanding of the dynamics of the masque. The term could mean "feigned, pretended, counterfeit," suggesting that the title means to undermine the notion that the noblewomen should be likened heretically to pagan gods. At the same time, the term denoted "of the nature of or resembling a person; embodied in a person; personified." In this way, the title implies that the women do in fact embody the spirit or characteristics of a goddess.

These various resonances offer a powerful dialectic for our discussion here. Performing a role onstage simultaneously reveals the distance between the actor and the character while it also reveals the similarity between the actor and character. Great acting transforms the player into someone new. As provocatively put by Zadie Smith, "It's what I believe actors and writers have in common: this personal sense of immateriality that becomes, perversely, more solid when they pretend to be someone else."[14] That is, acting reveals the inmost part of the actor. This theory of acting has antecedents in ancient criticism of drama and thus reflects the abiding uneasiness with the metamorphosis that the stage demands of performers.[15] These noblewomen are the best actors to play goddesses both because they are skilled at feigning and because their elevated social and stage statuses are tinged with the divine. As Bruce Heiden puts it in his study of ancient acting, "any successful performer acquires a certain aura that can be regarded as godlike or mythic, since the measure of his success is the audience's acceptance of him as a fulfillment of an impersonal paradigm, the role."[16] For royalty playing gods, the apotheosis into the role would be doubly felt.

The use of the term "vision" in the title of the play contributes to the interpretation of the masque as dramatizing this dialectic. "Vision" certainly describes the experience of the audience members who are seeing the spectacle, but the concept of looking also has a role within the narrative itself. The character of Sybilla is given a "prospective" by Iris, and we are to understand this as a device "wherein she might behold the figures of their deities and thereby describe them."[17] The meaning of "prospective" in early modern parlance is ambiguous, and scholars have debated whether the prop in the text of the masque is intended to be a scroll, mirror, or telescope. Iris gives the device to Sybilla and says, "take here this Prospective and therein note and tell what thou seest: for well may'st thou there observe their shadows."[18] If we look at the meanings of the term "shadow" that circulated during the period, we find intriguing possibilities for how one might interpret this scene. "Shadow" could denote "a reflected image," thereby supporting a reading where the vision of the goddesses reflects the vision of the true nature of these women. A now-obsolete use of the term linked it to theatrical performance in the seventeenth century. "Shadow" described "an actor or a play in contrast with the reality represented." We hear resonances of this in the well-known soliloquy by Macbeth:

> Life's but a walking shadow, a poor player
> That struts and frets his hour upon the stage
> And then is heard no more.
>
> 5.5.23–25

Here and in the masque, the term simultaneously points to the distance between the actor and the role. Sybilla, like the audience members, is supposed to see the actor and the character at once. In this way, "Personate" and "Vision" function together in the title to emphasize the double-nature of the performance. The actor acquires divine status because of her ability to convince us that she is something she clearly is not in nature: a goddess.

There is an additional, intriguing angle to this line of thinking. While "prospective" has the multiple meanings noted above, there is strong evidence to interpret the prop used in this particular performance as a mirror. The account of the masque written by the Spanish ambassador in attendance and later sent to King Phillip III of Spain recounts that Iris presents Sybilla with an *espejo prospectiuvo* (prospective mirror) where

> (not being permitted to contemplate the goddesses being present) she could see at her pleasure everything what was to happen, and looking in the mirror [*espejo*], the Sybil related the name of the goddesses, their costumes, figures and the blessings they brought with them.[19]

As we noted in the Introduction, Hamlet's notion that "the purpose of playing [...] was and is, to hold, as 'twere, the mirror up to / nature" (3.2.16–18) nicely captures the operations of presenting gods onstage. Here, in Daniel's masque, Hamlet's notion that the theater would "show virtue her feature" (3.2.18) finds fruition as the masque reveals the actual virtues inherent in these noblewomen. In the spirit of the stage holding a mirror up to nature, a character in the play holds up a mirror to see the true nature of these goddesses as noblewomen and vice versa. In fact, the ambassador's commentary is overt about the role of theatricality. He perceives that the character Sybilla cannot see the goddesses, though the audience would, and can only relate the trappings of their theatrical presentations.

What emerges in this case study is a strong sense of the transformative power of theater yet also the complex implications of likening actors to divine beings. Performing in a play in the court setting elevates these women to the status of gods but also reinforces what the court already knew: the noblewomen were of an elevated status and pagan imagery simply served the needs of the early modern artist. The mirror plays a crucial role in this process. "Metamorphosis," as Leonard Barkan remarks in his wide-ranging study of the Renaissance reception of the ancient pantheon, "becomes a means of creating self-consciousness because it establishes a tension between identity and form, and through this tension the individual is compelled to look in the mirror."[20] The masque walks a fine line in this regard. The pagan imaginary is put to work in order to reinforce the social hierarchies of the court, but the fact that this pantheon must be imaginary in both theatrical and Christian contexts consequently reveals such hierarchies as artifice. As Caroline Walker Bynum makes clear in her study of the influence of Ovid's epic poem upon later writers, metamorphosis is not a complete change from one thing to another but rather an operation of "hybridity, the two-in-one-ness of an entity."[21] In these noblewomen-turned-goddesses-turned-actors, we certainly see Bynum's notion of "a constantly new thing that is nonetheless the same."[22] The masque's staging of gods reveals the very human nature of its actors and the court within which they perform.

Acting as Artificial Life

A brief discussion of a second masque underscores how casting an actor as divine has ramifications for social power and lets us look even more deeply at the notion that classical gods imbue life into the theater. While the previous masque involves Juno, this one involves her husband Jupiter, or Jove.

The Masque of the Inner Temple and Gray's Inn was performed on a Saturday morning on February 20 in 1613, part of celebrations of the marriage of Princess Elizabeth, the daughter of James I, to Frederick V, future King of Bohemia. As noted by its title, the drama was presented by members of two of the four Inns at Court. These were schools and residences which would enroll students after they completed what we would today call "undergraduate" training. Not only were they schools that provided training for gentlemen in the early modern period but they were also sites of performance. "Revels" were held annually at the Inns of Court and featured masques, mock trials, and plays. Testifying to the political import of theater at the Inns of Court and of this masque in particular, the performance of *The Masque of the Inner Temple and Gray's Inn* had been postponed by one day to ensure that King James could be in attendance.

The action of the masque begins with a conflict between Mercury and Iris regarding how to best "do honour to the Marriage" (1–3), ultimately framing the messenger of the gods as the presenter and author of the masque. In the first section of the masque, Iris objects to Mercury's devising a "lifeless" dance of only men (146). Mercury counters Iris's complaint of the performance's lifelessness by retorting, "Stay light foot Iris, For thou strivest in vain" (56). Mercury's levity is underscored by the pun on "foot," being both Iris's pedestrian travel on land and also the extra poetic foot in Mercury's depiction of her. His next line, "My wings are nimbler than thy feet" (57), stresses that Mercury's movement requires less effort. He describes his own winged (poetic) feet as nimbler in hypometric terms, stressing that he can move more efficiently than she can. This suggests Mercury's superiority as a poet, speaker, and maker. As Sidney's *Defense of Poesie* reminds us, the poet is, by way of the term's origin in ancient Greek, a maker (216–22). The messenger god's poetic authority and alliance with the author-position is stressed when he tells Iris that he "could make thee dance," emphasizing his control over the action of the masque and Iris's (poetic) feet. The wit and subtle commentary on poetic form would be at home in the poetry of Ovid, whose *Amores* famously opens with a joke about Cupid's theft of a foot from the poet; though intending to write epic hexameters, he must now write, one foot shy, in elegiac couplets, the classical meter of erotic poetry.

Mercury continues his role as maker—as both actor and author—when the masque depicts an instance of startling procreation. Soon four Cupids arrive, "attired ... like naked Boys" (s.d. 152), who "first struck these Lovers with their equal darts" (150). Mercury continues directorial command by calling statues onto the stage. The statues are played by actors and are by no means static objects. These statues are alive, and that life is fueled by intermingled energies: poetic imagination, pagan divinity, and royal matrimony. Mercury announces:

> Behold the Statues, which wise Vulcan plac'd
> Under the Altar of Olympian Jove,
> And gave them an Artificial life,
> Shall Dance for joy of these great Nuptials:

> See how they move, drawn by this heavenly joy,
> Like the wilde trees, which follow'd Orpheus Harp!
>
> 159–64

These statues, placed by Vulcan and given "artificial life" as a dedication to Jove, offer compelling analogues for dramatic characters: created on paper and then breathed into life by actors. Vulcan creates the shell, and Jove imbues that shell with life. Some audience members may have interpreted the scene as an allusion to the statue coming to life in Shakespeare's *The Winter's Tale*, performed two years earlier. The passage's more overt allusion to Orpheus not only ties the scene to Ovidian myth but also ties the scene to poetry. The *Metamorphoses* relates the story of Orpheus' ability to command non-sentient objects with his music as well as his near-successful attempt to free his wife Euridice from the underworld. This ancient tale of change—from dead to living—tracks to the scene of statues coming to life. Tellingly, Orpheus was widely regarded in the Renaissance as the first poet and the artistic progenitor of writers during the period.

In the context of this display, we should not overlook how the artificial life created in the masque is linked to value and profit. The directions of the masque place strong emphasis on the statues' attire of silver and gold. The statues are supposed to resemble "solid images of metal," and what little clothing they wear, "small aprons of oaken leaves," has also been "carved or molded out of" silver and gold (168–73). This costuming anticipates Bacon's advice that masques favor bold colors and, by extrapolation, bold symbols.[23] The forging and production of precious metal suggests both the minting of coins and the value of mining operations in the New World. References to silver and gold appear numerous times throughout the remainder of the masque, and the masque was lavishly expensive. In this short text of only ten pages, the term "silver" appears thirteen times, and the term "gold" eight times. The summary of the masque notes that Mercury desires that the marriage of the rivers be celebrated with "both love and riches," embodied by the cupids and the statues.

Iris responds to Mercury's directed performance by saying that she will "match this show," introducing couples who are costumed for May-games: a May-Lord and May-Lady, Servingman and Chambermaid, Host and Hostess, and even a He-Baboon and She-Baboon. It is a parade of bodies dressed to impersonate paradigmatic characters or categories of being. Actors here are changed into people of a different class or job role, or into a different species. Mercury implores her:

> If Juno be the Queene
> Of Marriage, let her give happy way

> To what is done, in honor of the State
> She governs.
>
> 216–19

The masque concludes with knights and priests—each costumed with prominent silver—ascending the stage. The knights dance by themselves, then take ladies for a dance. Finally, the knights exit the stage, while the priests sing a final song. The priests' song, the final eight lines of the masque, address the "man" and "bride," wishing them "peace and silence." The promenade of representatives from these highly esteemed social categories—combined with the blessing from the ancient goddess of love and marriage—signals an alignment of past and present, as well as artistic inspiration and political power to bless the real-world marriage. This masque, like Daniel's staging of the goddesses, offers a compelling example of how the courtly aims of performance intersected with the use of gods onstage.[24]

Jupiter Made Flesh

As we noted above, the proem of Ovid's *Metamorphoses* announces his interest in divine, cosmic flux. The proem also signals Ovid's provocative engagement with the epic tradition, with its origins in the Greek hexameter adapted to Latin poetics, and prefigures his engagement with the mythological tradition, as he blends local Roman mythology syncretically with Greek mythology. One myth that Greek and Roman poets deployed as paradigmatic of a body's ability to change from mortal to immortal form is the myth of Heracles. Heracles, though divine on his father's side, inherited mortality from his mother Alcmene. The mortal part of Heracles, according to Ovid's version of the hero's apotheosis, burns away on the funeral pyre (9.250), and he loses his skin and mortal limbs (*mortales artus*) (9.266–68) before being transported by Jupiter to the heavens. The hero's apotheosis after his death speaks to the belief that bodies could transcend their terrestrial limitations and transform into a new, immortal form.

The life of Heracles has an intriguing symmetry of mortality and immortality, as we can see in Ovid's version of the conception of the hero of twelve labors, a story embedded in the tale of Arachne's weaving contest with Minerva. Arachne weaves into the tapestry the crimes of the gods:

> addidit, ut satyri celatus imagine pulchram
> Iuppiter inplerit gemino Nycteida fetu,
> Amphitryon fuerit, cum te, Tirynthia, cepit

> She added how, concealed by the image of a satyr, Jupiter filled the beautiful daughter of Nycteus, Antiope, with twin progeny, and he was Amphitryon when he seized you, Alcmena, mother of the Tirynthian hero Hercules.
>
> 6.110–12

Though Jupiter is said to have hidden himself (*celatus*) in the guise of a satyr, he actually became—he was (*fuerit*)—Amphitruo when he rapes Alcmene. Because Jupiter becomes a mortal, Heracles' life has its origins in a reversal of the metamorphosis that defines his end. Ovid's brief treatment of Heracles' life and death reveals its appeal to the dramatists, who, we argue, found the myth an evocative one for exploring the transformation of the mortal bodies of actors into temporarily divine figures on the stage. Thus, there is a curious overlap between the role of Jupiter bringing artificial life to the stage in the early modern *The Masque of the Inner Temple and Gray's Inn* and the supreme divinity's role in ancient myth, involved as he is with bringing Heracles (his mortal son destined to transcend his mortality) to life.

The myth of Heracles' birth and the preceding sexual encounter between Jupiter, or Zeus, and Alcmene, an encounter that was variously depicted in ancient terms as a rape or a seduction, was not uncommon on Greek stages. A few titles suggest such plots, including Euripides' tragedy *Alcmene*, Archippus' comedy *Amphitryon*, and Plato's comedy *Long Night*, but these plays survive only in a few fragments. From the Roman stage, however, we have Plautus' *Amphitruo*, the only comedy that comes to us from antiquity nearly intact with a mythological subject.[25] The play dresses the traditional plot of the domestic farces of Roman comedy—boy meets girl, boy falls in love with girl, boy encounters obstacle in relationship with girl, boy overcomes obstacle—in mythological garb, as it depicts Jupiter's deception of Alcmene by disguising himself as her husband Amphitruo, who is off on campaign, and tricking her into a sexual relationship.

Like Ovid, Plautus is interested in change. The god Mercury, who will play the part of the doppelgänger of Amphitruo's slave Sosia, delivers the prologue that, as usual, fills the audience in on the necessary details of the story. Atypically, it also promises to change the myth from tragic to comic fare:

> nunc quam rem oratum huc veni primum proloquar,
> post argumentum huius eloquar tragoediae.
> quid? contraxistis frontem, quia tragoediam
> dixi futuram hanc? deus sum, commutavero.
> eandem hanc, si voltis, faciam ex tragoedia
> comoedia ut sit omnibus isdem vorsibus.

utrum sit an non voltis? sed ego stultior,
quasi nesciam vos velle, qui divos siem.
teneo quid animi vostri super hac re siet:
faciam ut commixta sit: <sit> tragicomoedia;
nam me perpetuo facere ut sit comoedia,
reges quo veniant et di, non par arbitror.
quid igitur? quoniam hic servos quoque partes habet,
faciam sit, proinde ut dixi, tragicomoedia.

Now I'll say what I first came here to ask. Afterwards I will explain the plot of this tragedy. What? You've furrowed your brows because I said this will be a tragedy? I am a god. I'll change it. This same play, if you wish, I'll make a comedy from a tragedy with all the same lines. Is this what you want or not? But I'm being rather foolish, as if I don't know what you want, since I am a god. I grasp what your opinion on this matter is. I'll make it mixed: let it be a tragicomedy; for making it a nonstop comedy, where royalty and divinities appear, is not right, I think. So what then? Since it also has slave parts, I'll make it, as I said therefore, a tragicomedy.
50–63

Plautus' coinage of the word tragicomedy (*tragicomoedia*) here has often been taken as a programmatic statement about the composition of the *Amphitruo*, possibly adapted from a tragedy, and an announcement of its generic affiliation. The role of Mercury as introducing the drama places this narrative in a genealogy tied to *The Masque of the Inner Temple and Gray's Inn*, as does their shared connection to tragicomedy.[26]

While scholarly criticism of this passage has focused largely on Plautus' sources and the fungibility of tragic material for comedy, we wish to focus attention on how Plautus' simplification of generic conventions for comic effect puts special emphasis on bodies.[27] When Plautus claims that he will change the play from a tragedy to a comedy with all the same lines (*omnibus isdem vorsibus*, 55), those theater-goers with even little experience with both genres would greet this claim with skepticism. The bon mot that comedy is tragedy plus time was not on spectators' minds. Nor would they give much weight to Mercury's axiom about the cast of characters of the dramatic genres. Gods and heroes do not appear only in tragedy, even if that was the tendency, and though the highly memorable slave characters are an almost essential component of Roman comedy, they appear in tragedy as well. These comments, however, draw attention to Mercury's own body, a god in a slave's costume. If the joke is that the drama's verses will not change, his costume, whose features were strictly defined by generic convention, would humorously define the body as an essential marker of generic status. The prologue to Plautus' *Captivi* likewise notes the inappropriateness of the troupe performing a tragedy, dressed as they are for a comedy (61–62). Mercury of tragic garb is not the Mercury of comic garb.

This corporal curiosity continues in Mercury's discussion of the mutability of the body of the actor playing Jupiter. In the age of Plautus, actors seem to have been primarily slaves and foreigners, and the plays and other evidence suggest that the low social standing of actors in subsequent periods was found in Plautus' day as well.[28] Therefore, the change of a human body of a low social status in Roman society into powerful divinities, including the most powerful of Olympians, reveals the power of theater to render the impossible possible, though not perfunctory. While this social and ontological transcendence may be thrilling for some involved in Roman theater, particularly the performers and dramatists, to others, as Anne Duncan notes, there were "concerns about the power of acting to override class and status."[29] In a status-obsessed, rigidly hierarchical Rome, a Greek slave actor, for instance, playing a mythological king or even a free youth was probably unsettling for many Romans.

The very nature of the performer and of his relation to character animates Mercury's introduction of Jupiter. The prologue begins immediately on Mercury's own mercantile prerogatives (2) before turning to Jupiter himself:

> pater huc me misit ad vos oratum meus;
> tam etsi, pro imperio vobis quod dictum foret
> scibat facturos, quippe qui intellexerat
> vereri vos se et metuere, ita ut aequom est Iovem;
> verum profecto hoc petere me precario
> a vobis iussit, leniter, dictis bonis.
> etenim ille, quoius huc iussu venio, Iuppiter
> non minus quam vostrum quiuis formidat malum:
> humana matre natus, humano patre,
> mirari non est aequom sibi si praetimet;

> My father sent me here to beseech you; for although he knew that you all would do whatever was dictated to you because of his power, as, naturally, one who knew that you venerate and fear him, as is fair concerning Jove. Indeed really, he ordered me to petition you with this entreaty, gently with kind words. Because that one, by whose command I come here, Jupiter, no less than any of you, fears a beating: born from a mortal mother and a mortal father, it is fair not to be surprised if he fears for himself.

> 20–29

Mercury teases the apparently surprising appearance of Jupiter onstage in the body of a mortal actor. The focus begins on the god, *ille Iuppiter*. Mercury, however, abruptly shifts from discussing the formidable powers of Jupiter, who can intuit the fears of the audience, to his fear of a beating from them. His statement, in turn, blurs the distinction between the god and the actor. Jupiter, not the actor, recoils from a beating. The stakes for playing Jupiter, in particular, were quite high, according to the imperial satirist Lucian, who offers us one of the rare testimonia about acting in antiquity. According to this later satire, an actor who failed to portray a god convincingly and in a way worthy of the gods was flogged. "Portraying some slave or messenger not deftly is a small misstep," a character in the satire exclaims, "but to present Zeus or Heracles unworthily to the spectators: how ill-omened and shameful!" (οἰκέτην μὲν γάρ τινα ἢ ἄγγελον μὴ δεξιῶς ὑποκρίνασθαι μικρὸν τὸ πταῖσμα, τὸν Δία δὲ ἢ τὸν Ἡρακλέα μὴ κατ᾽ ἀξίαν ἐπιδείξασθαι τοῖς θεαταῖς, ἀποτρόπαιον ὡς αἰσχρόν, *The Fisherman* 33).

We can compare Jupiter's fear to that of Dionysus in a scene in Aristophanes' *Frogs*. In this comedy, Dionysus has disguised himself as Heracles and is accompanied by a slave Xanthias. In a scene that depicts "Heracles" being variously rewarded and whipped, the god's flesh is as susceptible to blows as that of the slave Xanthias. Dionysus criticizes Xanthias for thinking he could be (ἔσει) Heracles though he is a mortal slave (δοῦλος ὢν καὶ θνητός, 531). When Dionysus-as-Heracles is threatened with a beating, however, the god begs Xanthias to pretend to be Heracles, and Xanthias turns Dionysus' own words against him: "And how could I, a mere mortal slave, become the son of Alcmene?" (καὶ πῶς ἂν Ἀλκμήνης ἐγὼ / υἱὸς γενοίμην δοῦλος ἅμα καὶ θνητὸς ὤν, 582–83). The irony that Dionysus is himself played by a mortal actor is part of the joke, but underscores the problematic corporeality of divine bodies onstage.[30]

In the *Amphitruo*, Mercury's joke crescendos to the claim that Jupiter himself has both a mortal father and a mortal mother, not only foreshadowing the problems of Hercules' parentage but further syncopating the identity of the god and the mortal actor. Later in the play, Jupiter claims to be Amphitruo (*ego sum ille Amphitruo*, 861), a claim that is comparable to Ovid's account of the rape of Alcmene, in which Jupiter is Amphitruo. In Plautus' comedy, Jupiter is the actor. The actor is Jupiter. His ability to transform into Jupiter "whenever it is pleasing" (*fio Iuppiter quando lubet*, 864) nods to the role of the actor and, in fact, reverses what we might expect to be the standard formulation. One would expect Jupiter to claim to be able to turn into Amphitruo whenever he wants, but the stage Jupiter, marked by his special cap with a golden tassel to distinguish him from him mortal counterparts (cf. 142–45), claims Amphitruo as his typical identity and Jupiter only occasionally (*interdum*). Jupiter's speech here thus underscores the instability of physical identity that was so fundamental not only to myths treating Jupiter's affairs but also to the stage itself. As in the *Frogs*, the joke is that these are simply actors, not gods, but these passages reveal the underlying power of drama to turn even the lowest on the social ladder into a divine being, even if only for a few hours.

The actors plan to take advantage of their new identities. Mercury goes on to claim that, more than the other gods in tragedy—Neptune, Virtue, Victory, Mars, Bellona—he and Jupiter deserve the audience's attention for everything that he and his father have done on their behalf and on behalf of the republic (*de vobis et re publica*, 40). This plea for the audience's favor is typical of prologues in Roman comedies, but this time it has the weight of divine appeal behind it because Mercury, in a clever praeteritio, declines to enumerate the benefits they have received from his father as ruler of the gods (*deorum regnator*) and architect (*architectus*) (44–45). This striking word *architectus* is an apt description of Jupiter, or Zeus, in the ancient Greek and Roman pantheon. Though the supreme divinity of the universe does not, as in other religious traditions, create the cosmos, he does order it. In Hesiod's *Theogony*, Zeus is born into a world that is the product of both sexual and asexual reproduction, a process that has created profound disorder, but Zeus establishes his authority by structuring the universe around social order.[31]

But an *architectus* is also used in Plautine comedy for the managing of a plot. In his *Poenulus*, Milphio refers to himself as the *architectonem* (1110) of the love story. Mercury's formulation also recalls the roughly synonymous *artifex*, a word denoting a range of expertise, from the plastic arts to acting. The word, in fact, appears later in the prologue, when Mercury encourages the audience to be on the lookout for those actors and artists (*histrionibus ... artifici*, 69–70) who canvas for prizes. Both Plautus (*Poenulus* 37) and Terence (*Phormio* 259) use the word to connote a performer. This word *architectus* equates the very power of Jupiter as ruler of the cosmos with performance.

The actor's assumption of Jupiter's body, and divine powers, is put to good use for the actor himself. His request: that the play be observed fairly by the spectators. That claqueurs be discouraged. That unfair solicitation of prizes be made illegal. This is done through the order of Jupiter himself (*iussit ... Iuppiter*, 73), and so the wishes of the actor—a fair hearing for the play—becomes the decree of Jupiter that is fulfilled by the will of the audience on account of the past benefits of Jupiter. Now, the actor is imbued with the powers of Jupiter, rather than Jupiter being imbued with the mortal realities of the actor. Mercury anticipates that these divine dictates will appear suspect to the audience, and he assures them that Jupiter does, in fact, care about actors (86–90) because "Jupiter himself will perform here today" (*hic Iuppiter hodie ipse aget*, 94–95). Mercury's formulation of Jupiter's role expresses the feeling of empowerment that consumes an actor who possesses a role completely. Stanislavski articulates this notion elegantly in *An Actor Prepares*: "I felt at home in this room that had been prepared for Othello. By a great stretch of the imagination, I could recognize a certain similarity to my own room. But the minute the curtain rose, and the auditorium appeared before me, I again felt myself possessed by its power."[32] The space of theater allows for actors to convince themselves that they can inhabit another identity, but it is the dynamic between the actors and audience that subtends the new reality generated within the sphere of performance.

As we have seen, what animates Mercury's discussion of the actor becoming Jupiter is the usurpation of divine power as the power of the actor. Mercury's prologue puts a humorous twist on one of the fundamental principles of Roman and Greek religion: the idea that mortals made sacrifices and offerings to the gods in the hope that the gods, in turn, may offer far greater benefits, made possible by their divine nature, to human beings. We need only recall the first book of the *Iliad* when the Trojan priest Chryses begs Apollo to unleash his fury on the Greeks and, as part of his solicitation, reminds Apollo of the offerings the god has received from him. The *Amphitruo* playfully manipulates this dynamic of prayer through blurring the identities of Jupiter and of the actor: Jupiter seeks the favor of the audience for past benefits while the actor requests it in anticipation of the play presently on offer. The prologue of the *Amphitruo*, thus, draws attention to a fundamental question about the nature of acting and the donning of another identity for a brief duration of a drama in the small space of the theater.

Comic Conventions with Divine Force

Though dressed in mythological garb, the *Amphitruo* is typical fare for domestic farces that were so popular on Roman and Greek stages. Doubling, seduction plots, and mistaken identity were all standard as are the conventional metatheatricalities of, for example, the prologue and the actor's aside to the audience. But because Jupiter and Mercury receive top billing, these conventions of drama are attributed to and imbued with divine powers.

Florence Dupont has persuasively argued that Plautus made the myth of Amphitruo into what she calls a "theatrical 'myth'" in which "the two gods appear as masters of illusion, who deceive mortals by making them confuse image and reality."[33] Throughout the play, Jupiter's omnipotence, or near omnipotence, is the very power needed to create a non-illusory theatrical experience for his audience. As Niall Slater argues in his influential *Plautus in Performance*, "the Plautine stage [...] is a neutral stage, not bound by time, space, or realistic plausibility, a home to both illusory and non-illusory playing."[34] Slater goes on to emphasize that the theatrical illusion in Plautine drama depends upon the expectations of the audience, created through the recursive experience of spectating the conventions of Roman comedy and learning its stock characters, its typical scenes, its poetic register. Slater continues, "The success of such conventions [...] is not to be measured by their approximation to reality but by their effectiveness as communication."[35] It is our contention here that Plautus' *Amphitruo* subsumes the actors' part in creating the non-illusory experience of the theater under the power of the gods.[36]

The actor's voice as a tool for constructing the reality of the stage can be seen throughout the play, and in two notable passages, these powers are associated with those of the gods. To continue to draw on Slater's work, he has noted that Amphitruo attempts to convince Sosia that he only saw his double, Mercury posing as Sosia, in a state of dreaming (621–24). "The play is a dream," Slater observes, "sent by the gods."[37] Sosia claims that his state while seeing this doppelgänger Sosia is the same as his current state reporting it to Amphitruo: "Awake, I saw. Awake, just as I see now. Awake, I tell the story" (*vigilans vidi, vigilans nunc <ut> video, vigilans fabulor*, 623). The possible metatheatrical reading of the word "story" (*fabulor*), used also for narrating the plot, draws attention to the unreal space that the audience themselves observe.

The creation of the non-illusory space is accomplished by the seemingly simple narration of an actor, whose words construct the fictive space within the theater. For example, the slave Sosia helps set the scene at night when he says, "I believe that on this night Nocturnus has gone to sleep drunk" (*credo ego hac noctu Nocturnum obdormiuisse ebrium*, 272). The actor's statement about the time constructs the temporal reality of the theater, one in which the audience sits, surely, in the blazing Roman sunlight while the actors work at night. Yet while Sosia only comments on fictive time to create it, the actor playing Jupiter is, like the god himself, able to manipulate time as he pleases. In a moment depicting the famous elongation of the night to spend more time with Alcmene, Jupiter says:

> nunc te, nox, quae me mansisti, mitto ut concedas die,
> ut mortalis illucescat luce clara et candida.

atque quanto, nox, fuisti longior hac proxuma,
tanto brevior dies ut fiat faciam, ut aeque disparet;
i, dies e nocte accedat. ibo et Mercurium supsequar.

Now you, Night, you who waited for me, I send away so that you give way to day, so that day might shine on mortals with a clear and bright light. And, Night, by however much you were longer last night, I'll make the day that much shorter to compensate. Go, let day approach from night. I will go and follow Mercury.

546–50

With these remarkable lines, Jupiter not only hastens the night and the story but the actor playing Jupiter also manipulates the fictional temporality within the space of the theater. This verbal construction of time is a standard convention of stage drama. It is the physical space of the theater, not the necessities of the plot, that dictates certain sense perceptions on behalf of the audience. The plot, however, often demands that the audience should perceive a light, sound, or smell that is not present in the space or time of the physical theater, but the audience is invited to see, hear, or smell it by the words of the actors onstage. In this passage of the *Amphitruo*, the night extends and recedes because Jupiter says so. Because the actor says so.

We offer another convention of Roman drama that is attributed to the power of Jupiter. Characters in drama often appear onstage at precisely the right moment. Plautus plays this convention up for humorous effect in Jupiter's order to an absent Mercury:

nunc tu divine huc fac assis Sosia,
(audis quae dico, tam etsi praesens non ades),

Now you, divine Sosia, make yourself available here,
(you hear what I say, for although not present you are here),

976–77

The peculiarity of the situation is underscored by the address to the god Mercury as "divine Sosia" (*divine Sosia*) and the paradoxical "although not present you are here" (*etsi praesens non ades*). Heraclitus would find this a fitting paradox, but its significance for the theater is clear. All actors are present though absent, and they know when to appear because they have rehearsed and because they listen offstage. Here, Plautus cleverly equates this aspect of theater with the divine power of Jupiter to know the whereabouts of a distant Mercury.

The final line of the play returns to the prologue's interest in the embodiment of the divine Jupiter and the play's persistent efforts to compare the power of the actor to that of the gods. In a moment predicting Prospero's appeal to the audience at the end of *The Tempest*, Jupiter's double Amphitruo bids the audience to clap for the god: "Now, spectators, give a round of applause for the sake of the greatest Jupiter" (*nunc, spectatores, Iouis summi causa clare plaudite*, 1146). Who is truly being celebrated? The Olympian Jupiter, who has just helped to bring forth Heracles into the world, or the actor, who has brought Jupiter into it? The explicit breaking of the fourth wall in the address to the spectators invites the double reading, as do the conventions of Roman comedy. Though a request for applause is typical in Plautus' comedies (for example, the audience is ordered simply to clap, *plaudite*, at the end of the *Miles Gloriosus*, or *Braggart Soldier*), the *Amphitruo* is the only play in which applause is requested at the end of the play for a particular character.

Throughout the *Amphitruo*, Plautus has acknowledged the magic of the theater by attributing the power of Jupiter to the actor and the power of the actor to Jupiter. We see, then, an ancient antecedent of the tension of acting that we observed in the early modern period, when masques invited audiences to consider how acting transforms the player into someone new and reveals the inmost part of the actor. This dynamic is appropriate for the gods of the classical pantheon whom we characterized in Chapter 1 as "both force and counterforce" for the ways in which they embody contradictions. The differences between the classical, particularly Roman, and early modern examples should not pass us by either. A masque performed in a court by figures of the court is remarkably different from the rough and tumble atmosphere of which Roman comic productions seems to have been a part. Nor were Roman elites acting onstage. Despite these important differences, the productions that we have studied in this chapter reveal how becoming a god onstage speaks to the general power of an actor to ascend to an identity not one's own.

Zeus on the Greek Stage

Though these ancient dramatists explore the evocative intersection of the powers of gods and of actors, the mere presence of the supreme divinity of the cosmos onstage makes these plays, in fact, anomalies in the surviving dramatic corpus. In the classical and early modern periods, his presence is often felt and his will often fulfilled, but Jupiter, or Zeus, rarely appears as a character, at least on the tragic stage. We end this chapter on this curious but consistent absence.

To be sure, as the fragments of Greek comedy reveal, Zeus regularly appears *in propia persona*. One of the comedians' preferred subjects was myths depicting the affairs of Zeus. A number of titles, about thirty, indicate that these plays were popular at the end of the fifth century and throughout much of the fourth century.[38] Not all of the titles have corroborating evidence for Zeus' appearance, but several do, including Alcaeus' *Ganymede*, Aristophanes' *Daedalus*, Cratinus' *Nemesis*, and Sannyrion's *Danaë*. Depicting these affairs was so popular one ancient scholar lists a lecherous Zeus among the hackneyed figures of the Greek comic stage.[39]

There is little evidence suggesting that Zeus ever appeared onstage in tragedy. While Plautus' Mercury says that when actors summoned Jupiter in a recent tragedy, he came and helped (*venit, auxilio is fuit*, 92), Mercury could simply imply that Jupiter sent aid.[40] Though Zeus may have appeared as a character in Aeschylus' *Weighing of Souls*, the evidence for this is inconclusive. Though Zeus and his cosmic powers may be the closest analogue for the control of the dramatists over actors and plots, he rarely explicitly plays such a metatheatrical role in the poets' use of the gods as metaphors for their own power.

The evidence for Zeus on the comic stage, however, once again points to his metamorphic qualities. For example, in the *Danaë* of Sannyrion (a poet producing comedies about 400 BCE), Zeus plots his infiltration of Danaë's bedroom. In fr. 8, Zeus says:

τί οὖν γενόμενος εἰς ὀπὴν ἐνδύσομαι;
ζητητέον· φέρ' εἰ γενοίμην ⟨ ⟩ γαλῆ·
ἀλλ' Ἡγέλοχος ⟨εὐθύς⟩ με μηνύσειεν ⟨ἂν⟩
ὁ τραγικὸς ἀνακράγοι τ' ἂν εἰσιδὼν μέγα·
"ἐκ κυμάτων γὰρ αὖθις αὖ γαλῆν ὁρῶ."

What should I become and enter the chimney? Let's see. What if I become a weasel? But Hegelochus the tragic actor, seeing me, might immediately give me away and croak loudly, "For anew from the billows I see a weasel."

This is a joke about Hegelochus' notorious mis-accentuation during the production of Euripides' *Orestes*, so that rather than saying γαλήν' ὁρῶ ("I see a calm sailing"), he says γαλῆν ὁρῶ ("I see a weasel"). Once again, we see Zeus as a powerful but comically hapless enabler of transformation. He has the power to become a weasel, but an actor's simple howler has the power to render the disguise ineffective.

For one final example from the Greek stage, we turn to the evocative Phanagoria *chous* that reveals the mutability of character that was so fundamental to ancient stages.[41] Actors of Athenian dramas wore masks that allowed them to play multiple roles. Because the same troupe of actors performed the entire tragic trilogy, each actor would play multiple parts across the three plays, and even within a single tragedy or comedy, actors often played two or more roles. Thus, the ability to transform seamlessly from one person to another was an essential skill for actors on the Athenian stage.

This vase visualizes that mutability. The *chous* was produced about 400 BCE in Athens but found in a tomb on the Taman Peninsula of the Black Sea that was in the ancient colony of Phanagoria. It depicts five figures—three actors and two others who seem to be aulos-players who provided the musical accompaniment to dramas—and five masks, none of which are worn (Fig. 4). The actor seated in the center of the scene, whose lack of beard signifies that he is a young man, prepares for a performance. He is partly in costume, wearing the padded suit and leather phallus that mark him as a comic actor. He interacts with three different masks—perhaps he will play three different parts in the production—and the variety of the parts, which this artist has chosen to capture, speaks to his skill. The masks suggest that parts in this drama include three bearded men, a young man, and the god Zeus.

Given Zeus' common role in fifth-century Athenian comedy, Zeus' mask is charged with the significance of a figure of mischief and metamorphosis. This image of the god, like Jupiter in Plautus' *Amphitruo* and the gods in the early

Fig. 4 The Phanagoria Chous, *c.* 400 BCE. St. Petersburg. Fa. 1869–47. The State Hermitage Museum. Photograph © The State Hermitage Museum. Photo by Natalia Antonova, Inna Regentova.

modern masques, speaks to the power of an actor to transcend his own identity. But unlike the examples discussed earlier in this chapter, this vase confronts us directly with the metamorphic demands placed upon an actor, who may be called to play someone like himself, a person older than himself, and the supreme divinity of the cosmos in a single production.

Shakespeare's Jupiter and Social Transformation

Jupiter makes a stunning appearance in *Cymbeline*. The play takes place in ancient England during the time of the Pax Romana. In a striking scene, the god appears while the character Posthumus sleeps and joins a collection of ghosts, relatives of the young man who are looking over him during a time of danger. As we described briefly in the Introduction, the scene strikingly collides the character's personal past with England's pagan past. The result here, as with the *Amphitruo* and the early modern masques described above, is a reification of political power and an elevation of social status.

The ghosts first converse with each other and then summon the god Jupiter. Posthumus' deceased father calls out to the ancient god and pleads, "No more, thou thunder-master, show / Thy spite on mortal flies" (5.5.124–25). Posthumus, in prison and longing for death, has been punished unjustly. The ghost laments that he was not present to protect his son as he died while the baby was still in the womb. The child is named Posthumus as a nod to the fact that he was born after his mother's death. His mother laments that during the childbirth, "Lucina lent not me her aid, / But took me in my throes, / That from me was Posthumus ripped" (5.5.137–39). Though his mother blames Lucina, here the Roman goddess of childbirth, for not allowing her to live long enough to see her baby's birth, the dynamics of the haunted stage allow her to see her son as an adult. The ghosts seem to worship Jupiter as they beg him to "take off his miseries" and to "help" Posthumus (5.5.181, 5.5.185). The relatives pose a series of questions, challenging the "justice" of the god's treatment of Posthumus, querying why the god has inflicted "harsh and potent injuries" on a virtuous man and his "valiant race" (5.5. 177–78, 188).

When the god actually does descend to the stage, "*The ghosts fall on their knees*" (s.d. at 5.5.186). Jupiter addresses the family members as "you petty spirits of region low," admonishing them for their complaints and dismissing them:

> [. . .] How dare you ghosts
> Accuse the thunderer, whose bolt, you know,

> Sky-planted, batters all rebelling coasts?
> Poor shadows of Elysium, hence, and rest
> Upon your never-withering banks of flowers.
>
> 5.5.187–92

The dead relatives are "ghosts" here in the god's exclamations. But all of the characters represent ghosts in this imagined history of Britain, including this god. Although Jupiter boasts of his power over mortals, the human relatives are capable of summoning and manipulating Jupiter just as the playwright does. After this brief rant, Jupiter orders the ghosts to "Be content" because

> Your low-laid son our godhead will uplift.
> His comforts thrive, his trials well are spent.
> Our Jovial star reigned at his birth, and in
> Our temple was he married.
>
> 5.5.196–200

Once more, we see a classical god on the Renaissance stage being instrumental to raising someone's status. The "Jovial star" that blessed his birth has now returned as Jupiter pronounces that this young man will be "uplift[ed]" and will secure a place among the royal family.

The scene dramatizes that complex overlay of times that Carolyn Dinshaw characterizes as "the possibility of a fuller, denser, more crowded *now* that all sorts of theorists tell us is extant but that often eludes our temporal grasp."[42] Upon witnessing a Greco-Roman deity blessing the fortunes of an individual on the early modern stage and upon hearing the mention of the goddess of childbirth, some audience members might recognize a nod to Geoffrey Whitney's *Choice of Emblems* (1586), which describes Juno blessing the early modern poet Philip Sidney's birth. As we have seen in previous case studies, here a classical god works behind the scenes as architect of the action to follow in the play. Indeed, it is hard not to read this prophecy as stage directions for a forthcoming scene of reconciliation and reward, as the audience might imagine the actors engaging in the actions as Jupiter names them:

> [...] Rise, and fade.
> He shall be lord of Lady Innogen,
> And happier much by his affliction made.
> This tablet lay upon his breast, wherein
> Our pleasure his full fortune doth confine.
> And so, away.
>
> 5.5.200–5

The tablet suggests a line of transmission from the pagan, classical past to the recognizably English world of the present. Jupiter and those who worship him can appear onstage because they are safely located in the past. Posthumus' very name points to his connection to the dead, and this scene makes palpable that connection. The classical gods and the play's characters are placed on an even playing field as they are all cordoned off within the space of the afterlife and England's pagan past. For our present purposes in this chapter, Shakespeare's Jupiter, once again, reveals how the classical gods both reveal the undergirding social hierarchy of dramatic performance and fuel the ascension of those within it.

4

Authoring Gods in Aeschylus' *Oresteia* and Shakespeare's *Hamlet*

The ancient Greeks certainly conceived of the powers of the dramatists as equivalent to the powers of the gods. Deploying the language of theatrical productions, Euripides' *Bacchae* casts Dionysus as the director of the tragic carnage unfolding onstage, and the closing lines of the drama, which were attached—likely spuriously—to the ending of several dramas of Euripides, mingles together the gods' ability to surprise and Euripides' own penchant for mythological innovation:

> πολλαὶ μορφαὶ τῶν δαιμονίων,
> πολλὰ δ' ἀέλπτως κραίνουσι θεοί·
> καὶ τὰ δοκηθέντ' οὐκ ἐτελέσθη,
> τῶν δ' ἀδοκήτων πόρον ηὗρε θεός.
> τοιόνδ' ἀπέβη τόδε πρᾶγμα.
>
> There are many forms of divine miracles, and the gods accomplish many things unexpectedly. And what is imagined is not done, but a god finds a way for the unimaginable. Such an ending did this affair reach.
>
> *Bacchae* 1388–92[1]

Though this metaphor of "god as *didaskalos*" (producer)—to borrow, once again, Pat Easterling's formulation—is used more explicitly by Euripides than by the two other tragedians of the classical triumvirate, it pervades the Athenian stage.[2] When the prophecy in *Oedipus the King* shapes the narrative of Oedipus' life, for example, the invisible hands propelling Oedipus to his doom are those of Apollo and of Sophocles. In these instances, the use of the metaphor is constructive, by which we mean the metaphor allows the poets to articulate their own broad powers of dramaturgy in terms of the awesome powers of the divine.

Nevertheless, the ancient pantheons of Greek and Roman gods were not traditionally considered all-powerful beings able to dictate and direct the lives of human beings without limitations. The folly, short-sightedness, and self-interest of humans can disrupt, even if only momentarily, the will of the gods. In the opening scene of the *Odyssey*, Zeus laments in a divine assembly that mortals attribute all of their misfortune to the gods when, in reality, "on account of their own folly, mortals suffer beyond fate" (σφῇσιν ἀτασθαλίῃσιν ὑπὲρ μόρον ἄλγε' ἔχουσιν, 1.34). Even Zeus' decisions were subject to the mandates of fate, scrutiny of other gods, and, as Homer reveals in this episode, the unpredictable whims of human beings. The power of gods had limits.

What interests us in this chapter, therefore, is not the well-explored comparison of dramatists' control over the characters of their plays through metaphors of gods but rather how dramatists express the limits of their own power through such metaphors. Taking the *Oresteia* and *Hamlet* (two plays often discussed together in the study of classical receptions) as case studies, we trace two similar yet divergent trajectories in the deployment of this metaphor. In turn, we suggest that the different degrees to which the gods reassert themselves as divine authors—or find that role usurped by humans—point to differences in the periods' attitudes toward the divine nature of authors.

Deities as Dramatists, Dramatists as Deities

Despite the Protestant contexts in which they were written and performed, early modern English plays featured ancient gods providing direction onstage. Venus and Mercury set human characters on new paths in Marlowe's *Dido, Queen of Carthage* (1594), and Mercury enlists an ordinary human in order to deliver a prophecy to Mars in Robert Wilson's *The Cobbler's Prophesy* (1594). Recall, also, the moment in Shakespeare's *The Tempest* that was discussed in Chapter 1. Just after the moment when he commands spirits to play the roles of the Roman gods Ceres and Iris in a wedding entertainment, Prospero announces:

> Our revels now are ended. These our actors,
> As I foretold you, were all spirits, and
> Are melted into air, into thin air.
>
> 4.1.148–50

Prospero's display of power hinges on his ability to present the entire world on a small stage (and, as we noted in Chapter 1, with a nod to Shakespeare's own Globe Theatre when he refers to "the great globe itself"), and his capacity to command the gods' actions as they are presented by spirit-actors (who are in turn human actors). His speech underscores for his audience that the ancient gods whom they have seen are not real, all the while he stresses that human actors can play gods and that human producers of plays can display god-like power. *The Tempest* offers one of the most overt dramatizations of these ideas, but, as we will see, even a play without gods onstage contemplates these dynamics and their limitations.

We have chosen *Oresteia* and *Hamlet* as our case studies because, in addition to being two of the most well-known dramas from their respective historical periods, the latter is understood to be strongly influenced by the former.[3] Their tales of avenging sons naturally puts them in dialogue with each other, and our own interest in these plays lies in their depictions of gods and the gods' integral role in the plays' metatheatricalities. Both texts involve a supernatural figure instigating the action who then leaves events to play out. Both have the intervention of a human as central to turns in the plot. Both offer profound meditations on the nature of the theater. Yet, while their tragic ends are similar, the respective roles of the gods and humans are not.

Orestes' Divine Mandate

Aeschylus' *Oresteia*, that monumental trilogy of *Agamemnon*, *Libation Bearers*, and *Eumenides* produced in 458 BCE, depicts the return home of the triumphant general Agamemnon after the Trojan War and its catastrophic aftermath. During her husband's ten-year absence, Agamemnon's wife Clytemnestra has led the city and has plotted against the son of Atreus for his sacrificing their daughter Iphigenia, a sacrifice demanded by the gods before the Greek fleet could set sail for Troy. In the first play of the trilogy, Clytemnestra greets her husband warmly, yet deceptively, in order to lull him into the house where she will expiate the human sacrifice with a sword driven three times into her husband.

Our analysis begins in the second play, the *Libation Bearers*, when the tides of retribution that have wrecked the House of Atreus crescendo once more to a confrontation between Clytemnestra and her son Orestes. He is moments away from exacting the vengeance he has sought throughout the *Libation Bearers*. At the cusp of action, he pauses. As Clytemnestra bares her breast and begs clemency, Orestes hesitates, presaging Hamlet's famous hesitation to kill Claudius, and consults his friend: "Pylades, what should I do?" (Πυλάδη, τί δράσω, 899). The audience must have thought that this question would be met with the same silence that held Pylades during the rest of the drama. Throughout

Orestes' reunion with his sister Electra, their plotting of the assassination of Clytemnestra and her lover Aegisthus, and Orestes' infiltrating the palace, Pylades remains silent. Because of the three-actor rule of tragic drama, it would seem as if a mute actor played the role. Finally, however, Pylades speaks his only lines of the play:

> ποῦ δαὶ τὸ λοιπὸν Λοξίου μαντεύματα
> τὰ πυθόχρηστα, πιστά τ' εὐορκώματα;
> ἅπαντας ἐχθροὺς τῶν θεῶν ἡγοῦ πλέον.
>
> What, then, in the future will the prophetic oracles of Pythian Apollo and oaths of faith be? Consider all mortals your enemy, rather than the gods.
>
> 900–2[4]

Pylades' encouragement of his friend riffs on the conventional trope of "god as *didaskalos*." Though Orestes has been ordered by Apollo to kill his mother, his doubt and hesitation reveal the human potential to deviate from the gods' dictates. Apollo does not, as with Dionysus' paradigmatic role in Euripides' *Bacchae*, intervene by directing from the stage—at least not yet. His will, however, is expressed in the voice of Pylades and so ensures that the divine plot, in which the mortals have become ensnared, continues. Bernard M.W. Knox even declares Pylades' voice to be "the voice of Apollo himself."[5] The gods, seemingly, will not allow Orestes to go off their script.[6]

Pylades' injunction in the *Libation Bearers* is a pivotal moment in Aeschylus' rumination on divine involvement in human affairs as the gods play a gradually more direct role in the mortal realm throughout the trilogy. In the *Agamemnon*, the gods exert their wills at a great distance, and the characters' claims to have the gods on their sides reinforce their fantasies of autonomy and control. The gods ultimately snatch that fantasy away when Apollo and Athena claim to represent the will of Zeus in the *Eumenides*. The presence of Athena and Apollo, who compel human beings along the path to an ordered society, clarifies the nature of civic justice (*dikē*) passed down from Olympus to Athens. Indeed, the *Oresteia*'s narrative arc mirrors the major cosmological text of Greek mythology, Hesiod's *Theogony*, in which the universe begins in disorder and is tamed through Zeus' gradually increasing presence in the cosmos, as he defeats the Titans and creates civic society.[7] Order is thus divinely sanctioned, divinely articulated, and divinely modeled.

This narrative structure, from Olympian distance to Olympian presence, would seem to lend support to Anne Lebeck's argument that the play's trajectory is dominated by "movement from enigmatic utterance to clear statement, from riddle to solution."[8] Yet, as Simon Goldhill's influential study of the trilogy's language has shown, "The problem of *dikē* in this trilogy and its critical readings is not solved but endlessly re-stated."[9] The tragedy's language does not solve any riddle but creates its own Aeschylean enigma. The range of critical opinion about the nature of justice in the trilogy underscores Goldhill's point.[10] The nature of justice remains unsettled.

The lack of clarity is especially surprising given the presence of the Olympian gods Apollo and Athena, who serve as Zeus' proxies onstage. Would the direct intervention of the gods not clarify once and for all the ambiguity concerning the characters' actions and their enacting justice? In this chapter, however, we will draw attention to how the performance of the *Oresteia* works in conjunction with the language to undermine attempts to interpret Aeschylean justice. When a reader or playgoer encounters Pylades' injunction to his friend, Orestes' potential deviation from Apollo's will introduces the thrill of rebellion from the divine and its ensuing autonomy. It is not a mere coincidence that, simultaneously, Pylades' interjection deviates from the three-actor rule and thus rebels against the limits of tragic conventions. The intertwining of divine and human directorial powers reflects, we shall argue, Aeschylus' anxiety about tragedy's power to affect the audience in any prescribed way.

Performing Justice in the *Agamemnon*

Not only in Pylades' three lines but indeed throughout the *Oresteia*, Aeschylus draws attention to the problems of enacting divine scripts. The gods are not omnipotent. Time and time again, the mortal characters fail to interpret correctly and to enact divine will, and only direct intervention by Zeus' children ensures that his new Olympian justice will be established on earth. Thus, the *Oresteia* places special emphasis on the challenges of not only the interpretation of divine will but also imitation of it. By framing mortal justice within the play as mere mimesis of divine justice, Aeschylus projects concern about the limitations of his own mimetic performances.

The prologue of the *Agamemnon* inaugurates the radical dramaturgy of the *Oresteia* and Aeschylus' framing of mimesis in divine terms. Aeschylus' innovative use of the *skene*, whose rooftop served as the platform for the Watchman's prologue, required audience members to cast their eyes a few degrees higher than typical, and they heard a speech that explicitly refuses to recount the requisite mythological story as is typical in a dramatic prologue. "About other things," the Watchman says, "I remain quiet" (τὰ δ᾽ ἄλλα σιγῶ, 36). To those familiar with the story, his words could be an allusion to Clytemnestra's indignant anger about Agamemnon's sacrificing their daughter Iphigenia, or to Clytemnestra's ongoing affair, or to the curse on the house of Atreus. The paradigmatic tragic prologue elucidates rather than obscures the important mythological details by refusing to clarify them. The Watchman thereby presages the challenges of interpretation on which the *Oresteia*, like *Hamlet*, broods.

These interpretive dilemmas are introduced at the cosmic level and then telescoped into the play's action. The Watchman laments the tedium of his rooftop vigil for Clytemnestra's beacon fire, the "symbol of illumination" (λαμπάδος τὸ ξύμβολον, 8) that will "bring rumor from Troy" (φέρουσαν ἐκ Τροίας φάτιν, 9) signaling the Trojan War's end. While on this assignment, the Watchman has learned celestial cartography and the stars, those "luminous sovereigns" (λαμπροὺς δυνάστας, 6) that "bring winter and summer" (φέροντας χεῖμα καὶ θέρος, 5). The verbal echoes ("illumination," λαμπάδος; "luminous," λαμπρούς) reveal the parallel purposes of these fiery symbols. Yet while the stars are clear harbingers of the seasons, so much so that the stars are said not to signal but literally to usher in winter and summer, the beacon fire bears only a report of Troy's fall. Human imitation of divine signals lacks the clarity that gods can convey.

In the mortal sphere, divine messages become ambiguous, disputed, even corrupted. When Clytemnestra affirms that the credibility of the beacon could be undermined only by a god (μὴ δολώσαντος θεοῦ, 273), the Chorus assume that she has been convinced by an apparition in a dream (ὀνείρων φάσματ᾽, 274). They continue exchanging epistemological barbs. Clytemnestra claims Hephaestus, the god of forges and fire, to be the divine patron of her beacons (281), but the Chorus continue to contest the significance of that fire. The play abounds with such debates about the interpretation of divine signs, from the Chorus' recounting the prophecy ordering the sacrifice of Iphigenia, to Apollo's prophetic powers mediated by Cassandra's foreign speech and inarticulate interjections. Even the debate about the murder of Agamemnon is fought in terms of Zeus' will. Clytemnestra claims that the murder is for Hades, whom she calls Zeus of the underworld: "I struck a third blow, a votive favor for underworld Zeus, savior of the dead" (τρίτην ἐπενδίδωμι, τοῦ κατὰ χθονὸς / Διὸς νεκρῶν σωτῆρος εὐκταίαν χάριν, 1386–87). Clytemnestra's boast recalls the Chorus' positive portrayal of attributing victories to Zeus in the Hymn to Zeus (160– 83)[11] and reverberates through the *Eumenides*, particularly in Zeus' indirect support, via Athena and Apollo, of Orestes' acquittal of the homicide.[12] Zeus, however, has not sanctioned all of these actions.

In addition to previewing the play's disputes concerning how humans perceive and receive the will of the gods, the prologue introduces problems inherent to performance. The Watchman describes Clytemnestra as a woman with a man-plotting (*androboulon*, 11) heart. The root *andro-* can mean man or husband, and so the compound neologism could convey the idea that Clytemnestra is plotting against her husband or is plotting like a man or like her husband.[13] This famous word introduces the exploration of appropriate gender roles that occupies much of Aeschylus throughout the trilogy, not only the nature and status of women—consider Clytemnestra's as well as Athena's androgyny—but also the appropriate treatment and conduct of men such as Agamemnon, who warns his wife not to treat him like a woman (918), and Aegisthus, whom the Chorus disparage as a "woman" (1625).

Because in antiquity, as in early modern England, male actors played all of the roles in the public theater, describing Clytemnestra's heart as "man-plotting" nods to the nature of performance and, in particular, the duplicitousness that underlies the transformation of an actor into a character onstage. The Watchman's words create a tension between Clytemnestra's gender and her nature, her appearance and her mind. Despite the character's mask and costume, which mark her as a woman, her persona and her elaborate plan are the products of the Aeschylean imagination and the actor's performance.[14] The Chorus' later praise of Clytemnestra's manner of speaking according to a man's method (κατ' ἄνδρα, 351) reignites this metatheatrical reading sparked by the prologue. Clytemnestra's verbal assertiveness is, in the Greek imagination, characteristic of men, but her lines were also crafted by a man and spoken by a man. Aeschylus' successors in the Theater of Dionysus, Euripides and Aristophanes in particular, will shine a spotlight on this dramatic convention in gender-bending plays, such as *Medea*, *Women at the Thesmophoria*, and *Assemblywomen*. Aeschylus' metatheatricality works more subtly than that of Euripides and Aristophanes, and, for that matter, Shakespeare, but his treatment of Clytemnestra poses the very question at the heart of Hamlet's famous distinction between seeming ("'Seems', madam?") and being ("Nay, it is. I know not 'seems.'") as well as his obsession with performance (*Hamlet* 1.2.76). Being and seeming are also at the heart of the Nurse's condemnation of Clytemnestra's deceptive behavior after the murder of Agamemnon: "For the household slaves, she made her eyes melancholy, concealing internal laughter at the deeds that have turned out well for her" (πρὸς μὲν οἰκέτας / θέτο σκυθρωπῶν πένθος ὀμμάτων, γέλων / κεύθουσ' ἐπ' ἔργοις διαπεπραγμένοις καλῶς / κείνῃ, *Libation Bearers* 737–40). Her face, molded not to express her feelings but to conceal them, is like a dramatic mask. Because the actor would have worn only one mask throughout the play, its single countenance both hides her intentions from her husband and conveys her jubilation after his slaughter in the *Agamemnon*.

Aeschylus intermixes his exploration of performance and the interpretation of divine will at the end of the *Agamemnon*. After Clytemnestra's triumphant return to the stage, she boasts:

αὐχεῖς εἶναι τόδε τοὔργον ἐμόν,
τῇδ' ἐπιλεχθείς,
Ἀγαμεμνονίαν εἶναί μ' ἄλοχον·
φανταζόμενος δὲ γυναικὶ νεκροῦ
τοῦδ' ὁ παλαιὸς δριμὺς ἀλάστωρ
Ἀτρέως χαλεποῦ θοινατῆρος
τόνδ' ἀπέτεισεν.

You bellow that the deed is mine, proclaiming that I am the wife of Agamemnon. But appearing in this dead man's wife, the ancient, destructive avenger of cruel Atreus' feast has exacted vengeance from this man.

1497–1503

Perhaps Clytemnestra speaks entirely metaphorically. She becomes this powerful, supernatural entity, so to speak, by fulfilling its will that has haunted the house since the feast of Thyestes. Like Orestes in the *Libation Bearers*, she performs a divine prescription. Yet, the hyperbaton in the Greek, with the masculine participle "appearing" (φανταζόμενος) closer to the word "wife" or "woman" (γυναικὶ) than the noun it modifies, avenger (ἀλάστωρ), once again reinvigorates the gender dynamics of the play and of the Athenian stage. Something masculine, something male has seized the skin of Clytemnestra to enact vengeance. On this reading, the actor and Aeschylus himself are divine entities who reincarnate ancient heroes and heroines on the Athenian stage.[15] Because of the three-actor convention, a single actor could, like an avenging demon flitting from body to body, possess the role of other characters.

Like his mother before him, Orestes also claims divine sanction of his retribution, though his vengeance against his mother introduces new problems of interpreting the will of the gods.[16] Orestes claims that Apollo has ordered him to pursue the ones responsible for his father's death "in the same way" (τρόπον τὸν αὐτόν), which Orestes clarifies, "killing them in turn" (ἀνταποκτεῖναι) (*Libation Bearers* 274). The "in the same way" carries a deep ambiguity that relies significantly on Orestes' interpretation of the phrase. Does Apollo order the same treatment of Agamemnon's killers or does Apollo order the same method of murder used by Agamemnon's killers? Orestes' clarification seems to imply the former, that Apollo orders only the retributive murder, but the description of his plan reveals he will deceive as his mother deceived his father. He articulates his plan to his sister Electra and his companion Pylades:

> αἰνῶ δὲ κρύπτειν τάσδε συνθήκας ἐμάς,
> ὡς ἂν δόλῳ κτείναντες ἄνδρα τίμιον
> δόλῳ γε καὶ ληφθῶσιν, ἐν ταὐτῷ βρόχῳ
> θανόντες, ᾗ καὶ Λοξίας ἐφήμισεν,
> ἄναξ Ἀπόλλων, μάντις ἀψευδὴς τὸ πρίν.
>
> I urge you to conceal my plan, so that they who killed an honorable man through trickery be even themselves caught by trickery and die in the same net, in which Loxias, lord Apollo, a prophet who has not lied in the past, foretold.
>
> 555–59

What stands out here is the tension between the action on the mortal plane and the nature of Apollo. In the same breath, Orestes claims to be fulfilling the will of Apollo, who never lies, with deceit. Rhetorically, he casts his plan as equivalent to that of Clytemnestra, and he describes how he will infiltrate the palace:

> ξένῳ γὰρ εἰκώς, παντελῆ σαγὴν ἔχων,
> ἥξω σὺν ἀνδρὶ τῷδ᾽ ἐφ᾽ ἑρκείους πύλας
> Πυλάδῃ †ξένος τε† καὶ δορύξενος δόμων·
> ἄμφω δὲ φωνὴν ἥσομεν Παρνησσίδα,
> γλώσσης αὐτὴν Φωκίδος μιμουμένω.
>
> For, like a guest, carrying a panoply of baggage, I will approach the front gates with this man here, Pylades, a guest and ally of the household, and both of us, mimicking the sounds of the language of Phocius, will speak Parnessian.
>
> 560–64

Orestes will perform the role of another person, a foreigner, as part of his own deception. Though Orestes claims to re-enact the actions of his mother at the behest of Apollo, the problematic interpretation of divine will on display in the *Agamemnon* must cast some doubt on his actions in the *Libation Bearers*. In fact, the Chorus later in the play describe Apollo as the god whose prophecies clarify the obscure but, by their unintelligible nature, cast darkness over eyes (πόλλα δ' ἀλά᾽ ἔφανε χρῄζων, / ἄσκοπον δέ πως βλέπων / νυκτὸς προὐμμάτων σκότον φέρει, 815–17). Here, we have a god whose force deploys its own counter-force. He is a god of clarity and of obscurity. This is not the Apollo of Shakespeare's *The Winter's Tale*, whose pronouncement could not be more clear, despite the disorder it creates amongst the mortals.

The Disappearing Mother and the Epiphany of Athena

The structure of the *Agamemnon* permits any of the three actors to deliver the Watchman's prologue, and so the actor possessing Clytemnestra may play only this role, depending upon whether Aeschylus wished to give his lead actor the first line or to spare his voice. Therefore, the same voice that introduced the themes of divine interpretation in the prologue may have also been heard in Clytemnestra's boasting about the gods' sanctioning her actions.

Yet the story of the *Eumenides* allows us to consider an interesting feature of the division of roles in the only surviving tragic trilogy of antiquity. If, as is likely, the actor performing the role of Clytemnestra also plays her ghost in *Eumenides*, this actor must play the role of the goddess Athena, and this "residual shadow" of Clytemnestra, as C. W. Marshall describes it, informs our reading of Athena's role in conveying the will of Zeus onstage.[17] Athena's paternal preferences, her own masculine characteristics, and her resulting vote to acquit Orestes cast the goddess as Clytemnestra's counterpart and foil. Athena's claim that "no mother bore" her (736), because she sprung not from a womb but from Zeus, applies just as well to Clytemnestra, who was born from an egg according to the myth of complicated paternities involving Leda, Tyndareus, and Zeus. The actor's body and voice would have underscored the parallels between the goddess and the mortal. Therefore, when Orestes' mother recedes from the drama and the actor playing her becomes Athena, the complexities of interpreting and enacting divine will in the *Agamemnon* casts doubt on whatever confidence the epiphany of the Olympians onstage brings.

This doubt is projected onto the audience itself during the trial of Orestes. When the gods vest judicial authority in the Areopagus Council, which ultimately votes to acquit Orestes, a political body of contemporary Athens is brought anachronistically into the Mycenaean past, an example of theater's tendency to create a space of heterochrony as noted in Chapter 1. The present and the mythological past are blurred even further when Aeschylus explicitly frames the audience of the *Oresteia* as a future Areopagus Council. In a speech, Athena addresses the Athenian people (Ἀττικὸς λεώς, 681), a phrase that applies to both the Areopagus Council onstage and the Athenian citizens in the audience. Athena proceeds to offer advice about the Council in a speech that she says is to the citizens for the future: "I have drawn out this exhortation for my citizens into the future" (ταύτην μὲν ἐξέτειν᾽ ἐμοῖς παραίνεσιν / ἀστοῖσιν εἰς τὸ λοιπόν, 707–8). By proclaiming that the Athenians should maintain this homicide court, Athena invites the audience to see their own contemporary Council as re-enacting the same customs and procedures of the first Council that acquitted Orestes. As if holding a mirror to life, Aeschylus refracts the layers of shared identities among the fictional Council, played by citizen-actors, and the audience, some of whom were current Areopagites or could be in the future.

How are we to interpret Athena's mandate to these spectator-citizens of Athens? Anne Lebeck says, "The paradox of the trial is the paradox of Dike. In human destiny the just often seems unjust, the unjust just. Man, in the end, can only trust in Zeus."[18] Perhaps we can read the actor's portrayal of both Clytemnestra and of Athena as a signal of the play's treatment of clemency and forgiveness. But this teleological reading of the play, as Goldhill's study of the trilogy's language shows, is suspect.[19] Indeed, though Athena tries to assuage the Furies' anger by reminding them that the clear (λαμπρά) testimony was from Zeus, the entire weight of the audience's experience would give pause at this statement. In a brilliant echo of language so typical of this trilogy, the "clear" testimony recalls the Watchman's prologue (cf. "illumination," λαμπάδος, 8; "luminous," λαμπρούς, 6) that we noted earlier. Therefore, not only do the fallible interpretations of Clytemnestra's mortal voice reverberate through the mask of Athena, but also the prologue of the *Agamemnon* has shown how the clarity of divine signs is unlike that of mortals. Although gods appear, the audience is watching a play written, produced, and performed by mortals.

Therefore, although the trilogy seemingly resolves the problems of justice by depicting the gods' imprimatur of Orestes' acquittal, the issues of imitation and of interpretation that are introduced in the *Agamemnon* pervade the trilogy, and in the *Eumenides*, Athena casts these issues into the future, onto the members of the audience. Based on their own experience as jurors in the city's various judicial bodies, the citizens would have been aware that no trial presents clear testimony from Zeus. Defendants dissemble. Witnesses lie. Whatever the Aeschylean conception of justice may be, the *Oresteia* casts doubt on mortals' abilities, both onstage and in reality, to interpret and to imitate Olympian order.

The Gods Losing Grip: Hamlet and the Waning Power of the Father

Hamlet opens with a similar circumstance to that of Orestes' revenge. The action of Shakespeare's play, like the chain of events in Aeschylus' play, is instigated by an intervention from the supernatural realm. The ghost of Hamlet's father stirs his son to avenging action (Fig. 5). King Hamlet is not a god. Yet while no god appears onstage in this play, we will come to realize that Hamlet reveres his father as such. This reverence resonates through the son's extensive allusions to the classical gods and how this worship resonates with the early modern cultural context in which the household father is associated with the Christian god. As we will see, the ghost's injunction, "remember me" calls upon the prince to obey what can be understood as a divine command. Unlike the *Oresteia*, however, *Hamlet* evinces a dynamic in which the supernatural becomes more and more distant as humans must take on more agency and engage in—ultimately failed—direction of dramatic action.

Shakespeare's play was performed in a cultural context that made it easy to imagine the father as a god-like figure. In the early modern period, the father

Fig. 5 The power of the father invigorates the son. "Hamlet, Horatio, Marcellus, and the Ghost," Robert Thew (Engraver), after Henry Fuseli (1796). Reproduced by permission of The Metropolitan Museum of Art, New York.

functioned as the king and godly ruler for the household, just as the king functions as the Christian god's appointee on Earth. Consider this passage from *A Godly Form of Household Government* (1610), a treatise or "conduct book" written by two Protestant ministers with instruction for the management of the home:

> A household is as it were a little commonwealth, by the good government whereof God's glory may be advanced; the commonwealth, which standeth of several families, benefited; and all that live in that family may receive much comfort and commodity.[20]

The authors invite readers to imagine the family as functioning like a small nation, where the father rules over his wife and children as his subjects. A commonwealth such as England is then imagined as a constellation of these families, so that the fathers are subject to a ruler and the members of a household are subject to the father-as-ruler. Such a hierarchy, in turn, allows the father to imagine himself as the god-like ruler of a nation:

> He is reckoned worthy to rule a commonwealth that with such wisdom, discretion, and judgment doth rule and govern his own house, and that he may easily conserve and keep his citizens in peace and concord, that hath so well established the same in his own house and family. And on the other side, none will think or believe that he is able to be a ruler, or to keep peace and quietness in the town or city, who cannot live peaceably in his own house, where he is not only a ruler, but a King, and Lord of all.[21]

The text resonates with the notions of the Great Chain of Being and the Divine Right of Kings, where the term "Lord" here reinforces the beliefs that the Christian God was a loving father and that a loving father should be revered as a god. This framework of thinking becomes all the more concrete in *Hamlet* where the protagonist's father is indeed the ruler of the country. He is framed as a god-like figure both in his status as the ruler of a country and household as well as in his dramatic position, speaking from a supernatural space.

Though a play steeped in Protestant and Catholic themes, *Hamlet* takes place in pagan Denmark in a period that pre-dates the arrival of Christianity. Its pantheon would not be the Greek and Roman gods, but the play's characters nonetheless often choose these figures as paradigms when they describe divine power. Hamlet's initial description of his late father deploys references to ancient supernatural beings in order to capture the man's greatness. In Act I, we hear King Hamlet described in contrast to the new king, Claudius: "So excellent a king, that was to this / Hyperion to a satyr" (1.2.139–40). The binary crystallizes young Hamlet's impressions of the two men. Hyperion was an ancient Titan who helped overthrow Ouranos, only to be overthrown himself when the new Olympians (including Zeus) took control. Such a figure stands in stark comparison to a nameless satyr, whose half-human and half-goat figure embodied his decadence and gluttonous desire for food, sex, and wine. Via simile, King Hamlet is given the position of a classical god. Yet the allusion to Hyperion does double-work: it lionizes the king for his power but also admits to the inevitability of his Titan-esque downfall.

For an early modern English audience, it would not be surprising to hear a young prince—especially one who has just returned from study at a university—to draw upon classical figures as points of comparison. The humanist education was so deeply tied to the languages and ideas of classical antiquity that the ancient Titans would be an apt choice for describing the superlative qualities of a king. Nevertheless, given the pagan context of the play's Scandinavia, it might seem odd for Hamlet to choose the Greco-Roman pantheon. The arrival of the king's ghost, however, famously creates a setting where "time is out of joint" (1.5.186). The Denmark of *Hamlet*, like the Athens of the *Eumenides*, is a setting where time periods merge. The Shakespearean heterochrony is perhaps most startling in the ghost's announcement that he burns in Purgatory—that location specific to the Catholic faith that has no place in Shakespeare's Protestant London or medieval Denmark.

The notion that the father should be seen in his son's eyes as possessing the qualities of an ancient god has particular charge in a play that dwells upon the question of whether we can trust appearances. Even before he learns his father was murdered by his uncle, Hamlet is concerned about whether people's external appearances offer an inaccurate guiderule to their intentions. In an early speech, Hamlet makes clear that he is concerned about whether outward appearances match interior feelings. It is only a few lines before the likening of his father to Hyperion when Hamlet admonishes his mother this way:

"Seems," madam? Nay, it is. I know not "seems."
'Tis not alone my inky cloak, cold mother,
Nor customary suits of solemn black,
Nor windy suspiration of forced breath,
No, nor the fruitful river in the eye,
Nor the dejected havior of the visage,
Together with all forms, moods, shapes of grief,
That can denote me truly. These indeed seem,

> For they are actions that a man might play;
> But I have that within which passes show.
>
> 1.2.76–85

The overtly metatheatrical language of the lines, especially Hamlet's awareness that clothing and facial expressions are simply "actions that a man might play," points to his desire to discern between real human emotion and the appearance of those who are acting. This and other instances where Hamlet notes the difficulty in discerning sincere expression from the expressions of those who are simply *putting on an act*. This awareness of the work of deception and hypocrisy in everyday interactions points to the ways in which the social sphere and the theatrical stage operate by the same dynamics and even with the same descriptive language. In this case, while his claim that his deceased father had the god-like qualities of Hyperion seems grounded in his insight into true character, Hamlet's point in this speech is that we should doubt what we perceive in how others present themselves. John Kerrigan observes that "Hamlet never promises to revenge, only to remember."[22] However, his memory becomes blurred as he chooses divine analogues upon which to anchor his impressions of his father while alive.

In fact, Hamlet might choose to liken his father to the powerful Hyperion in order to shore up the pedestal upon which he has placed the former king. Montaigne posits in his *Essays* that "memory represents unto us not what we choose but what pleases her."[23] If there were negative recollections of the father or good reason not to mourn him, Hamlet may choose an allusion that can overpower other memories that might linger. Placing the image of Hyperion on "the visage" of his father would do much to mask the flawed man he may have been.

Before and after the ghost's edict to "remember me," Hamlet dwells on the nature of the former king. Perhaps in his process of remembering his father, he comes to doubt his father. In doubting his father, the prince loses his clarity about what to do. While his assiduous efforts to remember his father inform this confusion, it might be that Hamlet, as Heather Hirschfield argues, "fervently wishes *not* to remember" his mother's quick change of attitude and attraction to his uncle.[24] This depiction of selective memory ties the play once more to the *Oresteia*. In both narratives, a supernatural urging to remember—the ghost's edict to Hamlet and Pylades' mandate for Orestes to recollect what Apollo has ordered—drives the action of the plot. However, in both cases it is the humans who interpret and act upon the distant decrees from beyond the mortal realm. The prince tries to control his memory and, as we will see, he is equally invested in how he will be remembered.

Yet for all the power that Shakespeare imbues into this figure, King Hamlet becomes less and less present in the narrative after he sets the play's actions in motion. As things look more dire for the play's justice-seeking protagonist, the narrative dramatizes Freud's assertion that "man's helplessness remains and along with it his longing for his father, and the gods."[25] In Act 1, a group of people—including Hamlet's close friend Horatio—sees the ghost. In the specter's second appearance in Act 3, only Hamlet sees him. The scene opens with Hamlet handling a picture (or, in the words of the play, a "counterfeit") of the deceased king (3.4.52). Showing it to his mother, he invokes a formidable array of gods to impress upon her the formidability of her late husband:

> See what a grace was seated on this brow:
> Hyperion's curls, the front of Jove himself,
> An eye like Mars, to threaten and command,
> A station like the herald Mercury
> New lighted on a heaven-kissing hill.
>
> 3.4.53–57

The speech is meant to attest to the father's greatness, and once more we find the prince invoking classical gods. However, it is filled with language that recalls the prince's remarks about the deceptive capacity of outward appearances. As we saw in Hamlet's discussion of appearances, what lies at the heart of Hamlet's problem is a concern with how seeming differs from or obfuscates the reality of inward nature.

By opening the speech with the imperative "see," the prince demands that his mother look at the portrait while also pointing to the overt role of *seeing* in the experience of a play. Hamlet may present the god-like qualities of his father's appearances as true or revelatory. However, the playgoers know that we cannot trust what they see because actors wear masks, emulate facial expressions, or otherwise work to present themselves other than as they are on the inside. Here, in this speech, we learn the father was not Jove but only wore his "front." He did not possess the eyes of Mars but only ones "like" them. Similarly, King Hamlet's station was only "like" Mercury as the play returns to the theme of where *seeing* intimately relates to the mechanics of *seeming*. The end of the speech introduces a seeming paradox. Hamlet says:

> A combination and a form, indeed,
> Where every god did seem to set his seal
> To give the world assurance of a man.
>
> 3.4.58–60

It all sums up to a mask in which "every god did *seem* to set his seal" (our emphasis) in order to give "assurance." Once more we find ourselves in the territory of *seeming*, that territory where outward expression might not track to inward qualities. The compounding roll call of gods, too, only adds doubt to the "assurance" that it attempts to supply. As Stephen Greenblatt notes, "there is something oddly unconvincing about this perfervid elegy; the metamorphosis of a particular man into a painted combination of classical deities might alternatively be viewed as a way of forgetting."[26] Put another way: Hamlet begins to realize that the father he remembers as so great is in fact a composite of characters, just as an actor is. When we see an actor in multiple roles, we become more likely to see that individual as the actor rather than the character.[27]

Hamlet's growing doubt in the authority of his father's ghost corresponds with the retreating presence of the ghost himself. The gods—absent in this world that is presented as a hybrid of Christian and pagan beliefs—become less and less effective guiding models for behavior. Early on, Hamlet wonders why Gertrude is not like Niobe, the mythical figure who cried so much out of mourning that even when turned to stone, she wept unceasing waters from her petrified face. At the funeral of her late husband, she seemed to be "Like Niobe, all tears," but:

> Within a month,
> Ere yet the salt of most unrighteous tears
> Had left the flushing in her gallèd eyes,
> She married.
>
> 1.2.149, 153–56

On the one hand, the pagan supernatural offers a type of litmus test for whether someone is acting genuinely. A great father should tower above others as Hyperion did. A mourning mother should weep as Niobe did. But to act like a mythological figure would be impossible. So, once more we find similitic comparison. Gertrude is only "like" the legendary mother. Comparisons to deities or to mythological figures are effective rhetorical tools, but when we imagine a human as a god, we acknowledge that supernatural self can only be an illusion or mask.

Hamlet desires his mother to perform, it would seem. Consider Hamlet's famous advice to a group of players:

> Nor do not saw the air too
> much with your hand, thus, but use all gently. For in the very torrent,
> tempest, and as I may say, whirlwind of your passion, you must acquire
> and beget a temperance that may give it smoothness.
>
> 3.2.3–6

Hamlet considers moderation to lead to the most convincing of acting. However, in the case of his parents, he seems to long for excessive performance to convince him of truth. His mother must be an exaggerated, mythical figure whose tears abide after her metamorphosis into stone. Or he must wear black for months-on-end to show his state of mourning. The need for the mother to express a level of mourning of mythic proportions appears again, famously, in the second act when the prince asks a visiting player to perform a speech in which Hecuba laments the death of her husband and decries the gods for not preventing it. Hamlet may wish his mother would act more like a paradigmatic mother from the age of the classical gods, yet, in choosing this speech, he acknowledges that the gods were just as absent for Hecuba as they are for him.

The Friend as Author and as Audience

As the supernatural presence of his father retreats and the figures of the gods become less reliable analogues for those parents he once revered, the prince gradually shifts towards looking in the human world for direction as he seeks justice. He finds such direction in Horatio, that friend who is "more an antique Roman than a Dane" (5.2.299). Lars Engle has argued that Horatio is a profoundly "just" character because he proffers "theatrical mirroring that will reinforce the virtue of the good while harrowing the consciences of the bad."[28] Like Pylades and other paradigmatic classical friends to whom Engel likens him, Horatio (in Engle's words) "is the one living person whom Hamlet mirrors without negative critique, showing his virtue its own image."[29] As Hamlet recedes from using classical gods as models for how to act, he draws inspiration from the human friend whom he favorably compares to the ancients.

We can extend Engle's comment in order to link the classical model of friendship (which was highly lauded in Shakespeare's time) to Hamlet's esteem for the theater. If the theater can "hold, as 'twere, the mirror up to / nature," so too does the ideal friend (3.2.17–18). Hamlet speaks this line to describe the play that he directs in hopes that it will drive his uncle to reveal that he murdered the former king. Just before the performance, Hamlet tells Horatio that "we will both our judgments join" in order to observe the new king for any expression of guilt (3.2.73). The request signals that Hamlet trusts in his friend and also that he considers Horatio to be of one mind. Cicero's treatise on friendship, *De amicitia*, reiterates the notion that a true friend is another self (*verus amicus est [. . .] alter idem*) because it captures the way a man "searches after another whose soul he may mingle with his own so as almost to make one from two" (*alterum anquirit cuius animum ita cum suo misceat ut efficiat paene unum ex duobus*, 21). When describing ideal friendship, the dialogue invokes Pylades and Orestes as examples and goes on to underscore the power of their story by describing its reception in the context of dramatic performance. The dialogue recounts "What resounding approval there was from the whole theater recently during the new play of my guest and friend Marcus Pacuvius!" (*qui clamores tota cavea nuper in hospitis et amici mei Marci Pacuvi nova fabula!*, 24). Seeing the performance of friendship in drama stirs the audience to affirm the actions displayed by these famous friends. The description of "the whole theater" applauding suggests the shared emotional experience of playgoers reacting to the depiction, and, as if to emphasize how dramatic performance can be linked to shared emotion, the playwright is described as "my friend" (*amici mei*). For Shakespeare's Danish prince, too, the friend is a model for how to act and, as we will see, Horatio plays a crucial role in directing the dramatic conclusion of *Hamlet*.

Not only were the tenets of classical friendship well known to the early modern audiences but also the stories of these friends as well. It was commonplace in early modern writing to list pairs of classical friends as paradigms, and the pair from the *Oresteia* was a frequent inclusion. For example, Baldassare Castiglione's volume of advice for the aspiring nobleman entitled *The Book of the Courtier* (1528) showcases Pylades and Orestes. Francis Bacon's court masque entitled *Gesta Grayorum* (1594) highlights this pair in a parade of famous friends, and Robert Burton's medical treatise entitled *Anatomy of Melancholy* (1621) includes Pylades and Orestes as paradigms of the relation. Although *Hamlet* does not name this pair at any point, we can understand the paradigm that they represent to flow through the text.

At the end of the play, Hamlet transfers the power over the narrative to his friend and, in turn, to the audience. The knowledge that Horatio, as his other self, will reflect the truth of the prince's story in his retelling drives Hamlet's dying injunction:

> If thou didst ever hold me in thy heart,
> Absent thee from felicity a while,
> And in this harsh world draw thy breath in pain
> To tell my story.
>
> 5.2.304–7

Horatio thus represents the dramatist, re-telling and recirculating the story to later audiences, and thus keeping Hamlet's memory alive. The prince's dying wish constitutes an injunction to both Horatio and the audience to tell and relive the young Dane's story. The phrase "hold me in thy heart" points to the way that early modern friends were thought to share one mind and one heart. Furthermore, it points to the operations of theater where an actor hopes to communicate the character's feelings so compellingly that the playgoer will understand and even trans-affectively feel the emotions of the character. By the time we reach the word "story" in Hamlet's request, we realize that the prince has a sense of how the heightened nature of his experience will make for compelling fiction.

Horatio points to the metatheatricality of Hamlet's final wish when the friend greets the invading Prince Fortinbras in the final moments of the play:

> Give order that these bodies
> High on a stage be placèd to the view;
> And let me speak to th' yet unknowing world
> How these things came about.
>
> 5.2.336–39

The notion that he will "speak to the yet unknowing world / How these things come about" sets him up as a storyteller. When the rival prince Fortinbras arrives at the bloody scene, he will rely on Horatio to give him knowledge about events that have come to pass. Horatio's narrative will both describe the previous action and also give him the opportunity to comment on the action. The next thing he will say reads like a recipe for revenge tragedy. He continues:

> So shall you hear
> Of carnal, bloody, and unnatural acts,
> Of accidental judgments, casual slaughters,
> Of deaths put on by cunning, and for no cause;
> And in this upshot, purposes mistook,
> Fall'n on th'inventers' heads. All this can I
> Truly deliver.
>
> 5.2.339–45

When he calls for the placement of "these bodies / High on a stage," he invokes a macabre scene to be staged after the events of the play. He also suggests how the bodies of the characters will reanimate as the actors stand to take their bows as well as how the characters will return to life when the actors repeat their roles in subsequent performances. What theater makes possible for us, then, is the ability to experience emotions that confront death but also defy death. We hear this movingly in Arthur Schopenhauer's notion that "every parting gives a foretaste of death, every coming together again a foretaste of the resurrection."[30] The stage offers to the playgoer a place to witness mourning and to practice mourning with the knowledge that the losses experienced during the performances will be restored.

The theater is an engine for creation and for resurrection, and Hamlet's charge to Horatio places these capabilities squarely within the purview of the human. Yet such creation and resurrection is not without limits. As we saw above, the choice of figures and allusions that one deploys inevitably invoke cracks in logic. Mimesis, no matter how effectively it allows the theater to mirror reality, makes visible the gap between analogue and original. Further, performances rely on actors, props, and story recipes that have been inherited not just from the long history of literature but also embedded in the playgoer's own history as part of previous audiences. Will West observes, "each performance unfolds already scored by previous performances, which are recalled in part by props, scripts, recordings, and other mediations, but foremost the memories of the producers of theatre, the actors, and spectators."[31] West helps us see the dialectic inherent in theatrical production: the stage has the ability to parade convincing life before the audience but can only do so by rendering itself recognizable as theater.

As we have seen thus far in our study, such machinations of creation are rendered particularly visible when gods appear onstage. At the same time, the work of the theater has its divine valences. The resurrections seen night-after-night onstage are not divorced from religious connotations. Sean Benson argues that the revivification of characters and actors often reveals points where "Shakespeare gestures towards the Resurrection."[32] Benson is also careful to note that this need not lead us to disaggregate "Christianity and paganism" in the plays because the playwright "intermingles the two in the crucible of his art."[33] This art is neither the sole property of a God or of the author but rather is created by the entire resurrection and creation machine that is the theater. Fortinbras and the other late-arrivals to Elsinore will need Horatio's narration of "how these things came about," but the audience now has been informed and moved in a way that they will leave the theater and recount the extraordinary events witnessed on the stage.

While Pylades in Aeschylus' drama turns the protagonist's attention back to the gods to direct the narrative, Horatio accepts the protagonist's desire that the human friend control the narrative going forward. In a now classic formulation of textual theory, Roland Barthes described the "The Death of the Author" as that process by which the "Author-God" disappears in favor of the "rise of the reader."[34] Tracing the disappearing presence of gods, of god-the-father, and of any controller of events in this play gives way to a progression imagined by Barthes.[35] If any ordering does take place at the end of *Hamlet*, it is not through the intervention of a God but rather in the human friend's promise to tell the story of what has happened. But there is a slight wrinkle in the seeming straightforwardness of this interpretation. The words "author" and "actor" have a shared etymology and were used interchangeably in the Renaissance. Horatio assumes the author role here, but such a transition would seem natural—at least at the level of language—for Shakespeare's audience. The playwright himself had, in fact, started his career as an actor and some scholars believe he continued to act in his own productions.[36]

Ultimately, the *Oresteia* exhibits the same tension that *Hamlet* does—human actors trying to interpret and act in response to gods' or god-like figures' orders but also dealing with their absences. Though both contain their own ambiguities, the *Oresteia* brings the gods onstage to articulate their will. Hamlet has no such ending.

Conclusion: Hamlet and Other Actors as Dramatic Machines

We encounter an intriguing adaptation of Shakespeare's play that emphasizes the notion of the human actor taking on the role of author. Its very title nods to the idea that Hamlet has become the machine that resolves the narrative. Heiner Müller's *Hamletmachine* (German: *Die Hamletmaschine*, 1977) adapts *Hamlet* but also places itself in dialogue with the *Oresteia*.[37] While Ophelia is given as the name of a character who appears in the play, she exclaims, "Here speaks Electra" ("*Hier spricht Elektra*"). The moment points to the ways that Shakespeare's play is haunted by its classical predecessor and to the ways that later characters resurrect previous ones. The play presents itself as an odd hybrid of Shakespeare's and Aeschylus' tragedies but offers an ever more metatheatrical version of both. In what is arguably the climax of this bizarre play, the character named "Hamlet" removes his mask to speak directly to the audience as he refers to himself as the "Hamlet-actor" ("*Hamletdarsteller*"). He describes his role in the Hungarian revolution as one of being on both sides, and his disgust at his own status as a privileged person. He then tears up a photo of the play's author.

Heavy-handed as this all may seem, the ending of *Hamletmachine* captures vividly the operations that both connect *Hamlet* and the *Oresteia* as well as separate them. The destruction of the photo offers a single gesture that signifies the death of the author, which we could say characterized both the ancient play and the early modern play which show the gods' influence on human lives ebbing and flowing. Yet it shows us the extreme end of this dynamic as the human actor is able to divorce himself from the narrative in which he performs the tragic hero. The play goes beyond the commentary that the end of *Hamlet* makes. In the early modern play, the protagonist dies knowing that the re-telling of his story will be controlled by his friend. *Hamletmachine* ends by shattering the illusion of the theater yet reinforcing it. We see that it was a human in the machine of this drama all along. But the fact that this actor reveals himself to simply be another character in Müller's fictional drama underscores that there is still a god-like author behind the scenes after all.

5

To Die Is Human, To Act Is Divine

So the classical and Renaissance stages were spaces of transformation and possibility, and ones where apotheosis was considered and even made possible at the level of fantasy. Gods fueled creativity and directed action. Their presence onstage helped audience members make sense of theatrical experience. Actors performing gods point to the operations of theatrical illusion and artifice.

Roland Barthes remarks, "Since antiquity, the 'real' has been on History's side; but this was to help oppose the 'lifelike,' the 'plausible,' to oppose the very order of narrative (of imitation or 'poetry')."[1] What we have seen in this study is that one of the least lifelike or plausible elements in drama and one of the most charged—the epiphany of a god—reveals the verisimilitude of the performance as performance. Epiphanies of gods onstage, in part, lay bare the emotional and technical mechanics of theater and demand even deeper investment by playwrights, performers, and playgoers alike. Without such an investment, the diverse, fruitful roles that we have seen deities play across the case studies in this book would not be possible.

In some ways, this book has suggested that gods and humans are near-copies of one another. The functions of theater allow for the plausibility of humans performing gods, and divine powers and presences offer a particularly apt mechanism for unmasking the experiences of humans both within and even beyond the world of the theater. To be sure, gods and humans do differ starkly. One possesses immortality and supernatural powers. The other is marked by fragility in the face of impending death and limited autonomy. Yet a sepulchral epigram for Euripides captures the tensions between mortality and immortality that we have seen throughout the book:

σοὶ δ' οὐ τοῦτον ἐγὼ τίθεμαι τάφον, ἀλλὰ τὰ Βάκχου
βήματα καὶ σκηνὰς ἐμβάδι σειομένας.

I do not regard this as your tomb, but the steps of Bacchus and scene-buildings quaking with his entrance.

Adaeus 3.15–16 GP

Though Euripides' body has been interred, this epigram imagines his true resting place in the performances of his drama, a sentiment that reveals how the dramatist transcends his mortality through reperformance. In this chapter, we consider how the stage in many ways showcased and contemplated the differences between gods and humans, even if at times it undermined those differences. We end our discussion by exploring the immortalizing power of drama for the performers and playwrights themselves.

Far From the Gods

Consider Gloucester's well-known observation in *King Lear*, "As flies to th' wanton boys are we to th' gods: / They bite us for their sport" (4.1.35–36).[2] Consider, too, Homer's description of mortals "who, like leaves, now flame with vigor and eat the fruit of the field, now wither away lifeless" (οἳ φύλλοισιν ἐοικότες ἄλλοτε μέν τε / ζαφλεγέες τελέθουσιν, ἀρούρης καρπὸν ἔδοντες, / ἄλλοτε δὲ φθινύθουσιν ἀκήριοι, *Iliad* 21.464–66). This ancient claim from the mouth of the god Apollo reveals the ephemerality and triviality of human existence, just as Gloucester's lament movingly captures the stark difference between humans and immortals. This old nobleman lives in pre-Christian Britain, and though the gods he disdains—whatever pagan gods they were— would seem a distant fiction for the early modern audience, playgoers might nevertheless empathize with his lament. After all, might they also look at their own world and wonder about the logic of seemingly senseless tragedy? Despite the pagan focus of Gloucester's simile, Eric Mallin notes that it exemplifies the strong grip that the biblical story of Job had on the early modern imagination. He writes, "of the numerous Job echoes in the Shakespeare canon, none borrows more pointedly than *King Lear* the notion of relentlessly unintelligible and possibly hostile cosmic forces."[3] Gloucester admonishes the gods and laments their cruelty, and the analogue he has chosen to describe supernatural, casual cruelty is human behavior. Here we see yet another expression of one thread we have traced in this volume: if the gods are unknowable, the only way to make sense of them is to place them in human terms.

For Gloucester, his complaint about the gods being similar to youths can be interpreted, too, as a complaint about the behavior of human boys. It is the capriciousness of youth and of human immaturity more broadly that so concerns him, and, in particular, he fears the potential cruelty and recklessness of his own sons. In the narrative of the play, he will become convinced that one son conspires against him, but it will be the other son's forgery that manipulates him into believing this falsehood. The aging father's lament, therefore, is both metaphysical and personal.

While Gloucester's comment speaks to philosophical and religious debates regarding determinism and free will, it also speaks to the theater. Zora Neale Hurston captures so nicely how we, as humans in a world of suffering, recognize gods by their inscrutability:

> All gods who receive homage are cruel. All gods dispense suffering without reason. Otherwise they would not be worshipped. Through indiscriminate suffering men know fear and fear is the most divine emotion. It is the stones for altars and the beginning of wisdom. Half gods are worshipped in wine and flowers. Real gods require blood.[4]

This inscrutability, in turn, explains our inability to withstand their at-times punitive eccentricities. Stephen Halliwell's description of the religious ethos of Greek tragedy applies to Gloucester's tragic existence: "Deeply rooted in the habits of thought and feeling manifested by those who inhabit this tragic world is the conviction that their actions and sufferings are surrounded by, and stand open to, larger sources of significance."[5] And from our perspective as playgoers at *King Lear*, Gloucester cannot affect the outcomes of his own story; that ability belongs to the author of the play.

The stage was a place to contemplate the limits of human experience, from the tragic fall to the comedic play of everyday life. Martha Nussbaum remarks, "To be a good human being is to have a kind of openness to the world, an ability to trust uncertain things beyond your own control, that can lead you to be shattered in very extreme circumstances for which you were not to blame."[6] This is what good theater shows us and what the gods in theater show us: the limits of what humans can do; the sometimes catastrophic realization by people who are stymied by those limits; and the lighthearted, humorous embrace of the whims of fate completely outside of our comprehension and control.

Certainly, theatergoers' perceptions of their own limitations would be informed, in part, by the characteristics of Gloucester's own life, which would seem beyond the reach of most playgoers. Gloucester is a wealthy nobleman with close ties to the royal family. His life experiences—of being betrayed by a son through a forged letter, of being blinded by his enemies, of believing that he miraculously survived a fall from a high cliff—mark him as a larger-than-life figure on the early modern stage. His character embodies a sentiment found in ancient drama and criticism of it, from Aristotle's statement that tragedy depicts men who are greater than those living (*Poetics* 1448a16–18) to Plautus' crude definition of the cast of characters in comedy (slaves) and tragedy (royalty) in the *Amphitruo* that we observed in Chapter 3.[7] At the time, Gloucester's fall will be spectacular and it is preceded by wandering through nature with a seeming madman. This turn erodes the distinctions of class and status, positioning him as one of those anonymous flies that he describes as toys for children.

The actions of King Lear further illuminate how the play stages humans frustrated by their own powerlessness, often cast in terms of their relative nearness to or distance from the gods. The tragic rejection of his daughter Cordelia at the beginning of the play occurs in the context of affirming pagan belief:

> For by the sacred radiance of the sun,
> The mysteries of Hecate and the night,
> By all the operation of the orbs
> From whom we do exist and cease to be,
> Here I disclaim all my paternal care,
> Propinquity, and property of blood;
> And as a stranger to my heart and me
> Hold thee from this for ever.
>
> 1.1.94–101

The fact that the king swears upon his gods as he engages in this misguided act signifies another way in which humans struggle to understand their relationship to gods in this play. His deities provide no guidance about what should be done. Instead, they provide a framework for him to justify his own decision as a father as well as his divine right as king to direct the heirs of the country. William Elton suggests that the devoutly pagan Lear is a "complex analogue of the Jacobean Christian believer, the spectator of Shakespeare's play."[8] That is, the Protestant playgoer can identify with Lear because he is an ardent believer, even if he believes in other gods and makes errors in judgment. Later, when Cordelia finds him confused and ailing, Lear will say:

> You do me wrong to take me out o' th' grave.
> Thou art a soul in bliss, but I am bound
> Upon a wheel of fire, that mine own tears
> Do scald like molten lead.
>
> 4.7.43–46

Here the king imagines himself to have already arrived in the classical underworld. Yet he also senses that his painful situation is a human, earthly one. In this moment of the character's precipitous fall (a moment also deeply demanding of the actor and thereby marking the height of performance), Lear realizes that it is his falling tears—metonymically standing in for his tragic fall—that cause him pain and that they are only similically "like" molten lead. Part of Lear's tragedy, then, is his inability to see not just his errors in judgment but the very humanness of those errors.

Despite the tragic humanity of the character himself, Anthony Sher remarks in his memoir of playing the role for the Royal Shakespeare Company that "Lear is known as the Everest of Acting."[9] Part of what makes this role so challenging is that the king climbs to the heights of claiming himself to be at the level of the gods and then later imagines himself to be pathetically at their mercy. All the while, Lear's tragic fall coincides with the rise of the actor's reputation as he (or she) joins the immortal ranks of those who have successfully ascended to the role. As we will see in the rest of this chapter, dramas of both early modern and classical periods contemplate the potential immortality of performers and their art by, once again, turning to the gods.

Approaching Divinity

In another famous moment in Renaissance theater, Hamlet meditates, quite differently from Lear, on what makes a human being:

> What
> piece of work is a man! How noble in reason! How infinite in faculties!
> In form and moving, how express and admirable! In action, how like
> an angel! In apprehension, how like a god! The beauty of the world, the
> paragon of animals!
>
> 2.2.255–59

The Prince of Denmark expresses his amazement at humanity. Attaching terms such as "infinite," "admirable," and "paragon," he valorizes the human above all creatures and captures why mortal characters make for such fascinating objects of theatrical stories. He even goes as far as to liken humans to "a god" and "an angel." Yet his use of "like" here emphasizes that humans are not gods, not divine beings. Instead, we function in semblance to such immortal beings and no place is more reliant on semblance as the theater. Humans are how Hamlet approximates the divine. We are "the beauty of the world" and "the paragon of animals." By placing humans at the top of the earthly hierarchy, he emphasizes that mortals are the only available medium by which the theater can depict and humans can understand the divine.

Sophocles hits upon a similar sentiment in his famous "Ode to Man" in the *Antigone*. The Chorus sing:

πολλὰ τὰ δεινὰ κοὐδὲν ἀν-
θρώπου δεινότερον πέλει·

Many awesome things are but nothing more awesome than a human.

332–33

The ode contemplates how *deinos* human beings are, an adjective that we have rendered here as "awesome" but that carries a range of connotations—mighty, terrible, clever, strange—which the ode is keen to exploit. Human beings, Sophocles' Chorus say, have not only tamed animals but even wear away the immortal earth, highest of the gods (θεῶν / τε τὰν ὑπερτάταν, Γᾶν / ἄφθιτον, 337–39), by plowing. Among the greatest achievements is the mastery of language that allows humans to live cooperatively in a city, in a *polis*. Such statements capture humanity's audacity and its folly. Yet as in Hamlet's meditation, the Chorus clearly position human beings between animals and gods, whose justice the civilized—literally lofty-citied (ὑψίπολις, 370)—uphold, and once again, the audience is asked to contemplate the nature and the accomplishments of human beings *vis-à-vis* the divine.

Such sublime considerations, however, are not the only dramatic moments that invite comparison to divinity. In Aeschylus' *Agamemnon*, the titular hero, though returning triumphant from Troy, loathes to step on the tapestry that Clytemnestra has strewn before him because such honors suit gods (θεοῖς, 922), not mortals (θνητὸν, 923). "I say," he pleads with his wife, "worship me like a man, not a god" (λέγω κατ᾽ ἄνδρα, μὴ θεόν, σέβειν ἐμέ, 925). The verb "worship" here is quite striking in the context of Agamemnon's request, perhaps foreshadowing his present succumbing to Clytemnestra's verbal outflanking. It is also striking in the context of the production of the *Oresteia* and the eventual appearance of gods onstage played by mortals, as we observed in Chapter 4. Agamemnon's transgression—his momentary ascendency to quasi-godhead—suggests the mutability of especially powerful human beings in the Greek imagination. In a fragment from a comedy of Eupolis, a poet active in the 420s and 410s BCE, the speaker laments that current politicians pale in comparison to those of the past, to whom the people "prayed as if they were gods, because they were" (οἷς ὡσπερεὶ θεοῖσιν ηὐχόμεσθα· καὶ γὰρ ἦσαν, fr. 384.6). Eupolis wrote a number of topical comedies set in Athens, and so if this fragment comes in fact from a comedy about his own city, it would suggest that comparisons of politicians to divinities happened even outside the fictional space of the Theater of Dionysus.

These moments of transcending one's mortality occur even in its depiction of the mundane. For example, in the *Kottabos-Players* of Ameipsias, a comic poet of the last quarter of the fifth century, some character says, "For all of you I am Dionysus, five and two" (ἐγὼ δὲ Διόνυσος πᾶσιν ὑμῖν εἰμὶ πέντε καὶ δύο, fr. 4). Kottabos was a game that involved flicking wine-lees, the dregs at the bottom of a once-full wine glass, at symposia. There were a number of variants of the game, but the object was to move a plate or a saucer by hitting it with these lees. We are told that the game was for "drunks," and those who threw poorly lost their clothing (Athenaeus 666d). The association of the game with the god of wine is clear enough, but though one might assume Dionysus was a character in this drama that we know little about, the claim to be "Dionysus for all of you" suggests a figure of more limited power. We seem to have, then, the master of ceremonies who determined the ratio of water to wine that his fellow symposiasts would consume, but he temporarily claims the authority of the god Dionysus in the mundane affair of drinking. Not only could politicians strike at divinity as did the heroes of the mythological past, but so could the everyday citizen, the drinker.

A character of Plautus' *Curculio* displays the same tendency to elevate the quotidian to the divine. Phaedromus describes to his companion Palinurus the heady experience of seeing the enchanting Planesium:

Phaedromus   sum deus.

Palinurus   immo homo hau magni preti.

Phaedromus   quid uidisti aut quid uidebis magis dis aequiparabile?

Phaedromus   I am a god.

Palinurus   Rather you're a human of great trouble.

Phaedromus   What have or will you see more comparable to divinity?

167–68

Phaedromus' bold claim to divinity and his companion's explicit rejection of his divine status encapsulates the theater as an engine of mutability that we have explored throughout the book.[10] Phaedromus obviously does not become a god, but the experience of seeing Planesium makes the man feel as if he has transcended his human nature. In his own act of seeing Planesium, Phaedromus is a spectator from afar who sees his own Helen, as it were, and this act of spectating leads to a fleeting quibble with his companion about his apotheosis.

Like Marlowe's Doctor Faustus, this character believes that the spellbinding effects of gazing upon extreme beauty gives access to a supernatural experience. Yet Palinurus cuts his pal down to size and reminds him that he is only a human being (*homo*), thus underscoring the mundanity of the event and refuting Phaedromus' claims to divinity. Phaedromus' rebuttal, itself recalling the language of ancient prophecies concerning the past and the future, re-states his divine status, albeit a temporary one, in a humorous way.

To return to *Hamlet*, it should come as no surprise that the Prince of Denmark, who shows his love of acting throughout the play, thinks that humans can behave in ways as to make them approximate or resemble gods. Hamlet, however, breaks the spell in the last part of his speech. He continues, "And yet to me, what is this quintessence of dust?" (2.2.259). Though Hamlet is known for his indecisiveness, these opinions—that man is like a god and that man is simply made up of dust—are not antithetical. To Hamlet, humans aspire to divinity by striving for perfection as much as possible given the restraints of mortality. Tracing the ways in which the play is "subscribed to the biblical narrative in which man's life is rounded in dust," Margreta de Grazia finds that the essence of dust points to the importance of earth and earthly possessions that mark mortal lifetimes in the play.[11] That is, we find "man issues from earth, returns to it, and during the interim is involved in its acquisition (through inheritance, purchase, conquest) or working (gardeners, ditchers, grave-makers, pioneers)."[12]

The early modern audience would hear echoes here of Genesis 3:19, which the Geneva Bible (1560) renders as "for out of it wast thou taken, because thou art dust, and to dust shalt thou return."[13] Hamlet's words may point to the insignificance of human life, but they also point to the possibility of a return from death. His reference to "dust" here brings us back to the atomism discussed in Chapter 3: in the early modern period, it was believed that matter was never truly destroyed. Rather, things (including the dead) could be reduced to atoms and then reassembled. Within the play, his father seems to have returned from death and, as discussed in the previous chapter, his own character will be reincarnated in the space of the theater during subsequent re-tellings of his story.

Of Masks and Mortals

While human characters may express disdain for their mortality, it is in such roles that actors themselves achieve a type of immortality, we might say, even as their characters die onstage. While their characters were at the whim of the playwright's plot, those same characters might be shaped by the actor. Shakespeare's handling of one of his troupe's main actors is revealing. As the actor Richard Burbage aged, Shakespeare imagined new stage presences for him. As James Shapiro notes, the playwright "had already created such career-defining roles as Richard III, Hamlet, and Othello [and now] could expand his imaginative horizons and write plays that starred more grizzled and world-weary protagonists."[14] Ben Jonson proclaims the greatness of another Elizabethan actor, Edward Alleyn, this way:

> If Rome so great, and in her wisest age,
> Fear'd not to boast the glories of her stage,
> As skilful Roscius and grave Aesop, men,
> Yet crown'd with honors as with riches then;
> Who had no less a trumpet of their name
> Than Cicero, whose every breath was fame;
> How can so great example die in me,
> That, Alleyn's I should pause to publish thee?
> Who both their graces in thyself hast more
> Outstript, then they did all that went before;
> And present worth in all dost so contract,
> As others speak, but only thou dost act.
> Wear this renown: 'tis just, that did give
> So many Poets life, by one should live.[15]

Jonson places the actor on the same level of the author in terms of deserving enduring fame, a fame that is sustained by their reciprocal relationship. The poem names the great Roman actor Roscius and the ancient Greek fabulist Aesop as famous and cites Rome's theatrical stages as a place where men's fame was forged. Alleyn's acting, similarly, "did give / So many Poets life." Jonson interpolates himself into this equation when he asserts, "How can so great example die in me, / That, Alleyn's I should pause to publish thee?" In order for the actor's fame to endure, so too must Jonson's poem.

Actors engage with immortality when they take to the stage in other ways. Playing a role connects the actor to a character who has been played before, and the donning of the trappings of that character—whether in the form of a stylized mask in antiquity or a cape and crown of a king in the Renaissance—invokes the memory of personages whose lifetimes are elongated by cultural memory. In *De Oratore*, Cicero suggests that masks, *personae*, can help people remember. This happens at the level of a single performance, when an actor remembers a role by donning a stylized mask or a playgoer recalls a mask with a similar or even the same appearance on previous actors. And because the header *Dramatis Personae*

(Latin for "The Masks of the Play") preceded the list of characters in early modern printed plays, the very term *personae*, a key component in how the early modern theater remembers the theater of antiquity, suggests another mode of cultural memory. Frances Yates keys into this word used to describe a character:

> The use of the word *persona* [...] is interesting and curious. Does it imply that the memory image heightens its striking effect by exaggerating its tragic or comic aspect, as the actor does by wearing a mask? Does it suggest that the stage was a likely source of striking memory images?[16]

The stage is part of a circuit of immortality as it brings historical personages back to life and grants immortality to characters and to actors. As we heard earlier in the discussion of Helen, Bert O. States notes the "sense in which the actor remains in character—or, to put it a better way, the character remains in the actor, like a ghost. It is not at all a clean metamorphosis."[17] The mask, rather than completely obscuring the person behind it, ignites a sense of the dialectical collision between actor and character, between past and present performance.

Though it is not the omnipotent immortality of gods, actors can achieve a complex form of immortality, whether they are remembered by their roles or by their real identity. As Marvin Carlson observes, "even when an actor strives to vary his roles, he is, especially as his reputation grows, entrapped by the memories of his public, so that each new appearance requires a renegotiation of those memories."[18] And so characters such as Gloucester, their laments on the human condition, and the actors who rise to the challenge of playing such famous parts, provide remarkable opportunities for playgoers to reflect on what separates humans from the divine.

Mortal Characters, Immortal Roles

One of Shakespeare's plays set during antiquity brings into focus the metatheatrical elements of characters dramatizing the at-times nearness and at-times distance between gods and humans. In *Antony and Cleopatra*, we have a mention of a god who chooses not to participate in the action of the play. A soldier reports from the battlefield,

> 'Tis the god Hercules, whom Antony loved,
> Now leaves him.
>
> 4.3.15–16

Although the issue is left ambiguous, the play seems to imply that the actual Hercules abandons Antony, rather than a metaphorical reference to the man's strength. The petty human drama is not interesting to this god. The fact that Antony loved him and despite that love Hercules leaves him reinforces the hierarchy between the deity and the human. Dramatizing the complex interrelationship between gods and heroes, Antony believes himself to be loved by the gods yet the warrior-god leaves him when he needs him most. It is not that gods are indifferent to the humans in this case (and in Gloucester's estimation of relations between immortals and mortals), rather the god departs to signal the human's lone place in the theater of war.

As the events of the play begin to make clear the inevitable loss of Egypt to Roman hegemony as well as the ever-diminishing romantic bliss between Cleopatra and Antony, the queen attempts to control not only the terms of her own demise but also how that demise will be remembered. Toward the end of the play, Cleopatra sequesters herself in her tomb, which she has built for herself, in a moment that echoes the conflation of the tomb and the theater that we hear in the sepulchral epigram for Euripides above. She commands her servant to go and tell Antony that she has already died: "go tell him I have slain myself. / Say that the last I spoke was 'Antony'" (4.14.7–8). Ultimately, this will not actually be the last word she says, but we see here her desire not only for Antony to experience her passing as deeply personal but also – when she asks the servant to "bring me how he takes my death" (4.14.10)—to have the satisfaction of knowing how he will react to her demise.

When the servant relays to him the false news, Antony announces to his attendant, whose namesake is the Greek god of love: "Unarm, Eros. The long day's task is done, / And we must sleep" (4.15.34–35). We can understand Antony to address his servant as well as the god and abstraction of love here. The "long day" speaks not just to the day in the narrative but also to this performance of this play coming toward its end and to the wearying life he has led. Antony has been married before and so has Cleopatra. So, they both are familiar with love and its potential failings. A recent production at the National Theatre in London nicely captures the characters' mortal exhaustion. Sophie Okenodo and Ralph Fiennes spend much of the play drinking and railing, lamenting and reminiscing, reassuring each other and being propped up by servants when they teeter from exhaustion, intoxication, self-doubt, or a combination of these. We get a real sense that these two individuals are unable to withstand the overwhelming weight of the present and of their own mortality. No wonder one of them longs for a god's permission to finally "unarm" and achieve the everlasting "sleep" of death.

When Antony invites Eros – simultaneously his servant and the concept of love—to join him in suicide, he exclaims, "Eros!—I come, my queen.—Eros!" (4.15.49). His death onstage invokes a god and a feeling. It is an homage to a form of immortality but an immortality based in death. He will die for love and in love. Though the character and the historical figure will die, there is a sense that the play contributes to the celebrity of their affair and thus to the immortalization of their love. Antony and Cleopatra achieve immortal status, in part, because their very mortality makes their striving for love more noble and more fit for dramatization, and so they live on through the stage.

In this play about two of the most famous doomed lovers in history, the characters are all too-aware of the shortcomings that one might associate with mortality. When she encounters Antony dying, Cleopatra attempts to lift him up but finds herself too weak. At this peak in the tragic plot, the queen explicitly bewails the fact that she is not a god:

> Here's sport indeed. How heavy weighs my lord!
> Our strength is all gone into heaviness,
> That makes the weight. Had I great Juno's power
> The strong-winged Mercury should fetch thee up
> And set thee by Jove's side. Yet come a little.
> Wishers were ever fools. O come, come, come!
>
> 4.16.33–38

Her choice of the term "sport" recalls Gloucester's exclamation above, when he decries the gods' use of humans just as boys play with flies. Here, Cleopatra goes quickly from bewailing the tragic show of being unable to lift her lover to wishing she had the power of the gods and recognizing she does not. She is unable to lift Antony without the power of Mercury, and her lover too does not have the status to sit beside Jove. While these characters lament not being gods, in all of these cases they are celebrities. They are recognizable nobles from history who are more material and more knowable as icons than abstract deities can ever be. Playgoers may not want to have these personages' tragic ends, but they might wish to live their wealth, beauty, power, eloquence, or fame.

Cleopatra, all the while that she decries not being immortal, does have a sense that she will survive her own death by transforming into a literary character. However, she is none too happy about it. She remarks to her servant:

> Nay, 'tis most certain, Iras. Saucy lictors
> Will catch at us like strumpets, and scald rhymers
> Ballad us out o' tune. The quick comedians

> Extemporally will stage us, and present
> Our Alexandrian revels. Antony
> Shall be brought drunken forth, and I shall see
> Some squeaking Cleopatra boy my greatness
> I'th' posture of a whore.
>
> 5.2.210–17

Renaissance playgoers will know that they are seeing only an imitation of one of the world's most reputably beautiful women. Indeed, the audience in Shakespeare's time would be seeing such a "squeaking [...] boy" imitating the queen of Egypt in his high-pitched, pre-pubescent voice. Perhaps the great fear here is that performances will not capture the grand tragedy of this story and will not immortalize them properly. It is the "comedians" and "rhymers" who seem to trouble Cleopatra the most when she imagines her story foretold. One wonders how Shakespeare's Cleopatra would respond to her portrayal on the big screen by timeless icon Elizabeth Taylor alongside Richard Burton as Antony (Fig. 6). The same two actors also appear as Helen of Troy and Faustus in the film version of that early modern play where the scholar asks the divine beauty to "make me immortal with a kiss."

As we have begun to see, a character's longing for remembrance can be understood in terms of attaining a divine or quasi-divine status, but these desires speak also to the not uncomplicated potential fame of actors who perform the roles.[19] It is the memory of their audiences that propels a famous, talented actor toward immortality. This cultural memory finds various expressions in antiquity. When acting became more professionalized in classical Athens, a new prize

Fig. 6 Burton and Taylor secure their celebrity status. *Cleopatra*. Dir. Mankiewicz, Twentieth Century-Fox Film Corporation (1963).

(established in 449 BCE for tragic actors at the Dionysia festival; *c.* 440 BCE for comic actors) was awarded at each festival during which dramas were produced.[20] The leading actors, called the protagonists (literally, "first actors" in the original Greek), competed, and the winners' names were inscribed on stone victors' lists which offer a permanence that the actors' bodies cannot.

And, as we saw in Chapter 3, performances do impact the status of the actors in reality. Throughout Greece, actors were so popular that in some periods they were sacrosanct, enjoying sacred immunity and free passage, and so were used as ambassadors.[21] In the mid-fourth century, Athens used the tragic actor Neoptolemus as ambassador to King Philip of Macedon. Neoptolemus' performances made him popular in his own day, and his popularity contributed to a fame that would live longer than the actor himself. Because Neoptolemus performed for Philip on the day the king was assassinated, his role became associated with this significant moment in history. Indeed, Suetonius tells us in his biography of *Caligula* that on the day before the Roman emperor's death, the "pantomime actor Mnestor danced the tragedy that the tragic actor Neoptolemus once did at the games during which the King of Macedon Philip was killed" (57.4). The biographer of the Caesars thus draws attention not to the name of the parts played during these pivotal moments of history, only the men who played them. This episode also reveals the significance of recursive performance. The reperformance of Neoptolemus' role portends the monarch's death, which can be read as a reperformance of Philip's own assassination. Thus memory of the actors perpetuates because of their performances at historical events featuring players of tragic grandeur who suffer falls worthy of the tragic stage.

These episodes draw attention to a metafictional irony of those laments concerning human mortality voiced onstage. Though the character may die, the role itself could become a famous one across generations or success in the role might make the actor immortal in collective memory. The actor Neoptolemus, for example, achieved a kind of immortality through his performance at Philip's assassination, an event relived in Mnestor's re-enacting Neoptolemus' role. Cleopatra certainly sees the theater as an engine for her own immortality, albeit one defined by infamy and characterized by the cracking voice of an actor.

Immortalized Dramatists

Yet actors are not the only participants in the theater whose potential immortality is pondered and made possible by performance. Despite the ephemera of productions, the plays also consider the legacy of the playwrights themselves, who often recreate in the present a past when humans and gods mingle once again.

Thomas Heywood's play *The Golden Age* (1611) addresses this challenge explicitly by dramatizing how the theater might realize the ancient pastoral paradise of the Golden Age, a time when the Greek epic poet Hesiod claims that humans lived like gods (ὥστε θεοί, *Works and Days* 112).[22] Heywood has human lords onstage alongside gods such as Jupiter, Juno, and Diana as well as alongside satyrs and nymphs. Unlike most plays that feature a god onstage, in this drama the deities do not make brief appearances. They are the centers of action. The main storyline follows Jupiter and Saturn, though they do interact with humans along the way. At one point, the votaries of Diana sing of their virginity and also of their lives living amongst "shepherds, satyrs, nymphs, and fauns" (2.1.256).[23] It is a pure vision of the golden age: a pastoral existence lived aside gods, worshipping them and having few cares.

Despite the focus on the gods, however, the play overtly reveals the pantheon to be a fiction created by the human imagination. At the inception of the play, Homer appears onstage, introducing the drama this way:

> The Gods of Greece, whose deities I rais'd
> Out of the earth, gave them divinity,
> The attributes of Sacrifice and Prayer
> Have given old Homer leave to view the world
> And make his own presentment. I am he
> That by my pen gave heaven to Jupiter,
> Made Neptune's Trident calm, the curled waves,
> Gave Aeolus Lordship over the warring winds;
> Created black hair'd Pluto King of Ghosts,
> And regent over the Kingdoms fixt below.
> By me Mars wars, and fluent Mercury
> Speaks from my tongue. I plac'd divine Apollo
> Within the Sun's bright Chariot. I made Venus
> Goddess of Love, and to her winged son
> Gave several arrows, tipt with Gold and lead.
>
> 1.1.1–15

Not only does the ancient poet state that he lays claim to the divine genealogy of "Greece, whose deities I rais'd / Out of the earth" but he also "gave them divinity." The assertion is interestingly ambiguous. Did Homer create the gods in his imagination or did he resurrect them from obscurity because they were forgotten? Are they gods who died or are they simply old characters from literature? And what are we to make of his claim that he granted them "divinity"? Is this Homer's claim to poetic authority?

The ancient poet, who has set himself up as the presenter of the play, continues in the lines that follow to contrast the present Iron Age with the Golden Age, when the world was newly born. This underscores the notion of the artist as god, both because it portrays him as immortal and because he claims to have created language itself. Note in this second half of his speech how we find even bolder claims regarding the power of the poet and his ability to grant gods divinity:

> What hath not Homer done, to make his name
> Live to eternity? I was the man
> That flourish'd in the world's first infancy:
> When it was young, and knew not how to speak,
> I taught it speech, and understanding both
> Even in the Cradle: Oh then suffer me,
> You that are in the worlds decrepit Age,
> When it is near his universal grave,
> To sing an old song; and in this Iron Age
> Show you the state of the first golden world,
> I was the Muses' Patron, learning's spring,
> And you shall once more hear blind Homer sing.
>
> 1.1.16–27

Homer lived in the "world's first infancy," a claim which casts doubt on the veracity of any tales of the gods. He seems to have been present at the birth of the world, and in turn he gave birth to the gods. Further, his aggrandizing claim to be the "Muses' Patron" makes him not only the progenitor of the gods but the engine behind those divine inspirers of the creative arts. By resurrecting Homer on his stage, Heywood in turn can make claims to his own authority by noting that it is by his power that the audience can "once more hear blind Homer sing." This playwright's poetic craft is a reprisal of earlier voices and roles, but it is his backward-looking gaze that fuels his forward-looking aspirations toward literary immortality. When the oldest bard claims his name lives "to eternity," Heywood reveals his own literary aspirations.

Ben Jonson's courtly masque *The Golden Age Restored* (1615) returns to the rich mythological territory resurrected and re-mapped by Heywood's plays. Athena and Astraea, the goddess of innocence and justice, appear onstage, announcing that they have arrived at the behest of Jove to do away with an evil age marked by fear, hate, pain, and strife. They call forth a group of gentleman actors, referred to as "Phoebus' sons" (102).[24] Each man plays the part of a famous poet from history, including Geoffrey Chaucer, John Gower, John Lydgate, and Edmund Spenser. Athena summons the poets this way:

> You far fam'd spirits of this happy Isle,
> That, for your sacred songs have gain'd the style
> Of Phoebus' sons: whose notes the air aspire
> Of th' old Egyptian, or the Thracian lyre,
> That Chaucer, Gower, Lydgate, Spenser height
> Put on your better flames, and larger light,
> To wait upon the age that shall your names new nourish,
> Since virtue pressed shall grow, and buried arts shall flourish.
>
> 100–7

With the resurrection of these poets and their "buried arts," Athena predicts a restoration of the Golden Age. Such rhetoric affirms both the power of English, post-classical writers and the necessity of classical culture to undergird the power of such writers. Yet the desire to resuscitate the wisdom and purity of the Golden Age here is not simply an engine for fiction. It also reflects political urgency. Martin Butler and David Lindley argue that this masque's "1616 audience would not have been able to regard *The Golden Age Restored* as a mere ceremonial celebration of the politics of the moment, but must have recognized it as a political intervention in its own right."[25] The drama acknowledges the corruption of the court all the while that it expresses a nostalgia for the past—both the recent past of the poet-courtiers it stages and the ancient epoch it valorizes.

It is a move we have seen before. In Chapter 3, we saw how the gods designated courtly women as possessing likeness to goddesses in *The Vision of the Twelve Goddesses* and how the gods imbued noblemen with social mobility in *The Masque of the Inner Temple and Gray's Inn*. All of these masques deploy a strategy whereby they render ambiguous whether the story takes place in the classical past or in the Renaissance present. In doing so, they seize upon dynamics inherent in the early modern re-staging of classical figures such that, as Steven Mullaney puts it, "theatrical performance offered a way to bring alternative forms of civil society to mind, to reimagine community, and, as a consequence, to crystallize new powers of critical, embodied social thought into historical actuality."[26] Here, though, the god's blessing does dual work. It signals the noble status of the gentlemen masquers, as we saw in the previous discussion of masques, and the designation of the men as poets elevates the status of the author. After Chaucer, Gower, Lydgate, and Spenser are summoned, Athena declares:

> That for their living good, now semi-gods are made,
> And went away from earth, as if but tam'd with sleep:
> These we must join to wake; for these are of the strain
> That justice dare defend, and will the age sustain.
>
> 113–16

Poets attain quasi-divinity as they become "semi-gods," an ambiguous status that places them above other humans but not quite at the level of Olympians. Still, they achieve immortality even though they, or their bodies, have died ("went away from earth, as if but tamed with sleep") and will return now in a second Golden Age. We once more find a celebration of the power of art. The poets possess the power to defend justice by using their drama to reawaken the values of the Golden Age in the later Iron Age. Echoing scenes we have encountered before, it is the power of this performance—and of Jonson as its author—to bring figures of the past to life. Further, it is these human poets—not the gods about which they have written—who can attain a new age of peace and immortality for the world.

The idea that fame represents access to immortality is not a new one, but it does play out in intriguing ways in the context of theatrical fame. Thomas Nashe, one of Shakespeare's contemporaries, speaks to this very notion in his remarks that "There is no immorality given a man on earth like unto plays."[27] The examples that we have already seen in this chapter suggest that dramatists consider their own immortality through the immortality of their predecessors and colleagues, and reperformance can be seen as the revivification of a famous actor.[28]

There are other ways to immortalize a poet. In Shakespeare's case, colleagues contributed prefatory poems to his collected works that depict him as attaining immortality.[29] Leonard Digges' opening poem portrays the plays as a living entity and as a timeless landmark to the playwright's life:

> And time dissolves thy Stratford monument,
> Here we alive shall view thee still. This Book,
> When Brass and Marble fade, shall make thee look
> Fresh to all ages:
>
> 4–7

The poem echoes a sentiment in Shakespeare's Sonnet 55, where he emphasizes that "Not marble nor the gilded monuments / Of princes shall outlive this

Fig. 7 Signaling the link between playwriting and eternal life, a cupid offers the nymph the classical masks of comedy and tragedy. "Nymph of Immortality, Attended by the Loves, Crowning Shakespeare," Francesco Bartolozzi (1784). Reproduced by permission of The Metropolitan Museum of Art, New York.

powerful rhyme" (55.1–2). Digges ends the poem: "Be sure, our Shakespeare, thou canst never die, / But crown'd with laurel, live eternally." The poet's lines are predictive of an Italian illustration where ancient laurels do signify Shakespeare's immortal fame (Fig. 7). These lines locate the responsibility upon the living ("our") to keep Shakespeare alive (21–22). Expressing similar sentiments, Hugh Holland closes his dedication: "For though his line of life went soon about, / The life yet of his lines shall never out" (13–14). The poem separates the playwright from his work, suggesting that Shakespeare's human body will perish but his body of work will live on. The ideas here recall Ben Jonson's famous claim from the poem that we quoted at the beginning of this book: "He was not of an age, but for all time" (43). In this line, Shakespeare seems to live outside of normative temporality, just as the gods do.

Of course, it is writers who secure immortality for other writers, thus reinforcing (in a somewhat self-serving way) the idea that literature is the means by which individuals can achieve an apotheosis. Consider again a recollection of seeing a play recorded in Cicero's *De Amicitia*: "What resounding approval there was from the whole theater recently during the new play of my guest and friend Marcus Pacuvius!" (*qui clamores tota cavea nuper in hospitis et amici mei Marci Pacuvi nova fabula*, 24). Seeing the performance of excellent drama spurred playgoers to affirm the work and, in turn, spurred stories of its success. The audience's applause, though temporarily heard, has been permanently captured in Cicero's treatise. Recall also that it was audience applause that could free Prospero from his cell in *The Tempest*. The audience's immortalizing power appears in one of the dedicatory poems to the 1632 collection of Shakespeare's work, or "Second Folio." James Mabbe captures the life-granting magic of many hands clapping: "We thought thee dead, but this thy printed worth, / Tells thy Spectators, that thou went'st but forth / to enter with applause" (3–5). As we saw in the Introduction, Ben Jonson's memorial poem imagined summoning ancient dramatists to life in order to witness one of Shakespeare's plays. Here, we see a vision of future readers as new spectators as Mabbe wants us to see that Shakespeare's printed work represents a second performance for an audience still waiting to see more Shakespeare. We find even more overt language that suggests a deification of Shakespeare in the Second Folio. John Warren's dedicatory poem describes the playwright as "again revived," "twice lived," and "immortal" within the pages of the book (1, 2, 6).

Returning to Aristophanes' *Frogs* one final time, we note the comedian's interest in literary criticism and in his interest in the transcendent nature of poetry. This comedy, which pits Aeschylus against Euripides in the underworld, evaluates tragedy on a number of criteria, not only language and style but also its influence on contemporary audiences. In the comic battle between two of the preeminent poets of Athenian drama, Aeschylus and Euripides debate tragedy's didacticism. A significant aspect of the debate centers around the role of the producer of drama, the *didaskalos*, and Aeschylus claims:

> ἀλλ' ἀποκρύπτειν χρὴ τὸ πονηρὸν τόν γε ποιητήν,
> καὶ μὴ παράγειν μηδὲ διδάσκειν. τοῖς μὲν γὰρ παιδαρίοισιν
> ἐστὶ διδάσκαλος ὅστις φράζει, τοῖσιν δ' ἡβῶσι ποιηταί.

But the poet ought to conceal the depraved, and not stage or teach (*didaskein*) it. For children, is it the teacher (*didaskalos*) who instructs, but for young men, it's the poets.

1053–55

The Greek here and throughout this passage (cf. 1026, 1069) plays on a pun in *didaskalos*, which means both teacher and the producer of a play.

Euripides does not disagree about the role of the producer but argues that Aeschylus' pompously elevated (literally mountainous) style obscures his didactic objectives. His plays ought to have been composed, Euripides charges, in a human way (ἀνθρωπείως, 1058).[30] If his plays were not composed in a human way, how were they composed? Perhaps the criticism is that Aeschylus wrote his plays in the fashion of a wild beast. Yet the charge is not so much that his plays are nonsensical but that their message is inscrutable. We can understand Aristophanes' Euripides, therefore, to mean that Aeschylean language is like divine, oracular language that can be and often is misinterpreted by the very people for whom the oracles are meant.

Though this is intended to be a jab at his imperceptible language, the joke invites us to consider not only the divinity of Aeschylus' language but also Aeschylus and his art. At the beginning of the contest between Aeschylus and Euripides, Aeschylus complains: "because my poetry hasn't died with me, but his has so that he'll be able to read it" (ὅτι ἡ ποίησις οὐχὶ συντέθνηκέ μοι, / τούτῳ δὲ συντέθνηκεν, ὥσθ' ἕξει λέγειν, 868–69). The joke is that a tragic trilogy was composed for a single performance at a dramatic festival, but sometime after the death of Aeschylus in 456, a decree was passed to allow, for the first time, the reproduction of Aeschylus' tragedies as part of the dramatic competitions. Hence, Aeschylus' dramas are still "alive," but the same honor had not yet been granted to the recently deceased Euripides (or Sophocles for that matter). Thus, the dramatist's poetry provides him a kind of immortality unattainable for the poet himself.

In a move characteristic of Aristophanic comedy, the metaphorical immortality becomes a literal one as Dionysus chooses to bring Aeschylus back from the underworld, back from the dead. After the god of drama makes his selection, Euripides says:

ΕΥΡΙΠΙΔΗΣ ὦ σχέτλιε, περιόψει με δὴ τεθνηκότα;

ΔΙΟΝΥΣΟΣ τίς δ᾽ οἶδεν εἰ τὸ ζῆν μέν ἐστι κατθανεῖν, τὸ πνεῖν δὲ δειπνεῖν, τὸ δὲ καθεύδειν κῴδιον;

Euripides You scum, will you overlook that I, of all people, am dead?
Dionysus Who knows if living is dying, if drinking is eating, if sleeping is a sheepskin blanket?

1476–78

Had Euripides been chosen the winner, he suggests that he would no longer be dead. Instead, Aeschylus himself will return to life. Dionysus does not answer Euripides' question directly but rather responds by adapting a line of Euripides' own fragmentary *Polyidus* (fr. 638). Are these opposites, in fact, opposites? Is Aeschylus, in fact, alive? Is Euripides dead? The subsequent decree by the city to allow performances not only of Aeschylean dramas but of those by Euripides and Sophocles as well started these poets on the road to apotheosis of their own.[31] As the epitaph of Euripides cited at the beginning of this chapter reveals, the dramatist has no physical tomb if his dramas live on through production. Though the epitaph claims a metaphorical tomb in reproductions of his dramas—literally "the steps of Bacchus and scene-buildings quaking with his entrance"—Euripides becomes, in a sense, revivified himself in the footsteps of the god of theater.

Afterword: Entertaining Gods in Zimmerman's *Metamorphoses*

While the scope of our book ends just before the eighteenth century, the story certainly does not end there. Classical gods appear onstage many times since the age of Shakespeare, and they are often pointing to the work of dramatic performance.

One particularly evocative example on the theatrical stage in recent years is Mary Zimmerman's *Metamorphoses*, which premiered in 1996 at Northwestern University. Zimmerman is a playwright with deep interest in the classics and has written adaptations for the stage, including *Odyssey* and *Argonautika*, and she has directed plays set in antiquity by Shakespeare that include *Cymbeline* and *Pericles, Prince of Tyre*. Her dramaturgical flair and talents often push the limits of theatricality. Her *Metamorphoses* does just that. While the play began as an on-campus production at Zimmerman's home academic institution, it eventually transferred to Broadway in 2002 and won the 2002 Drama Desk, Drama League, and Lucille Lortel Awards for Best Play. It was nominated for the Tony Award for Best Play, and it won the Tony Award for Best Direction of a Play.

Her *Metamorphoses* dramatizes a handful of tales from Ovid's epic of the same name as well as one myth from Apuleius' *Metamorphoses*, a novel also known as *The Golden Ass*.[1] As Zimmerman notes, a limited cast plays the dozens of characters who appear in the play. The original cast of five women and five men played the more than seventy-five parts. The play's opening lines, spoken by a character identified as Woman, adapt the proem of Ovid's epic:

> Bodies, I have in mind, and how they change to assume
> new shapes—I ask the help of the gods, who know the trick:
> change me, and let me glimpse the secret and speak,
> better than I know how, of the world's birthing,
> and the creation of all things, from the first to the very latest.[2]

From the beginning of the play, then, Zimmerman ties the gods to elements of the performance itself, as the actress both notes the power of the gods to take on new shapes and begs their help to change her. On first reading, her plea suggests that the gods "change" her mind by conveying that which is unattainable for human beings: knowledge about the creation of the cosmos. The duality of bodies and minds, however, introduced in the first few words, and the nature of this performance, in which the actors play multiple parts, reveal that actors have the same power as the gods to transform into new shapes.[3]

The flux and flow of identity, inherent to theatrical spectacle, is reified by the set itself of *Metamorphoses*. A wooden deck surrounds a 1500-gallon pool of water. We can understand the pool as a metaphor for change as well as for reflection at work in the theater and in Ovid's epic poem. The water is used several times in the performance as a surface in which characters will see their own reflections and serves as a constant reminder that tales of the past, featuring gods and heroes of myth, are ones in which humans can see their own lives reflected. Yet the experimental techniques used in *Metamorphoses* will dispel notions of unified voices, identities, and selves. If Hamlet's thinly veiled dramatization of his uncle murdering King Hamlet was the proof point for the notion that "the purpose of playing [...] was and is to hold, as 'twere, the mirror up to / nature" (3.2.16–18), Zimmerman's play wants to show us a different purpose. In its innovative approaches, the play embodies the ways in which Marvin Carlson sees postmodern theater moving "ever further from even the illusion of an unmediated reality to which theatre could hold up its mirror."[4] Zimmerman's play and its massive pool of water do not seek to mirror the reality of playgoers' lived experience in the social sphere. Instead, they seek to refract an audience's experience of theatrical performance.

Our focus here is on one of these myths told in the play: the tale of Baucis and Philemon. Though the myth of Baucis and Philemon was not dramatized onstage in the classical period, Ovid features the story in his *Metamorphoses* (8.611–724).[5] In the tale, Jupiter and Mercury disguise themselves as mortal beggars and visit a town in order to test whether the inhabitants are following the rule of *xenia*, those ancient mandates for hospitality over which Zeus or Jupiter himself prevails. In violation of these rules, the two gods are dismissed from every household until they come upon the home of an elderly couple who welcome and entertain them. Ovid draws special attention to the old couple's poverty: they lived "in a small house, indeed, thatched with straw and reed from the marsh" (*parva quidem, stipulis et canna tecta palustri*, 8.630). Their accommodations only draw attention to the extreme generosity shown for their divine visitors disguised as beggars.

The very language of the story captures the notions of reciprocity and disguise that will prove to be so important for Zimmerman's conception of theatrical performance. The poem describes the entrance of the god into the old couple's little room: "Therefore when the celestial-dwelling gods reached the small, humble entrance, they entered the door with their heads lowered" (*ergo ubi caelicolae parvos tetigere penates / summissoque humiles intrarunt vertice postes,*

8.637–38). As is typical of the Ovidian style, the intricate language conveys subtitles so difficult to render in a translation. The word for gods here, *penates*, is typically used of familial gods of the household not Olympians, and so Jupiter and Mercury unusually, proleptically become protectors of this house even before they enter. The adjective *humiles* ("humble"), because of its ambiguous grammatical ending, could modify the object of the sentence, "the door," or the subject of the sentence, "the gods." This single word, therefore, reminds the audience of the gods' disguises and foreshadows the reciprocal generosity that both pairs will show one another.

The offerings of Baucis and Philemon are meager, but they miraculously find their pitcher of wine constantly full. Realizing that the two visitors are gods, the old couple raise their hands in supplication (Fig. 8). The gods then ask the couple to leave the town and not look back while it is destroyed by a flood. In reward for their hospitality, the humans are granted one request: to die together in the same moment. Upon their deaths, the gods transform them into a pair of intertwining trees. The story ends on an uplifting note, one of reciprocity and this time a kind

Fig. 8 Baucis and Philemon offer the gods the same supplication that the beggars, now posed as theatrical audience members, had offered them earlier. *Jupiter and Mercury in the House of Baucis and Philemon*, Hyacinthe Collin de Vermont (eighteenth century). Reproduced by permission of The Metropolitan Museum of Art, New York.

of reciprocal divinity focused on Baucis and Philemon: "Let those mindful of the gods be gods, and let those who have worshipped be worshipped" (*cura deum di sint, et, qui coluere, colantur*, 8.724). In Ovid's version of the myth, the old couple themselves become divinities for their attention to the affairs of the gods.

As is typical of metamorphoses in Ovid's epic, however, the transformation of the old couple opens up ambiguities that underlie any corporeal change, and Baucis and Philemon are bestowed a kind of vexed immortality that Zimmerman also captures. As Andrew Feldherr says, of the Ovidian epic, the Roman poet's treatment of transformation points toward an "exposure of the flux, change, and victimization that underlies" the cosmos.[6] Baucis and Philemon are no longer human or even, like Zeus and Hermes onstage, anthropomorphic. Their transformations and the very persistence of their story offer an immortality that they did not request.

As this short summary makes clear, the dramatized tale is plentiful with theatrical elements: acting, disguise, magical object-props, and ritualist performance in the social sphere.[7] Indeed, the play's interest in language, genre, metatheatricality, and change is encapsulated in the transition from the penultimate myth, the myth of Cupid and Psyche, to this last one. Psyche says to the audience, "If you will indulge us, we have one more tale to tell: a coda, if you will."[8] The actress breaks the fourth wall with the direct address to the audience and acknowledges the audience's role in theatrical spectacle. The audience must be a willing participant and "indulge" the actors, an idea that we saw presented in Euripides' *Helen* and Marlowe's *Doctor Faustus* as well as in Prospero's request to be set free in the Epilogue of Shakespeare's *The Tempest*. The "we" in Psyche's line points to the mutability of actors, particularly in this play, the limited cast of which performs, in the ancient fashion, multiple roles. The alliterative "tale to tell" draws attention to the joke in "a coda," coda deriving from the Latin *cauda* or tail. The punchline is not only in tale-tail but also Zimmerman's literary source of the Cupid and Psyche myth: Apuleius' *Metamorphoses* or *The Golden Ass*, a story about the metamorphosis of the protagonist into a donkey and his quest to regain his human form. The donkey's tail thus undergirds the joke. It is an appropriately subtle note of humor before the depiction of the myth of Baucis and Philemon, which, in Zimmerman's telling, blends the tragic and the comic to end the play on a poignant yet joyous note.

Among all the stories in Zimmerman's play, the tale of the old couple most explicitly wrestles with the transformative capacities of role-playing and dramatic action. This Zeus is about creation and vivification, just as we saw with early modern examples in Chapter 3. An onstage narrator describes the action as it happens, beginning by telling us that Zeus and Hermes "disguised themselves as two old beggars, filthy and poor, ragged and filthy."[9] The omniscience of the narrator thus expels any questions about the identity of the gods in disguise and helps to position the audience themselves closer to the gods' perspective than the humans who are tested in the final myth of the play. Zeus and Hermes further adopt the station of mortals through their colloquial diction. Zeus: "Hello, do you have any spare—"[10] Hermes: "Hello, we're tired, we live on the street, and we hoped that you might—"[11] Yet the gods are met only with quotidian callousness of the humans on whose doors they knock to request aid.

What distinguishes Baucis and Philemon from the other mortals is their immediate hospitality for the disguised gods. In this metatheatrical production, *xenia*, those rules of hospitality so important to Greek social relations, serves as a powerful analogue for theater, which requires the audience not only to accept but to embrace the identities of unknown figures. "Do you know us?," Zeus asks. "Of course," Philemon responds, "... You are the children of God."[12] Several moments in Greek drama presage this association of *xenia* and deceptive mimesis. For example, in Euripides' *Electra*, Electra's husband, a poor farmer, immediately accepts Orestes in disguise as one who brings a report about Orestes himself and invites him into their house to offer hospitality. The farmer says, "In return for your useful words, you will find as much hospitality (*xenia*) as my house contains" (ἀντὶ γὰρ χρηστῶν λόγων / ξενίων κυρήσεθ', οἷ' ἐμὸς κεύθει δόμος, 358–59). The exchange of stories for hospitality is deeply rooted in Greek culture and an evocative metaphor for the relationship between actors and audiences. This relationship was, for example, formalized between the people of the Greek island Samos and one of the most celebrated actors of antiquity, Polos of Aegina. In a decree of circa 306 (*SEG* 1.362), the actor was granted the status of guest-friend of the people (*proxenos*, 21) in acknowledgment of his generously accepting lower fees for his theatrical performance. Thus, even in antiquity, performance had been linked to the reciprocity of *xenia*.

Zimmerman draws attention to the importance of reciprocity in her production through performative gestures. The stage directions tell us that "Zeus *knocks on the surface of the deck. Both adopt supplicating poses.*"[13] The stance will be replicated by the human characters when they realize the true, divine nature of their visitors. When Baucis and Philemon welcome the disguised deities into their home, "*the narrative divides among several members of the company*" and "*the entire surface of the water becomes the 'table' being set with illuminated candles.*"[14] When the couple realizes that their visitors are gods, all of the narrators say, "And then they knew" just before all of the narrators exit the stage.[15] Julia Reinhard Lupton has traced the overlap between the experience of hospitality and the experience of theater, noting that "because entertainment as a social art involves sumptuary shifts and ceremonial extemporizing in spaces that invite welcoming and display, hospitality also bears immediately upon the stage."[16] The older couple's acceptance of these disguised strangers into their home and the staging of the home as a space to legitimize their interactions mirrors the experience of the audience members in the theater.

The metamorphoses within the tale also speak to Zimmerman's interest in the significance of change for the theater. At the end of this story, the original narrator then returns to the stage and tells the audience:

> Suddenly, everything was changing. The poor little house, their simple cottage, was becoming grander and grander, a glittering marble-columned temple. The straw and reeds of the thatched roof metamorphosed into gold, and gates with elaborate carvings sprang up, as ground gave way to marble paving stones.[17]

What the narrator describes here does not occur onstage, at least in the sense of what playgoers can see. However, the playgoers can imagine it nonetheless as *Metamorphoses* has continually made clear its overt metatheatrical valences. If a pool of water has already been an elderly couple's dining table (and, in earlier moments, the sea, a bed, and a therapist's couch), then certainly it can now be a grand temple. The couple, as in Ovid's version, are also transformed upon their deaths. The narrator of Zimmerman's play says, "Walking down the street at night, when you're all alone, you can still hear, stirring in the intermingled branches of trees above, the ardent prayer of Baucis and Philemon."[18] Among their whispered petitions, "Let me die still loving, and so, never die."[19] The tale thus captures the ambiguity of immortality available to human beings, who live on only through love for one another and through the whispers that invite a retelling of their story.

Further underscoring the inherent themes of fluidity and theatricality that *Metamorphoses* exposes in the tale, the actors who play Zeus and Hermes have played human characters throughout the presentation. In the original production, the actor playing Zeus played seven other characters, inducing three human ones and the narrator of one of the stories. The actor playing Hermes had four other roles, including a human character as well as that of the god Vertumnus, who himself wears a series of human disguises in the play.[20] The story has a special place in Zimmerman's play, too, as it ends the drama and ties to the opening, in which a character simply known as "Scientist" narrates the origins of the universe and Zeus mimics the introduction of light into the amorphous, chaotic cosmos by lighting a cigarette. Zeus notes one theory of the origins of humankind: "Some say that god perfected the world, / creating of his divine substance the race of humans."[21] Thus, the creation of humankind from divine material gestures toward the divine flux of identity as well as the imitation of divinity via the flesh of human beings.

Though Zimmerman does not explicitly draw on the early modern tradition, Shakespeare, too, found the story of Baucis and Philemon to be a flashpoint for discussing the nature of theatricality in two of his plays.[22] In *Much Ado About Nothing*, The Prince, named Don Pedro, courts Hero on behalf of his friend Claudio. Her name already points to the metatheatricality of the play. We are rooting for the hero, named Hero, and we know the play will involve high dramatics, "much ado," about events with few consequences, "nothing." At the beginning of the second act, the characters all gather at a masked ball, and so they become actors playing characters disguising themselves as other figures. We do not have a description of the masks, but we do know that the disguises still allow the characters to recognize each other. In this way, theatergoers see themselves in the characters who witness others playing roles. The scene takes us once more into a space where the spectator (now, a character in the play) sees both the actor and the character at once.

Yet while Hero certainly sees Don Pedro and his masked persona at once, he asks her to see other figures haunting his appearance. He invokes Ovid's tale and two of its characters when he remarks, "My visor is Philemon's roof. Within the house is Jove" (2.1.70). It is an allusion that does much work in the play. His appearance may be unassuming but it obscures greatness within. The mention of the tale of *theoxenia*, a welcoming of divine figures, overlays a narrative upon their interpersonal interaction, using literary history as a shorthand to define how they might relate to each other at this social gathering. The Ovidian metaphor frames Don Pedro as trustworthy, given the kindness that Philemon pays to his divine guests and his long-time marriage to his wife Baucis. It also portrays the Prince as playing a role. Within the metaphor, his outward appearance is that of a kind, older man (Philemon-like) while his internal identity is one possessing great authority (Jove-like). Yet, as a go-between for his friend and his friend's beloved, The Prince appears to be himself but speaks for another.

Ovid's tale does a different kind of work in a scene from *As You Like It*, though it also points to the operations of disguise and the inheritances of literary history that play a role in drama.[23] Several of its exiled characters take new names and identities as they navigate the forest world. In the middle of the play, we find the clown Touchstone wooing the country maiden Audrey, with a side comment by the court wit Jaques:

> **Touchstone**   I am here with thee, and thy goats, as the most capricious poet, honest Ovid, was among the Goths.
>
> **Jaques** (*aside*)   O, knowledge ill-inhabited, worse than Jove in a thatched house.
>
> **Touchstone**   When a man's verses cannot be understood, nor a man's good wit seconded with the forward child, understanding, it strikes a man more dead than a great reckoning in a little room. Truly, I would the gods had made thee poetical.
>
> **Audrey**   I do not know what "poetical" is. Is it honest in deed and word? Is it a true thing?
>
> **Touchstone**   No, truly; for the truest poetry is the most feigning, and lovers are given to poetry, and what they swear in poetry may be said as lovers, they do feign.
>
> 3.3.5–17

Touchstone compares his exile from the court to that of Ovid, when the Roman poet lived in Tomis by order of the Emperor Augustus. The exchange here is key for our discussion on several levels. It nods to the theme of hospitality. Though in spaces of strangers, both the clown and the ancient poet find a new home. Jaques' quip suggests how unqualified the interlocutors might be to discuss ancient poetry, yet both Touchstone's knowledge of Ovid's exile and Jaques' allusion to the disguised Zeus testify to their (and their audience's) knowledge of the culture and literature of classical antiquity. The clown places himself in the shadow of literary history, inviting us to see "goats" as "Goths" and his own wooing as guided by the ancient poet's advice for lovers.[24]

In some ways, this scene's use of Ovid's tale does the opposite work of the scene in *Much Ado About Nothing*. Jaques' aside asks us to doubt the clown's authority. Touchstone may know about Ovid, but this does not suggest we should trust that authority should be given to his thoughts and words. What joins the two scenes is that they both use the story of Baucis and Philemon to discuss how disguise functions to differentiate between external appearances and internal ones while reminding us to see both at once. Such is the function of theater and of suspension of disbelief. Within Touchstone's light-hearted claim, "the truest poetry is the most feigning," we find a nice articulation of one of the central conundrums explored in our own book. It is often in the depiction of the impossible that we find the most convincing performance. This might be an event as supernatural as the appearance of a god onstage or might be a natural and everyday occasion such as believing every word that emerges from a wooer's mouth.

Given the metatheatrical implications of this scene from Shakespeare's often-performed comedy, it is perhaps not surprising that Bert O. States chooses a line from this dialogue as the title for one of his most important studies. As we noted in the introduction to this book, *Great Reckonings in Little Rooms* gives us much to think about in terms of how the actor embodies and subsequently becomes the character. States elegantly captures the spirit of our exploration: "It is the *truth* of the god that arrives on the stage and not the stage that refers to a *real* god beyond it, existing in some unavailable form."[25] States would like us to imagine the realness of a god onstage derives from the realness of the fictional world into which that god emerges, divorcing the character from an abstract power in which audience members may or may not believe. We have extended such an argument by showing how the presence of gods onstage also reveals the true machinery behind the theatrical fiction. All the while, this revelation only deepens actors' and playgoers' engagements with the experience of creating theater. The realness of these gods manifests itself through the communal, co-constitutive experience of spectating, producing, and acting.

"A great reckoning in a little room." Has a better phrase ever described the work and experience of theater?

Baucis and Philemon certainly have their reckoning when they meet their gods in their small house, only to have that house turned into a majestic temple. Zimmerman's play not only shows us this couple's reckoning with the divine but also challenges us to embrace the divinity inherent in theatrical spectacle. The tale of Baucis and Philemon, like all the others, interacts with a massive pool of water in the center of the stage. This pool is a site of change and of reflection. Though the pool of water serves an important function throughout the play, there is a peculiar silence about another feature of the set that Zimmerman has imagined for the play. She describes a large painting of the sky "above which gods and goddesses might appear."[26] Thus, Zimmerman aims to depict the gods with their celestial grandeur, physically above the actors playing the parts of human beings. But the "Note on the Staging" mandates that the audience "look down at the playing space in such a way that the entire surface of the water is visible."[27] This painting, suggesting the loftiness of the gods, positions the audience as kind of divine spectators, looking down, as the gods do, on the interactions of human beings, all the while the audience also sees themselves within the stage itself, within the play.

A great reckoning, indeed.

Notes

Introduction

1. The festival featured 37 plays performed in 37 languages. Ninagawa was well known for his adaptations of Shakespeare. After his death in 2016, Gregory Doran, the artistic director of the Royal Shakespeare Company, praised Ninagawa as "a great interpreter of Shakespeare," and Catherine Mallyon, the organization's executive director, praised "Ninagawa's innovative take on classical theatre and eye for stunning staging." Quoted in Gil Sutherland, "'Great Interpreter of Shakespeare' Yukio Ninagawa Dies," *Stratford-Upon-Avon Herald* (May 13, 2016), https://www.stratford-herald.com/52307-great-interpreter-shakespeare-yukio-ninagawa-dies.html (accessed June 15, 2020).
2. We were thrilled to find this image for our book cover. It captures so nicely the artificiality of theatrical performance but also the way that sheer artificiality counter-intuitively generates the reality effect of drama. As Artaud puts it, "The theater, which is in no thing, but makes use of everything—gestures, sounds, words, screams, light, darkness—rediscovers itself at precisely the point where the mind requires a language to express its manifestations. To break through language in order to touch life is to create or recreate the theatre." Antonin Artaud, *The Theatre and its Double* (New York: Grove Press, 2013), 12–13.
3. John Lavagnino, "Year of Shakespeare: *Cymbeline* at the Barbican," *Blogging Shakespeare from the Shakespeare Birthplace Trust* (June 6, 2012), https://www.bloggingshakespeare.com/year-of-shakespeare-cymbeline-at-the-barbican (accessed June 1, 2020).
4. Lavagnino, cited above, praised the delivery as "expected" and "theatrically impressive." However, Howard Loxton found that "Jupiter was also a little disappointing: despite his thunder and lightning, which punctuates some scenes, he makes a very subdued delivery despite being borne through the air on a huge eagle." Howard Loxton, "Cymbeline," *British Theatre Guide* (n.d.), https://www.britishtheatreguide.info/reviews/cymbeline-barbican-theatr-7559 (accessed June 1, 2020).
5. Jean-Paul Sartre, "The Work of Art," in *The Imaginary: A Phenomenological Psychology of the Imagination*, ed. and trans. Jonathan Webber (London: Routledge, 2015), 191.
6. Ismene Lada-Richards, "Greek Tragedy and Western Perceptions of Actors and Acting," in *A Companion to Greek Tragedy*, ed. Justina Gregory (Oxford: Blackwell, 2005), 459.

7 Georg Wilhelm Friedrich Hegel, *Hegel on Tragedy*, ed. Anne Paolucci and Henry Paolucci (New York: Doubleday, 1962), 312.
8 Denis Feeney, *The Gods in Epic: Poets and Critics of the Classical Tradition* (New York: Oxford University Press, 1991), 5–56.
9 An older study but still a useful starting point for how myths were collected and presented in the period is DeWitt T. Starnes and Ernest William Talbert, *Classical Myth and Legend and Renaissance Dictionaries* (Chapel Hill: University of North Carolina Press, 1955). A shorter, more comprehensive overview of how ancient myth became so pervasive in the English imagination is Angus Smith, "Myth and Legend," in *The Ashgate Research Companion to Popular Culture in Early Modern England*, ed. Andrew Hadfield, Matthew Dimmock, and Abigail Shinn (New York: Routledge, 2016), 103–18.
10 Edgar Wind, *Pagan Mysteries in the Renaissance* (New York: Penguin, 1967), 26.
11 Alison Findlay and Vassiliki Markidou, "Introduction," in *Shakespeare and Greece*, ed. Alison Findlay and Vassiliki Markidou (London: Bloomsbury Arden Shakespeare, 2017), 1.
12 Leonard Barkan, *The Gods Made Flesh: Metamorphosis and the Pursuit of Paganism* (New Haven: Yale University Press, 1990), 183.
13 Don Cameron Allen, *Mysteriously Meant: The Rediscovery of Pagan Symbolism and Allegorical Interpretation in the Renaissance* (Baltimore: Johns Hopkins University Press, 1980), 1.
14 Erich Auerbach, *Mimesis: The Representation of Reality in Western Literature* (Princeton: Princeton University Press, 2013), xxvii.
15 On the hybridity of the present and the past, see Caroline Walker Bynum, *Metamorphosis and Identity* (New York: Zone Books, 2005); Johannes Fabian, *Time and the Other: How Anthropology Makes Its Object* (New York: Columbia University Press, 2002); Jonathan Gil Harris, *Untimely Matter in the Time of Shakespeare* (Philadelphia: University of Pennsylvania Press, 2011); and Reinhart Koselleck, *Futures Past: On the Semantics of Historical Time* (New York: Columbia University Press, 2004).
16 William Shakespeare, *Mr. William Shakespeare's Comedies, Histories, & Tragedies* (London: Printed by Isaac Jaggard and Edward Blount, 1623), A4–A5v. For an assessment of Shakespeare's knowledge of Latin, Greek, and ancient sources more broadly, an excellent overview is Jonathan Bate, *How the Classics Made Shakespeare* (Princeton: Princeton University Press, 2019). Other important works on the influence of Greek and Roman drama on Shakespeare and his contemporaries include: Robert Miola, *Shakespeare and Classical Tragedy: The Influence of Seneca* (Oxford: Clarendon Press, 1992) and *Shakespeare and Classical Comedy: The Influence of Plautus and Terence* (Oxford: Clarendon Press, 1995); Matthew Steggle, "Aristophanes in Early Modern England," in *Aristophanes in Performance 421 BC–AD*

2007: Peace, Birds, and Frogs, ed. Edith Hall and Amanda Wrigley (London: Legenda, 2007); David Hopkins, *Conversing with Antiquity: English Poets and the Classics, from Shakespeare to Pope* (Oxford: Oxford University Press, 2010); Helen Slaney, *The Senecan Aesthetic: A Performance History* (New York: Oxford University Press, 2016); Tania Demetriou and Tanya Pollard, "Homer and Greek Tragedy in Early Modern England's Theatres: An Introduction," *Classical Receptions Journal* 9.1 (2017): 1–35; and Curtis Perry, *Shakespeare and Senecan Tragedy* (Cambridge: Cambridge University Press, 2020)

17 Greek does occur in Shakespeare's poetry, however; cf. the Greek *threnos* in *The Phoenix and the Turtle*.

18 Michael Silk, "Shakespeare and Greek Tragedy: Strange Relationship," in *Shakespeare and the Classics*, ed. Charles Martindale and Anthony B. Taylor (Cambridge: Cambridge University Press, 2004), 241.

19 Colin Burrow, *Shakespeare and Classical Antiquity* (Oxford: Oxford University Press, 2013), 1–2.

20 For studies of classical learning in the early modern schoolroom, see Lynn Enterline, *Shakespeare's Schoolroom: Rhetoric, Discipline, Emotion* (Philadelphia: University of Pennsylvania Press, 2012) and Walter Ong, *Rhetoric, Romance, and Technology: Studies in the Interaction of Expression and Culture* (Ithaca: Cornell University Press, 2012), 1–112.

21 Micha Lazarus, "Greek Literacy in Sixteenth-Century England," *Renaissance Studies* 29 (2014): 433–58.

22 Key studies include Colin Burrow, *Shakespeare and Classical Antiquity* (Oxford: Oxford University Press, 2013); Tanya Pollard, *Greek Tragic Women on Shakespearean Stages* (Oxford: Oxford University Press, 2017); and Leah Whittington, *Renaissance Suppliants: Poetry, Antiquity, Reconciliation* (Oxford: Oxford University Press, 2016). Another excellent starting place is Sean Keilen and Nick Moschovakis, *The Routledge Research Companion to Shakespeare and Classical Literature* (Abingdon: Routledge, 2017).

23 Excellent starting points for understanding the influence of Ovid on English Renaissance culture include *Shakespeare's Ovid*, ed. Anthony B. Taylor (Cambridge: Cambridge University Press, 2000); Lynn Enterline, *The Rhetoric of the Body from Ovid to Shakespeare* (Cambridge: Cambridge University Press, 2000); *Ovid and Masculinity in English Renaissance Literature*, ed. John S. Garrison and Goran Stanivukovic (Montreal: McGill-Queen's University Press, 2020); and Raphael Lyne, *Ovid's Changing Worlds: English Metamorphoses 1567–1632* (Oxford: Oxford University Press, 2001).

24 Oliver Taplin, *Greek Tragedy in Action* (London: Routledge, 2003), 1.

25 See Martin Revermann, *Comic Business: Theatricality, Dramatic Technique, and Performance Contexts of Aristophanic Comedy* (Oxford: Oxford University Press,

2006); Alan Hughes, *Performing Greek Comedy* (Cambridge: Cambridge University Press, 2012); Pat Easterling and Edith Hall (eds.), *Greek and Roman Actors: Aspects of an Ancient Profession* (New York: Cambridge University Press, 2002); and Eric Csapo, *Actors and Icons of the Ancient Theater* (Oxford: Wiley-Blackwell, 2014). We also note here Eric Csapo and William Slater's *The Context of Ancient Drama* (Ann Arbor: University of Michigan Press, 2009), which presents much of the primary evidence about actors in translation with brief analyses.

26 Richard Schechner, *Between Theater and Anthropology* (Philadelphia: University of Pennsylvania Press, 1985), 35.

27 Quotations of Shakespeare come from *The Complete Works: Modern Critical Edition*, ed. Gary Taylor, John Jowett, Terri Bourus, and Gabriel Egan (New York: Oxford University Press, 2016).

28 Two other foundational thinkers in this area are Victor Turner, and his notion of "social drama" and Singer, with his notion of "cultural performance." See Victor Turner, *Schism and Continuity in an African Society. A Study of Ndembu Village Life* (Manchester: University of Manchester Press, 1957) and Milton Singer (ed.), *Traditional India: Structure and Change* (Philadelphia: American Folklore Society, 1958).

29 Erving Goffman, *The Presentation of the Self in Everyday Life* (London: Allen Lane, 1969), 19.

30 John J. MacAloon, "Introduction: Cultural Performances, Cultural Theory," in *Rite, Drama, Festival, Spectacle*, ed. John J. MacAloon (Philadelphia: Institute of the Study of Human Issues, 1984), 9.

31 Nova Myhill and Jennifer A. Low, "Introduction: Audience and Audiences," in *Imagining the Audience in Early Modern Drama, 1558–1642*, ed. Nova Myhill and Jennifer A. Low (New York: Palgrave Macmillan, 2011), 10.

32 Vaughan's book discusses allusions to six ancient gods: Ceres, Diana, Hercules, Mars, Jupiter, and Venus. Virginia Mason Vaughan, *Shakespeare and the Gods* (London: Bloomsbury Arden Shakespeare, 2019), 221.

33 Vaughan (2019: 2).

34 Lisa Maurice, *Screening Divinity* (Edinburgh: Edinburgh University Press, 2019), 202.

35 Jon D. Mikalson, *Honor Thy Gods: Popular Religion in Greek Tragedy* (Chapel Hill: University of North Carolina Press, 1992), 5.

36 Christiane Sourvinou-Inwood, *Tragedy and Athenian Religion* (Lanham: Lexington Books, 2003), 460, 514–15.

37 Christiane Sourvinou-Inwood, "Tragedy and Religion: Constructs and Readings," in *Greek Tragedy and the Historian*, ed. Christopher Pelling (Oxford: Oxford University Press, 1997), 182. Mary Lefkowitz, *Euripides and the Gods* (New York: Oxford University Press, 2016).

38 Pat Easterling, "Gods on Stage in Greek Tragedy," in *Religio Graeco-Romana: Festschrift für Walter Pötscher*, ed. Joachim Dalfen, Gerhard Petersmann, Franz Ferdinand Schwarz (Horn: F. Berger, 1993), 81.
39 Robert Parker, *Polytheism and Society at Athens* (Oxford: Oxford University Press, 2007), 152. Parker's chapter on the gods in the Greek theater provides a clear introduction to current debates.
40 Sarah Miles, "Gods and Heroes in Comic Space: A Stretch of the Imagination?," *Dionysus ex Machina* 2 (2011): 109–33.
41 Anna Clark, "Gods and Roman Comedy," in *The Cambridge Companion to Roman Comedy*, ed. Martin T. Dinter (Cambridge: Cambridge University Press, 2019), 219. Her essay is an excellent starting point on the gods in Roman comedy; those readers with Latin will find useful John A. Hanson, "Plautus as a Source Book for Roman Religion," *TAPA* 90 (1959): 48–101.
42 Jean Seznec, *The Survival of the Pagan Gods: The Mythological Tradition and its Place in Renaissance Humanism and Art*, trans. Barbara F. Sessions (New York: Pantheon Books, 1953), 13.
43 Jon Whitman, *Interpretation and Allegory: Antiquity to the Modern Period* (Boston: Brill Academic, 2003), 358.
44 Frances Yates, *Giordano Bruno and the Hermetic Tradition* (Chicago: University of Chicago Press, 1964), vi.
45 David Scott Kastan, *A Will to Believe: Shakespeare and Religion* (Oxford: Oxford University Press, 2014), 6.
46 Kastan describes the function of religion throughout Shakespeare's work in *A Will to Believe: Shakespeare and Religion*. Among other helpful resources, *Spiritual Shakespeares*, ed. Ewan Fernie (London: Routledge, 2005) contains essays that examine religious belief from a presentist perspective. Eric S. Mallin's *Godless Shakespeare* (London: Continuum, 2007) finds Shakespeare's characters exhibiting skepticism and unbelief rather than the pious beliefs popularized by his time. Anthony Baker's *Shakespeare, Theology, and the Unstaged God* (New York: Routledge, 2019) considers the apparent absence of religion in the plays from a different angle more focused on performance. He notes that the absence of God from the plays does not necessarily signal an atheistic outlook. Rather, he considers God to be an unseen actor-figure that expresses itself through the human wit in dialogue.
47 Kastan (2014), 6.
48 In the recent *Shakespeare and the Gods* (2019), Virginia Mason Vaughan inventories appearances or references to classical deities, providing in-depth discussion of six: Jupiter, Diana, Venus, Mars, Hercules, and Ceres. The present book, however, differs in two important ways from these recent studies: we focus more attention on performance than Lefkowitz does, and we discuss in detail dramatists from other genres (comedy) and other traditions (ancient Rome and Renaissance England). We

focus very little on allusion and the meanings with which particular gods would resonate with later audiences familiar with myth, as Vaughan does, and focus instead onto the questions that staged gods raise for theatricality.

49 Daryl Kaytor, "Shakespeare's Gods," *Literature and Theology* 29.1 (March 2015): 3.
50 Steven Mullaney, *The Reformation of Emotions in the Age of Shakespeare* (Chicago: University of Chicago Press, 2015), 62.
51 Rebecca Schneider, *Performing Remains: Art and War in Times of Theatrical Reenactment* (New York: Routledge, 2011), 6.
52 For example, see Csapo's critique of the periodization of Greek drama. "From Aristophanes to Menander? Genre Transformation in Greek Comedy," in *Matrices of Genre: Authors, Canons, and Society*, ed. Mary Depew and Dirk Obbink (Cambridge: Harvard University Press, 2000).
53 William B. Worthen, *Shakespeare Performance Studies* (Cambridge: Cambridge University Press, 2014), 18.
54 We use "performative" here in the theatrical sense, but Marlowe's play also serves as a thought-provoking case study for the broader philosophical notion of a speech-act as "performative." See Andrew Sofer, "How to Do Things with Demons: Conjuring Performatives in Doctor Faustus," *Theatre Journal* 61.1 (March 2009): 1–21.
55 Vaughan (2019: 8).

Chapter 1

1 For an excellent introduction to the term and overview of the reception of the practice in theater, see "Deus ex Machina," in *The Classical Tradition*, ed. Anthony Grafton, Glenn W. Most, and Salvatore Settis (Boston: Harvard University Press, 2010), 263–64.
2 The date of the first use of the *mechane* in the fifth century is controversial. On the evidence for its introduction and function, see Donald Mastronarde, "Actors on High: The Skene Roof, the Crane, and the Gods in Attic Drama," *Classical Antiquity* 9 (1990): 247–94. See also Francis M. Dunn, *Tragedy's End: Closure and Innovation in Euripidean Drama* (New York: Oxford University Press, 1996).
3 Victor Turner made these remarks in an address given in 1980. Quoted in Richard Schechner and Willa Appel, "Introduction," in *Means of Performance: Intercultural Studies of Theatre and Ritual*, eds. Richard Schechner and Willa Appel (Cambridge: Cambridge University Press, 1990), 1.
4 The plays are Sophocles' *Ajax* and Euripides' *Andromache, Bacchae, Electra, Helen, Hippolytus, Ion, Iphigenia Among the Taurians, Orestes, Suppliant Women* as well as the *Rhesus*, a play that is likely not by Euripides but attributed to him.

5 Lada-Richards (2005: 466) has suggested that the theme of madness in Greek drama aligns "the stage-player and the madman in a manner reminiscent of European puritan anti-theatricality."
6 On whether Athena appears on the stage or on the roof of the stage building, see Patrick Finglass, *Sophocles: Ajax* (Cambridge: Cambridge University Press, 2011), 137–38.
7 Easterling (1993: 82).
8 For an insightful discussion of Apollo's appearance in *The Winter's Tale*, as well as in George Peele's *The Arraignment of Paris* (1584), Robert Wilson's *The Cobbler's Prophesy* (1594), Thomas Heywood's *The Golden Age* (1611), the anonymous *The Maid's Metamorphosis* (1600), and John Lyly's *Midas* (1589), see David Bergeron, "The Apollo Mission in *The Winter's Tale*," in *The Winter's Tale: Critical Essays*, ed. Maurice Hunt (New York: Routledge, 1995), 361–82.
9 John L. Austin, *How to Do Things With Words* (Oxford: Oxford University Press, 1975), 12.
10 For two excellent collections of and reflections upon this and other enduring myths (e.g., that productions of *Macbeth* ["the Scottish play"] are haunted, that Shakespeare was Catholic), see Laurie Maguire and Emma Smith, *30 Great Myths About Shakespeare* (Oxford: Wiley-Blackwell, 2013); and Stanley Wells, *Is It True What They Say About Shakespeare?* (Ebrington: Long Barn Books, 2007).
11 The mixing of the ancient Greek and Roman names might be interpreted as a nod towards the ways that the early modern present is itself a hybrid that intermingles classical elements. Or, more playfully, might imply that Ariel does not know his mythology that well.
12 By watching a group of spectators, the theatrical audience members are invited to reflect on their shared experience of heightened emotion. Francis Bacon remarks that "the minds of men in company are more open to affections and impressions than when alone." See Francis Bacon, *The Advancement of Learning*, ed. J. Devey (New York: P.F. Collier & Son, 1901), 97.
13 Alison P. Hopgood, *Passionate Playgoing in Early Modern England* (Cambridge: Cambridge University Press, 2014), 28.
14 Elizabeth Spiller, "Shakespeare and the Making of Early Modern Science: Resituating Prospero's Art," *South Central Review* 26 (2009): 25.
15 Spiller (2009: 25).
16 The reference to the "globe" may also nod to the stage globe in Jonson's *Hymenaei*, and the "rack" may refer to the cloud effect in that same masque. See David Bevington, "*The Tempest* and the Jacobean Court Masque," in *The Politics of the Stuart Court Masque,* ed. David Bevington and Peter Holbrook (Cambridge: Cambridge University Press, 1998), 239. For an edition of the play with excellent notes, see Ben Jonson, "*Hymenaei*, or the Solemnities of Masque and Barriers at a

Marriage," in *Ben Jonson: Selected Masques*, ed. Stephen Orgel (New Haven Yale University Press, 1970), 47–78.
17 Sarah Beckwith, *Shakespeare and the Grammar of Forgiveness* (Ithaca: Cornell University, 2011), 170. In Chapter 4, we return to the question of when and how humans (rather than the gods) resolve classical and early modern dramas.
18 Brian W. Schneider, *The Framing Text in Early Modern English Drama: 'Whining' Prologues and Armed Epilogues* (London: Routledge, 2016), 6, argues that epilogues represent porous boundaries of the theatre "in which real life and dramatic imagination tended to merge."
19 William Arrowsmith, "Aristophanes' *Birds*: The Fantasy Politics of Eros," *Arion* 1 (1973): 162–64.
20 There is little room for overlap between *caritas* and *cupiditas* in the early modern Christian morality scheme. Indeed, in his influential discussion of *caritas* and *cupiditas*, the Christian theologian Thomas Aquinas celebrated *caritas* exclusively: *est autem alia cupiditas venialis peccati, quae semper diminuitur per caritatem: sed tamen talis cupiditas caritatem diminuere non potest, ratione iam dicta.* See Thomas Aquinas, *Summa Theologica*, vol. 34, ed. Thomas Gilby (New York: McGraw-Hill, 1964–1981), 68.
21 The header is composed by Philemon Holland, the editor and translator of the early modern collection of Plutarch, *The Philosophie, Commonly Called the Morals* (London: Arnold Hatfield, 1603), 83.
22 Jane Kingsley-Smith, *Cupid in Early Modern Literature and Culture* (Cambridge: Cambridge University Press, 2010), 2.
23 Thomas Heywood, "The Apology for Actors (1612)," in *Reader in Tragedy: An Anthology of Classical Criticism to Contemporary Theory*, ed. Marcus Nevitt and Tanya Pollard (London: Bloomsbury, 2019), 71.
24 Heywood (2019: 71).
25 Kathryn Schwarz, *Tough Love: Amazon Encounters in the English Renaissance* (Durham: Duke University Press, 2000), 131.
26 On this episode, see Françoise Frontisi-Ducroux, "The Invention of the Erinyes," in *Visualizing the Tragic: Drama, Myth, and Ritual in Greek Art and Literature: Essays in Honour of Froma Zeitlin*, ed. Christina S. Kraus (Oxford: Oxford University Press, 2007), 165–76.
27 Stephen Gosson, "Plays Confuted in Five Actions," in *The Broadview Anthology of Sixteenth-Century Poetry and Prose*, ed. Marie Loughlin, Sandra Bell, and Patricia Brace (Buffalo: Broadview Press, 2012), 451.
28 Philip Sidney, "The Defense for Poesy," in *The Broadview Anthology of Sixteenth-Century Poetry and Prose*, ed. Marie Loughlin, Sandra Bell, and Patricia Brace (Buffalo: Broadview Press, 2012), 718.

29 Stephen Halliwell, *Between Ecstasy and Truth: Interpretations of Greek Poetics from Homer to Longinus* (Oxford and New York: Oxford University Press, 2011), 6.
30 For more on the peculiar temporality of play performance, see Pat E. Easterling "Anachronism in Greek Tragedy," *JHS* 105 (1985): 1–10; Matthew D. Wagner, *Shakespeare, Theatre, and Time* (New York: Routledge, 2012); David Wiles, *Theatre and Time* (New York: Palgrave, 2014); Scott Maisano, "Now," in *Early Modern Theatricality*, ed. Henry S. Turner (Oxford: Oxford University Press, 2013), 368–87; Margreta de Grazia, "Anachronism," in *Cultural Reformations: Medieval and Renaissance in Literary History*, ed. Brian Cummings and James Simpson (Oxford: Oxford University Press, 2010), 15.
31 Nicely capturing the complexity of her own play based on Ovidian myth, she says, "It has been said that the myth is a public dream, dreams are private myths. Unfortunately we give our mythic side scant attention these days. As a result, a great deal escapes us and we no longer understand our own actions. So it remains important and salutary to speak not only of the rational and easily understood, but also of enigmatic things: the irrational and the ambiguous." Mary Zimmerman, *Metamorphoses* (Evanston: Northwestern University Press, 2002), 67–68.
32 On this philosophical tradition, see Feeney (1991: 5–56).
33 Mary Lefkowitz, "'Impiety' and 'Atheism' in Euripides' Dramas," *CQ* 39 (1989): 70–82. See also Tim Whitmarsh, *Battling the Gods: Atheism in the Ancient World* (New York: Knopf Doubleday, 2015).
34 Christopher Marlowe, *Dido, Queen of Carthage* (London: Thomas Woodcocke, 1594), s.d. 1.1.1.
35 Stephen Orgel, *Impersonations: The Performance of Gender in Shakespeare's England* (Cambridge: Cambridge University Press, 1996), 70.
36 Milton invokes Bellerophon's flight as a cautionary tale (*Paradise Lost* 7.16–20).
37 The weddings could just as easily be performed by an available human character. Kenneth Branagh makes this change in his film version of the play. *As You Like It*, directed by Kenneth Branagh (London and New York: BBC Films and HBO Films, 2006), DVD.
38 Gosson responds to Thomas Lodge's *Defense of Poetry, Music, and Stage Plays* (1579), which itself was a response to Gosson's treatise published in the same year, *The School of Abuse*. Stephen Gosson ("Plays Confuted in Five Actions," 2012: 451).
39 Kendall L. Walton, *Mimesis as Make-believe: On the Foundations of the Representational Arts* (Cambridge: Harvard University Press, 1990), 27.
40 Shakespeare 1623, S2v. Emphasis added.
41 Jeffrey Masten, *Queer Philologies: Sex, Language, and Affect in Shakespeare's Time* (Philadelphia: University of Pennsylvania Press, 2016), 62–63.
42 In this case, though the marriage was arranged by James I, it notably ended in annulment several years later. See *Ben Jonson: Selected Masques* (New Haven: Yale

University Press, 1970) and Edmund Kerchever Chambers, *The Elizabethan Stage*, vol. I (of 4 vols) (Oxford: Oxford University Press, 1923), 172–73.
43 Walter Benjamin, "The Storyteller: Reflections on the Works of Nikolai Leskov," in *Illuminations: Essays and Reflections*, ed. Hannah Arendt (London: Fontana, 1982), 109.
44 Richard McCoy, "Awakening Faith in *The Winter's Tale*," in *Shakespeare and Early Modern Religion*, ed. David Loewenstein and Michael Witmore (Cambridge: Cambridge University Press, 2015), 215.

Chapter 2

1 Bread, "If," released March 1971, track 4 on *Manna* (Hollywood: Elektra, 1971).
2 These anecdotes and other sources on Zeuxis are gathered in Jerome Pollitt, *The Art of Ancient Greece: Sources and Documents* (Cambridge: Cambridge University Press, 2001), 149–51.
3 On Helen from antiquity to the present, see Bettany Hughes, *Helen of Troy: The Story Behind the Most Beautiful Woman in the World* (New York: Vintage, 2007), esp. 298–307; Laurie Maguire, *Helen of Troy: From Homer to Hollywood* (Hoboken: Wiley-Blackwell, 2009); Ruby Blondell, *Helen of Troy: Beauty, Myth, Devastation* (New York: Oxford University Press, 2016); and Lowell Edmunds, *Stealing Helen: The Myth of the Abducted Wife in Comparative Perspective* (Princeton: Princeton University Press, 2016), esp. 197–235. Hughes has a short chapter on Marlowe's play, which Blondell and Edmunds discuss only briefly. On the reception of Greek drama in the work of Marlowe, see Charles Martindale, "Marlowe," in *The Oxford History of Classical Reception in English*, vol. II, ed. P. Cheney and P. Hardie (New York: Oxford University Press, 2015).
4 Anne Duncan, *Performance and Identity in the Classical World* (New York: Cambridge University Press, 2006), 12–13, discusses three ancient "*de facto* theor[ies] of acting" that explain how audiences "coped with the threat of theatrical deception"; according to these theories, an actor played a character similar to his own nature, or the actor was temporarily possessed by the character, or the technical skill of actors permitted them to take on the persona of different characters. Richard Green, "Towards a Reconstruction of Performance Style," in *Greek and Roman Actors: Aspects of an Ancient Profession*, ed. Pat Easterling and Edith Hall (Cambridge: Cambridge University Press, 2002), 93–94, suggests that the inexperience of ancient audiences explains their tendency to see performance as "real."
5 Easterling (1993: 81).
6 Michael Silk, "Heracles and Greek Tragedy," *G&R* 32 (1985): 6.

7 Those readers familiar with Stephen Halliwell will note throughout this chapter an affinity with his conception of ecstasy in Greek poetics. He (2011: 6) describes ecstasy as "being outside oneself" as "experienced in direct encounter with song or poetry."
8 See William Allan (ed.), *Euripides: Helen* (Cambridge: Cambridge University Press, 2008), 10–28.
9 See Alfred Heubeck et al., *A Commentary on Homer's Odyssey*, vol. I (Oxford: Clarendon Press, 1988), *ad Od.* 4.279 on the scholiast and on the disputed authenticity of the line.
10 Froma I. Zeitlin, "Travesties of Gender and Genre in Aristophanes' *Thesmophoriazousae*," *Critical Inquiry* 8 (1981): 322.
11 On Helen's voice in Homeric epic, see Nancy Worman, "This Voice Which Is Not One: Helen's Verbal Guises in Homeric Epic," in *Making Silence Speak: Women's Voices in Greek Literature and Society*, ed. A. Lardinois and L. McClure (Princeton: Princeton University Press, 2001). Worman (2001: 30) notes that when Helen asks whether she should tell Telemachus truth or lies (*Od.* 4.140), her statement "recall[s] the power that the Muses possess" (cf. Hesiod's *Theogony* 27).
12 Leah Rissman, *Love as War: Homeric Allusion in the Poetry of Sappho* (Königstein: Hain, 1983); John Winkler, "Double Consciousness in Sappho's Lyrics," in *The Constraints of Desire: The Anthropology of Sex and Gender in Ancient Greece* (New York: Routledge, 1990), 162–87.
13 Gorgias says that *logos* accomplishes the most divine deeds (θειότατα ἔργα, 8) and that the sight of bodies is effective either because *eros* is a malady and sickness of the soul (ἀνθρώπινον νόσημα καὶ ψυχῆς ἀγνόημα, 19) or because *eros* is a god with the divine power of gods (θεὸς <ὢν ἔχει> θεῶν θείαν δύναμιν, 19) to drive them from rational thinking (φρόνημα, νόημα, 17); see Zeitlin (1981: 324–27), Nancy Worman, "The Body as Argument: Helen in Four Greek Texts," *CA* 16 (1997): 171–80, and Charles Segal, "Gorgias and the Psychology of the Logos," *HSCP* 66 (1962): esp. 120–21. See also Gorgias fr. B23 on tragedy and deception.
14 On representations of this myth in art, see Lilly Kahil, "Helene," *LIMC* 4.1 (1988): 559–61.
15 See generally Isabelle Torrance, *Metapoetry in Euripides* (New York: Oxford University Press, 2013); on the metatheatrical qualities of *Helen*, see Anne N. Pippin, "Euripides' *Helen*: A Comedy of Ideas," *CPh* 55 (1960): 151–63; and Charles Segal, "The Two Worlds of Euripides' *Helen*," *TAPA* 102 (1971): 553–614.
16 Donald J. Mastronarde, *The Art of Euripides* (New York: Cambridge University Press, 2010), 170.
17 Froma Zeitlin, "Playing the Other: Theater, Theatricality, and the Feminine in Greek Drama," in *Nothing to Do with Dionysos? Athenian Drama in its Social Context*, ed.

John Winkler and Froma I. Zeitlin (Princeton: Princeton University Press, 1992), 71. See also Worman (1997: 151–203).

18 On the religious experience of spectatorship in Attic drama, see Easterling 1993, Sourvinou-Inwood 2003, Mastronarde 2010, and Lefkowitz 2016.

19 The antecedents of Euripides' eidolon are found in Stesichorus' *Palinode*. Herodotus tells a similar version of Helen in Troy, though he does not mention the eidolon (2.118–19). See Matthew Wright, *Euripides' Escape-Tragedies: A Study of Helen, Andromeda and Iphigenia Among the Taurians* (New York: Oxford University Press, 2005), 56–157 and Allan (2008: 18–28).

20 Eric Downing, "Apatê, Agôn, and Literary Self-Reflexivity in Euripides' *Helen*," in *Cabinet of the Muses: Essays on Classical and Comparative Literature in Honor of Thomas G. Rosenmeyer*, eds. M. Griffith and Donald J. Mastronarde (Atlanta: Scholars Press, 1990).

21 Helen tells a syncopated account of her birth. The full account, that Zeus has ordered Aphrodite to transform into an eagle and pursue him, was likely told in Cratinus' lost comedy *Nemesis* of 431. See Jeffrey Henderson, "Pursuing Nemesis: Cratinus and Mythological Comedy," in *No Laughing Matter: New Studies in Old Comedy*, ed. C.W. Marshall and G.A. Kovacs (London: Bloomsbury, 2012).

22 Some editors have suggested deleting these lines. David Kovacs, *Euripides: Helen. Phoenician Women. Orestes* (Cambridge: Harvard University Press, 2002), deletes 20–21. James Diggle, *Euripidis Fabulae*, vol. 3 (Oxford: Oxford University Press, 1994) and Richard Kannicht, *Euripides: Helena*, 2 vols. (Heidelberg: Winter, 1969), delete 257–59. Allan (2008, *ad* 257–59) rightly defends their retention: "As in her prologue-speech, [Helen's] tone of skepticism at the details of her birth ... highlights her sense of abandonment by the gods."

23 Friedrich Solmsen, "ΟΝΟΜΑ and ΠΡΑΓΜΑ in Euripides' *Helen*," *CR* 48 (1934): 119–21; Karen Bassi, "The Somatics of the Past: Helen and the Body of Tragedy," in *Acting on the Past: Historical Performance Across the Disciplines*, eds. M. Franko and A. Richards (Hanover: Wesleyan University Press, 2000).

24 Later the Chorus call it Hera's sacred eidolon (εἴδωλον ἱερὸν Ἥρας, 1136).

25 Cf. the Dioscuri's description of Helen's path from Sparta to Egypt via the heavens (τὸν κατ' οὐρανὸν δρόμον, 1671).

26 Allan (2008: *ad* 35–36).

27 As Segal (1971: 561) notes, "*Helen* [...] has a more epistemological and ontological focus than" his *Medea*, *Hippolytus*, and even *Bacchae*.

28 Ekplexis is discussed in Gorgias' theory of *opsis* (cf. *Encomium of Helen* 16); see Segal (1962: 131–35).

29 Cf. Halliwell (2011: 169–80).

30 Gregory Dobrov, *Figures of Play: Greek Drama and Metafictional Poetics* (New York: Oxford University Press, 2001), 75; on the metatheatricality of the *Bacchae*, see also

Charles Segal, *Dionysiac Poetics and Euripides'* Bacchae (Princeton: Princeton University Press, 1997) and Helene Foley, "The Masque of Dionysus," *TAPA* 110 (1980): 107–33.

31 Zeitlin (1992: 88) suggests that Euripides' *Helen*, and his *Bacchae*, "'feminized' tragedy."

32 On the idea that gods in theater are the gods of cult, in addition to Sourvinou-Inwood 2003 see Sourvinou-Inwood 1997. For an opposing view, see Mikalson 1992.

33 For a more extensive discussion of how Faustus' encounter with Helen speaks to questions of the early modern cultural memory of classical antiquity, see John S. Garrison, "Marlowe's Helen and the Erotics of Cultural Memory," in *Sexuality and Memory in Early Modern England: Literature and the Erotics of Recollection*, ed. John S. Garrison and Kyle Pivetti (London: Routledge, 2016), 120–27. The analysis of Helen here draws from and extends that earlier thinking.

34 Quotations from the play are drawn from Christopher Marlowe, "The Tragical History of Doctor Faustus," in *English Renaissance Drama: A Norton Anthology*, ed. D. Bevington, L. Engle, K.E. Maus, and E. Rasmussen (New York: W.W. Norton, 2002), 250–85.

35 Bert O. States, *Great Reckonings in Little Rooms: On the Phenomenology of Theater* (Berkeley: University of California Press, 1985), 159.

36 Bassi (2000: 26).

37 For an intriguing discussion of a series of choices in portraying Helen by the Royal Shakespeare Company since the 1960s, see Laura Godwin, "'There is nothin' like a Dame': Christopher Marlowe's Helen of Troy at the Royal Shakespeare Company," *Shakespeare Bulletin* 27 (2009): 69–79. For a useful history of arguments regarding whether or not Faustus sins by kissing a demonic Helen and a discussion of whether we should place this Helen in the literary tradition of depicting the succubus, see Nicolas Kiessling, "Faustus and the Sin of Demoniality," *Studies in English Literature 1500–1900* 15 (1975): 205–11.

38 For a modern edition of the play, see John Lyly, "The Descent of Euphues," in *Three Elizabethan Romance Stories*, ed. J. Winny (Cambridge: Cambridge University Press, 2015), 1.

39 See Lyly (2015: 1)

40 Arthur Golding, *The xv bookes of P. Ovidius Naso, entytled Metamorphosis, translated oute of Latin into English meeter* (London: William Seres, 1567), 15.255–56.

41 Lyly is not necessarily an innovator in imagining Helen in this way. The "blemished" appearance of Helen shows up at the end of Euripides' play, where she changes masks to signify her mourning of Menelaus' fake death (cf. *Helen* 1186–90).

42 The *OED* notes that several definitions of the noun "spoils" circulated in the fifteenth and sixteenth centuries. In addition to our more familiar usage of the term as "goods, esp. such as are valuable, taken from an enemy or captured city in time of war," a

now-rare usage indicated "damage, harm, impairment, or injury, esp. of a serious or complete kind."
43 Marvin Carlson, *The Haunted Stage: The Theater as Memory Machine* (Ann Arbor: University of Michigan Press, 2003), 9.
44 States (1985: 199).
45 Quoted in Edmund K. Chambers, *The Elizabethan Stage*, vol. III (Oxford: Oxford University Press, 1923), 424.
46 William Prynne, *Histriomastix: The Player's Scourge, or Actor's Tragedy* (London: 1633), 556r.
47 The stage directions once more refer to the character as "Helen" when she re-enters at s.d. 5.1.89.
48 Although he famously advocates for ascertaining veracity of phenomena through repetition of experiments by multiple natural philosophers, Bacon also warns that "the minds of men in company are more open to affections and impressions than when alone." In the early modern imagination, this scene of a group of men stunned by a woman's beauty may in fact discredit the objective nature of their observations. That is, we see here a scene of closet drama not of the laboratory. See Bacon (1901 [1605]: 116).
49 This tension may be emblematic of a wider matrix of seemingly binary tensions that drive the dialectic energies of the play. Thomas Cartelli, *Marlowe, Shakespeare, and the Economy of Theatrical Experience* (Philadelphia: University of Pennsylvania Press, 1991), 122, suggests that "In *Doctor Faustus,* his most celebrated achievement, we again find Marlowe casting about in seemingly opposed directions at one and the same time."
50 This reading, though often favored by scholars because of Faustus' claim that "Her lips sucks forth my soul," seems unlikely to be the perception of early modern playgoers. Keith Thomas, *Religion and the Decline of Magic: Studies in Popular Beliefs in Sixteenth- and Seventeenth-Century England* (London: Penguin, 1971), 529, notes that a belief in incubus and succubus (demons who prey upon humans by engaging in sexual relations with them) was rare in early modern England (as opposed to continental Europe or medieval England) and that accusations of such were almost entirely initiated by the English witchfinder Matthew Hopkins.
51 Stephen Gosson, *Playes Confuted in Five Actions* (London: 1582), B4r.
52 Gosson (1582: D4v).
53 Garrett Sullivan, *Memory and Forgetting in English Renaissance Drama: Shakespeare, Marlowe, Webster* (Cambridge: Cambridge University Press, 2005), 77.
54 This fantasy of joining the age of heroes seems consciously only that: a fantasy. Anthony Dawson singles out Marlowe for "his awareness of theatrical poverty—the problem of representing on stage the grand images of past heroism and defeat." All the while that the theater may offer early modern audiences the only venue in which

to see figures from antiquity in action, it only emphasizes that those visions are figures of imagination. Dawson adds, "Performance is a form of remembering just as remembering is a form of repetition: both hark back to a past that is originary and yet inaccessible." See Anthony Dawson, "Priamus is Dead: Memorial Repetition in Marlowe and Shakespeare," in *Shakespeare, Memory, and Performance*, ed. Peter Holland (Cambridge: Cambridge University Press, 2006), 65.

55 Michael Keefer, "Fairer than the Evening Air: Marlowe's Gnostic Helen of Troy and the Tropes of Belatedness of Historical Mediation," in *Fantasies of Troy: Classical Tales and the Social Imaginary in Medieval and Early Modern Europe*, ed. A. Shepard and S.D. Powell (Toronto: Centre for Reformation and Renaissance Studies, 2004), 48.
56 Pollard (2017: 3).
57 M.L. Stapleton, *Marlowe's Ovid: The Elegies in the Marlowe Canon* (Farnham: Ashgate, 2014), 191.
58 Jan Frans van Dijkhuizen, *Devil Theatre: Demonic Possession and Exorcism in English Renaissance Drama, 1558–1642* (Cambridge: D.S. Brewer, 2007), 47 n. 45.
59 George Peele, *A Tale of Troy* (London: I.C., 1589), B3v.
60 George Seferis, "Helen," in *George Seferis: Collected Poems*, ed. and trans. Edmund Keeley and Philip Sherrard (Princeton: Princeton University Press, 1995), 178.
61 Carlson (2003: 65).
62 Neil Rhodes, "Marlowe and the Greeks," *Renaissance Studies* 27 (2011): 199–218.
63 On the importance of considering the possible mediations in the process of reception, see Charles Martindale, "Afterword: Greek Texts and the Early Modern Stage," *CRJ* 9 (2017): 166–76.
64 Erasmus, *Luciani Erasmo interprete Dialogi & alia emuncta* (Paris: Ascensius, 1514), 93.
65 On Lucian and Greek drama, see Orestis Karavas, *Lucien et la tragédie* (Berlin: De Gruyter, 2005), and Thomas Schmitz, "A Sophist's Drama: Lucian and Classical Tragedy," in *Beyond the Fifth Century: Interactions with Greek Tragedy from the Fourth Century BCE to the Middle Ages*, ed. I. Gildenhard and M. Revermann (Berlin: De Gruyter, 2010); on the literary history of Marlowe's line, see Maguire (2009: 160–64).
66 Erasmus (1514: 93) translated the pun *ossa ... calvariasque carnibus renudatas*.

Chapter 3

1 Consider, for example, the recent obituary headline: "Ian Holm, Malleable Actor Who Played Lear and Bilbo, Dies at 88" (Mel Gussow, *New York Times*, June 19, 2020). Great actors are celebrated for their ability to change into and adopt new

identities. A complication to this claim might be the question of the stock-character or type-casting. On the one hand, Stanislavski claims that "the most ardent partisans of the custom of type-casting are the poorly endowed actors, whose range is rather not broad but one-sided." However, we need not dismiss the greatness of actors who seem to come from (what we today would term) central casting to play a stock character. Stanley Cavell remarks, "what makes someone a type is not his similarity with other members of that type but his striking separateness from other people"; see Stanley Cavell, *The World Viewed: Reflections on the Ontology of Film* (Cambridge: Harvard University Press, 1979), 33; and Constantin Stanislavski, "Types of Actors," in *Stanislavski's Legacy: A Collection of Comments on a Variety of Aspects of an Actor's Art and Life*, trans. Elizabeth Reynolds Hapgood (New York: Routledge, 1999), 16.

2 David Giles, *Illusions of Immortality: A Psychology of Fame* (New York: Palgrave Macmillan, 2000), 32.

3 See, especially, Lyne 2001, as well as the discussion of scholarship on Ovidian receptions in our Introduction. For a widely popular (though not uncriticized) account of the far-reaching effects of Lucretius' text, see Stephen Greenblatt, *The Swerve: How the World Became Modern* (New York: W.W. Norton, 2011). Another account that is focused on Renaissance receptions of the text is Jonathan Goldberg, *The Seeds of Things: Theorizing Sexuality and Materiality in Renaissance Representations* (New York: Fordham University Press, 2009). See also David A. Hedrich Hirsch, "Donne's Atomies and Anatomies: Deconstructed Bodies and the Resurrection of Atomic Theory," *Studies in English Literature* 31.1 (1991): 69–94. For the influence of Lucretius on yet another canonical author, see Jessie Hock, "'The Mind Is Its Own Place': Lucretian Moral Philosophy in *Paradise Lost*," in *Milton's Modernities: Poetry, Philosophy, and History from the Seventeenth Century to the Present*, ed. Patrick Fadely and Feisal G. Mohammed (Evanston: Northwestern University Press, 2017).

4 Edmund Spenser, *The Faerie Queene* (London: Printed by H.L. for Matthew Lownes, 1609), Hh4.

5 Thomas Heywood, "The Prologue to the Stage, at the Cocke-pit," in Christopher Marlowe's *The Famous Tragedy of the Rich Jew of Malta* (London: J.B., 1633), A4v. For a broader discussion of the use of Proteus in the early modern literature, see A. Bartlett Giamatti, "Proteus Unbound: Some Versions of the Sea God in the Renaissance," in *The Disciplines of Criticism*, ed. Peter Demetz, Thomas Greene, and Lowry Nelson, Jr. (New Haven: Yale University Press, 1968), 437–75.

6 Jonas A. Barish, *The Antitheatrical Prejudice* (Berkeley: University of California Press, 1981), 106–7, traces other ways in which Proteus came to be associated with creative expression in the Renaissance. In his discussion of anti-theatrical tracts, the author notes that Aliciati's emblem books has Proteus as the embodiment of poesy and that

Tasso's play *Aminta* presents the shape-changing deity as the divine overseer of theater.

7   Francis Beaumont, "The Masque of the Inner Temple and Gray's Inn," in *The Dramatic Works in the Beaumont and Fletcher Canon*, vol. I, ed. Fredson Bowers (Cambridge: Cambridge University Press, 2008), line 161.

8   Francis Bacon, "Of Masques and Triumphs," in *Francis Bacon, The Major Works*, ed. Brian Vickers (Oxford: Oxford University Press, 2008), 416.

9   Martin Butler, "Courtly Negotiations," in *Politics of the Stuart Court Masque*, ed. David Bevington and Peter Holbrook (Cambridge: Cambridge University Press, 1999), 21.

10 For an excellent history of the performance, including textual variations in extant copies and evidence of how the masque was funded, see John Pitcher, "Samuel Daniel's Masque 'The Vision of the Twelve Goddesses': Texts and Payments," *Medieval and Renaissance Drama in England* 26 (2013): 17–42.

11 Samuel Daniel, *The Vision of the Twelve Goddesses*, ed. Joan Rees, in *A Book of Masques; in honour of Allardyce Nicoll*, ed. T.J.B. Spencer and Stanley Wells (London: Cambridge University Press, 1967), lines 353, 363, and 366.

12 Amanda Bailey and Mario DiGangi, "Introduction," in *Affect Theory and Early Modern Texts: Politics, Ecologies, and Form*, ed. Amanda Bailey and Mario DiGangi (New York: Palgrave Macmillan, 2017), 16.

13 The Goddesses were Juno, Pallas Athena, and Venus; Diana, Vesta, and Proserpine; Macaria, Concordia, and Astrasa; and Flora, Ceres, and Tethys. The queen played Pallas Athena, rather than, as we might expect, the wife of Jupiter, Juno.

14 Zadie Smith, *Feel Free* (London: Penguin Books, 2018), 245.

15 See Ismene Lada-Richards, "The Subjectivity of Greek Performance," in *Greek and Roman Actors: Aspects of an Ancient Profession*, ed. Pat Easterling and Edith Hall (New York: Cambridge University Press, 2002); Duncan (2006: esp. 9–12).

16 Bruce Heiden, "Emotion, Acting, and the Athenian *ethos*," in *Tragedy, Comedy and the Polis: Papers from the Greek Drama Conference, Nottingham, 18–20 July 1990*, ed. Alan H. Sommerstein, Stephen Halliwell, Jeffrey Henderson, and Bernhard Zimmermann (Bari: Levante editori, 1993), 148–49.

17 Daniel (*The Vision of the Twelve Goddesses* 1967: lines 147–48).

18 Daniel (1967: 274–75).

19 Quoted in Pitcher (2013: 26). See also Berta Cano-Echevarría and Mark Hutchings, "The Spanish Ambassador and Samuel Daniel's *Vision of the Twelve Goddesses*: A New Document," *English Literary Renaissance* 24 (2012): 223–57.

20 Barkan (1990: 46).

21 Bynum (2005: 161).

22 Bynum (2005: 189).

23 See Vickers' edition (2008: 416–17) of Bacon's work.

24 Other intriguing examples exist, including John Lyly's *Endymion* (1588). It adapts the story of a shepherd with whom the moon falls in love. Because Endymion returns the moon's adoration in the form of divine worship, he is granted immortality through ageless sleep. The queen in Lyly's play is named Cynthia, which would resonate with the audience as both an alternate name for the goddess Diana and for Queen Elizabeth. The play was performed with the virgin queen as an audience in 1588. The moon signifies for Endymion a model for immortality as she "being in her fullness, decayeth" as she waxes and wanes yet does not perish (1.1.51–52). Lyrical depictions of the animal kingdom in the play mirror the language that Lyly uses elsewhere to valorize Elizabeth's victory over her Catholic enemies in 1569. See John Lyly, "*Endymion*," in *English Renaissance Drama: A Norton Anthology*, ed. David Bevington, Katharine Eisaman Maus, and Eric Rasmussen (London: W.W. Norton, 2002), 80–128; and David Bevington, "Endymion: Introduction," in *English Renaissance Drama: A Norton Anthology*, ed. David Bevington, Katharine Eisaman Maus, and Eric Rasmussen (London: W.W. Norton, 2002), 77.

25 On the possible influence of Plautus' *Amphitruo* on the *Metamorphoses*, see Mathias Hanses, "*Plautinisches im Ovid*: The *Amphitruo* and the *Metamorphoses*," in *Plautine Trends: Studies in Plautine Comedy and Its Reception*, ed. Ioannis N. Perysinakis and Evangelos Karakasis (Berlin: De Gruyter, 2014).

26 Gary A. Schmidt, *Renaissance Hybrids: Culture and Genre in Early Modern England* (London: Routledge, 2013), 210–13, places the Jacobean masque in the history he traces regarding the rise of tragicomedy as a popular genre in Renaissance England.

27 For a survey of the scholarly debates about this passage, see David Christenson, *Plautus: Amphitruo* (Cambridge: Cambridge University Press, 2000), 50–55. To his survey, we can add Hayden Pelliccia, "Unlocking *Aeneid* 6.460: Plautus' *Amphitryon*, Euripides' *Protesilaus* and the Referents of Callimachus' *Coma*," *CJ* 106 (2010): 149–219, who has argued that the *Amphitruo* is an adaptation of Euripides' *Bacchae*, *Alcmene*, and *Protesilaus*.

28 See Peter G. McC. Brown, "Actors and actor-managers at Rome in the time of Plautus and Terence," in *Greek and Roman Actors: Aspects of an Ancient Profession*, ed. Pat Easterling and Edith Hall (New York: Cambridge University Press, 2002), 225–37; Duncan (2006: 162–65).

29 Duncan (2006: 161).

30 This scene raises further questions about divine bodies. Dionysus is terrified of the threats against him and asks for a sponge for his heart, a request that prompts a question from Xanthias about where the golden gods keep their hearts and a brief statement from Dionysus on the psychosomatic effects of fear on a god's colon (481–84). After a ribbing from Xanthias, Dionysus urges him, if he is such a tough

guy, to take the costume of Heracles and "become me" (σὺ μὲν γενοῦ 'γώ, 495). A quick costume change is all that is required for Xanthias' apotheosis on the stage into Herakleioxanthias (Ἡρακλειοξανθίαν, 499).

31 On this political reading of the *Theogony*, see Stephen Scully, *Hesiod's* Theogony: *From Near Eastern Creation Myths to* Paradise Lost (New York: Oxford University Press, 2015), esp. 30–50.

32 Constantin Stanislavski, *An Actor Prepares*, trans. Elizabeth Reynolds Hapgood (New York: Routledge, 1989), 8.

33 Florence Dupont, "The Theatrical Significance of Duplication in Plautus' *Amphitruo*," in *Oxford Readings in Menander, Plautus, and Terence*, ed. Erich Segal (New York: Oxford University Press, 2001), 188.

34 Niall Slater, *Plautus in Performance: The Theater of the Mind* (Princeton: Princeton University Press, 1985), 11.

35 Slater (1985: 11).

36 Elsewhere, Slater argues that the *dei ex machina* "divinize theater," though not strictly in the sense that we would mean here. Slater suggests that the standard conventions of Roman comedy are given a divine twist by playing with the established visual codes of drama via a double *dei ex machina*, one by Mercury to abuse Amphitruo and the other by Jupiter at the end of the play. See Niall Slater, "Gods On High, Gods Down Low: Romanizing Epiphany," in *Plautine Trends: Studies in Plautine Comedy and Its Reception*, ed. Ioannis N. Perysinakis and Evangelos Karakasis (Berlin: De Gruyter, 2014), 61.

37 Slater (1985: 171).

38 These are Alcaeus' *Callisto, Ganymede*; Alexis' *Tyndareus*; Amphis' *Callisto*; Anaxandrides' *Io*; Anaxila's *Io*; Antiphanes' *Ganymede*; Apollophanes' *Danaë*; Archippus' *Amphitryon*; Aristophanes' *Daedalus*; Crates' *Lamia*; Cratinus' *Nemesis*; Epicharmus' *Dictues, Hip Joint*; Eubulus' *Antiope, Danaë, Europa, Ganymede, Spartans or Leda, Semele or Dionysus*; Hermippus' *Europa*; Platon's *Daedalus, Europa, Long Night, Io*; Polyzelus' *Demos-Tyndareus*; Sannyrion's *Danaë, Io*; Sophilus's *Tyndareus or Leda*.

39 The comment is made by a scholiast to Aristophanes' *Peace* (Σ 741b).

40 This line may refer to a recent staging or adaptation of Euripides' now fragmentary *Alcmene*. We follow Ussing 1875 and Leo 1895 in bracketing the clumsy line 93: "And he certainly appears in tragedy" (*praeterea certo prodit in tragoedia*).

41 On this vase, see Jeffrey Rusten, "The Phanagoria *Chous*: Comic Art in Miniature in a Luxury Tomb in the Cimmerian Bosporus," in *Ancient Theatre and Performance Culture Around the Black Sea*, ed. David Braund, Edith Hall, and Rosie Wyles (Cambridge: Cambridge University Press, 2019), 59–81.

42 Carolyn Dinshaw, *How Soon is Now? Medieval Texts, Amateur Readers, and the Queerness of Time* (Durham: Duke University Press, 2012), 4.

Chapter 4

1. Cf. the endings of *Alcestis, Andromache, Helen,* and *Medea*. On the metatheatricality of the *Bacchae*, see Foley (1980: 107–33); Segal 1997.
2. Easterling (1993: 77–86, 80).
3. As Burrow (2013: 13) notes, "The stories of Orestes and of Oedipus were available to [Shakespeare] through Latin sources and through English translations of those sources, as well as through dictionaries and mythographical handbooks." Inga-Stina Ewbank remarks, "evidence seems to mount up that some form of first-hand contact with Aeschylus has left traces in Shakespeare's dramatic imagination"; see Inga-Stina Ewbank, "'Striking too short at Greeks': The Transmission of *Agamemnon* to the English Renaissance Stage," in *Agamemnon in Performance: 458 BC to AD 2004*, ed. Fiona Macintosh, Pantelis Michelakis, Edith Hall, and Oliver Taplin (Oxford: Oxford University Press, 2005), 52. See also Louise Schleiner, "Latinized Greek Drama in Shakespeare's Writing of *Hamlet*," *Shakespeare Quarterly* 41 (1990): 29–48; Martin Mueller, "Hamlet and the World of Ancient Tragedy," *Arion: A Journal of Humanities and the Classics* 5 (1997): 22–45. Pollard 2017 notes that at least three plays that dramatize Orestes' story circulated in England before Hamlet was written—John Pickering's *Horestes* (c. 1550–67), a performance of Euripides' *Orestes* by Westminster schoolboys in 1567, and the performance of a play entitled *Orestes Furies* at the Rose Theatre in 1599. She also notes a manuscript of a play called *Pylades and Orestes*, "probably from around the turn of the century" (2017: 132). For a much longer history of the reception of Aeschylus' cycle in England, see J. Michael Walton, "Benson, Mushri, and the First English 'Oresteia,'" *Arion: A Journal of Humanities and the Classics* 14 (2006): 49–68.
4. On the issue of the fourth actor in this scene, see C.W. Marshall, "Casting the *Oresteia*," *Classical Journal* 98 (2003): 270.
5. Bernard M.W. Knox, "Aeschylus and the Third Actor," *AJP* 93 (1972): 109. This moment is so memorable and surprising that Euripides turns it into a joke in his *Orestes*. Pylades is a full participant in the drama until he is asked about his part in the murder. He remains silent and Orestes answers for him (1591–92).
6. On Apollo's oracle instructing Orestes, cf. *Libation Bearers* 269–74, 555–59.
7. On the *Oresteia* as cosmogony, see Nancy S. Rabinowitz, "From Force to Persuasion: Aeschylus' *Oresteia* as Cosmogonic Myth," *Ramus* 10 (1981): 159–91; Scully (2015: 159–91).
8. Anne Lebeck, *The Oresteia: a Study in Language and Structure* (Washington, DC: Center for Hellenic Studies, 1971), 2.
9. Simon Goldhill, *Reading Greek Tragedy* (New York: Cambridge University Press, 1986), 56.

10 Angus M. Bowie, "Religion and Politics in Aeschylus' Oresteia," in *Oxford Readings in Classical Studies: Aeschylus*, ed. M. Lloyd (Oxford: Oxford University Press, 2007), 323–26, surveys the opinions of critics.
11 Cf. the Chorus' statement that "the one who is forward thinking and resounds victory of Zeus will hit the mark wisely in every way" (Ζῆνα δέ τις προφρόνως ἐπινίκια κλάζων / τεύξεται φρενῶν τὸ πᾶν, 174–75).
12 Cf. esp. *Eumenides* 796–99.
13 Clytemnestra is Agamemnon's equal in a metaphor comparing Aegisthus to a wolf, Agamemnon to a lion, and Clytemnestra to a lioness (1258–59).
14 Andrea Blasina has argued that Clytemnestra is a kind of tragic poet orchestrating the action onstage; see Andrea Blasina, *Eschilo in scena: Dramma e spettacolo nell' Orestea* (Stuttgart: Metzler, 2003), 49–75.
15 We note here the tantalizing possibility that Aeschylus may have acted in his own plays. The *Life* of Aeschylus records the names of two actors whom Aeschylus employed: Kleandros and Mynniskos (*TrGF* 4, T 78). Aeschylus may have indeed been the third if the notice that Sophocles was the first to abandon the practice of acting in his own dramas (*Life* of Sophocles *TrGF* 4, T 1.4) is correct. See Arthur Pickard-Cambridge, *The Dramatic Festivals of Athens*, 2nd edition (Oxford: Oxford University Press, 1998), 93–95.
16 The Chorus of the *Agamemnon* also attribute the murder of Agamemnon to Zeus' will (1481–88).
17 Marshall (2003: 271). See this essay on the possible division of roles across the trilogy. See also Reginald P. Winnington-Ingram, "Clytemnestra and the Vote of Athena," *Journal of Hellenic Studies* 68 (1948): 141, who reminds us that "amid the debates of the gods we shall do well to remember the woman of the earlier plays."
18 Lebeck (1971: 137).
19 Goldhill 1986.
20 John Dod and Robert Cleaver, *A Godly Form of Household Government* (London: R. Field for Thomas Man, 1610), 13.
21 Dod and Cleaver (1610: 175–76).
22 John Kerrigan, "Hieronimo, Hamlet, and Remembrance," *Essays in Criticism* 31 (1981): 114.
23 Although the English translation of Montaigne's essays did not appear until after *Hamlet* was written, the French version of the collected volume appeared in 1580. Its ideas circulated widely in early modern English culture. Michel de Montaigne, *The Essayes or Morall, Politike and Militarie Discourses of Lord Michaell de Montaigne*, trans. John Florio (London: Edward Blount, 1603), 286.
24 Heather Hirschfield, *The End of Satisfaction: Drama and Repentance in the Age of Shakespeare* (Ithaca: Cornell University Press, 2003), 81.

25 Sigmund Freud, *The Future of an Illusion,* ed. James Strachey (London and New York: W. W. Norton & Company, 1961), 22.
26 Stephen Greenblatt, *Hamlet in Purgatory* (Princeton: Princeton University Press, 2001), 222.
27 We see another instance of how amalgamation leads to mis-identification in *Cymbeline*. Innogen mistakes the headless body of Cloten for Posthumus as she declares, "A headless man? The garments of Posthumus? / I know the shape of's leg; this is his hand, / His foot Mercurial, his Martial thigh, / The brawns of Hercules; but his Jovial face" (4.2.310–13). She mis-identifies the man partly because she sees him as many mythical gods and men.
28 Lars Engle, "How Is Horatio Just? How Just Is Horatio?," *Shakespeare Quarterly* 62.2 (2011): 258.
29 Engle (2011: 258).
30 Arthur Schopenhauer, *Studies in Pessimism* (Whitefish: Kessinger Publishing, 2010), 65.
31 William N. West, "Replaying Early Modern Performances," in *New Directions in Renaissance Drama and Performance Studies*, ed. Sarah Werner (Basingstoke: Palgrave Macmillan, 2010), 35.
32 Sean Benson, *Shakespearean Resurrection: The Art of Almost Raising the Dead* (Pittsburgh: Duquesne University Press, 2009), 2.
33 Benson (2009: 164).
34 Barthes uses the term more than once. Elsewhere, he states "We know that a text does not consist of a line of words, releasing a single 'theological' meaning (the 'message' of the Author-God), but is a space of many dimensions." Roland Barthes, "The Death of the Author," in *Image-Music-Text*, trans. Stephen Heath (London: Fontana, 1993), 146.
35 Tanya Pollard (2017: 133) suggests that "Hamlet serves crucially as observer of tragedy," rather than playing an active role in much of the drama and thus we can see "Shakespeare reflecting on the genre's consequences on audiences."
36 The notion that the ghost is directing stage action perhaps contributes to the belief that Shakespeare himself played King Hamlet in some productions.
37 The text quoted here is drawn from a full edition of the play printed as Heiner Müller, "The Hamletmachine," *Performing Arts Journal* 4.3 (1980): 141–46.

Chapter 5

1 Roland Barthes, "The Reality Effect," in *The Rustle of Language*, ed. Francois Wahl and trans. Richard Howard (Berkeley: University of California Press, 1989), 147.

2 Even though New Oxford Shakespeare has "bite us," the standard line in other editions is "kill us." The verb "bite" might be interpreted to portray the gods as monstrous and animalistic, or even more cruel if they bite their prey but allow it to keep suffering.
3 Mallin (2007: 14–15).
4 Zora Neale Hurston, *Their Eyes Were Watching God* (Urbana: University of Illinois Press, 1978), 215–16.
5 Stephen Halliwell, "Human Limits and the Religion of Greek Tragedy," *Literature and Theology* 4 (1990): 169.
6 The philosopher here reflects on Euripides' *Hecuba*. Martha Nussbaum, "Applying the Lessons of Ancient Greece," interview with Bill Moyers, *A World of Ideas* (November 16, 1988), Moyers on Democracy.
7 We think also of Euripides' statement in Aristophanes' *Frogs* that he made tragedy more democratic by giving more prominent roles to women and slaves (948–52). Aristophanes here is certainly pushing the differences between Euripidean and Aeschylean tragedy to extremes (Aeschylus also featured women and slaves in his dramas), but Euripides' claim to have democratized theater does suggest the perception that the characters and the scenarios of the royalty of the mythological past do not have significant purchase to the Athenian audience.
8 William R. Elton, *King Lear and the Gods* (Lexington: University Press of Kentucky, 1988), 173.
9 Anthony Sher, *Year of the Mad King: The Lear Diaries* (London: Nick Hern Books, 2018), 9.
10 On other such claims to divinity in Plautine comedy, see Hanson (1959: 51–53).
11 Margreta de Grazia, *Hamlet without Hamlet* (Cambridge: Cambridge University Press, 2007), 43.
12 De Grazia (2007: 43).
13 The King James Version (1611) reads similarly, "till thou return unto the ground; for out of it wast thou taken: for dust thou art, and unto dust shalt thou return" (Gen. 3:19).
14 James Shapiro, *The Year of Lear: Shakespeare in 1606* (London: Simon & Schuster, 2015), 26.
15 Ben Jonson, "To Edward Allen (Alleyne)," in *The Oxford Book of Seventeenth Century Verse*, ed. H.J.C. Grierson and G. Bollough (Oxford: Clarendon Press, 1934), 152.
16 Frances Yates, *The Art of Memory* (London: Routledge, 1966), 34.
17 States (1985: 199).
18 Carlson (2003: 9).
19 As we have traced through this book, to play a human who lives amongst gods or to play a god gives an actor access to an immortality in several senses: the performer seems to live in an era not their own; the performer merges into a long genealogy of

those who have played that role; and the performer may achieve fame that will outlive their physical lifetime. For a discussion of personal fame as a desired form of immortality or afterlife in the early modern period, see Keith Thomas, *The Ends of Life: Roads to Fulfilment in Early Modern England* (Oxford: Oxford University Press, 2009), 252–62, and John S. Garrison, *Shakespeare and the Afterlife* (Oxford: Oxford University Press, 2018), 114–15 and 120–5.

20 On the rise of the acting profession in Athens, see Niall Slater, "The Idea of the Actor," in *Nothing to do with Dionysos? Athenian Drama in its Social Context*, ed. John J. Winkler and Froma I. Zeitlin (Princeton: Princeton University Press, 1992), 385–96.

21 See Csapo and Slater (2009: 223–24).

22 Heywood's *Ages* (1611–1632) include *The Golden Age, The Silver Age, The Brazen Age*, and *The Iron Age* (parts 1 and 2). Offering an interesting perspective on the transmission of stories of ancient gods, Liz Oakley-Brown argues that Heywood's plays fundamentally engage with Ovid's *Metamorphoses* not in terms of re-telling its tales but rather by imitating the structure of those tales; see Liz Oakley-Brown, "The Golden Age Rescored? Ovid's *Metamorphoses* and Thomas Heywood's *The Ages*," in *Ovid and Adaptation in Early Modern English Theatre*, ed. Lisa S. Starks (Edinburgh: Edinburgh University Press, 2019), 221–37.

23 Thomas Heywood, *The Golden Age. Or The Lives of Jupiter and Saturn, with the defining of the Heathen Gods* (London: William Barrenger, 1611).

24 Ben Jonson, "The Golden Age Restored," in *The Workes of Benjamin Jonson* (London: William Stansby, 1616), 1010–15.

25 Martin Butler and David Lindley, "Restoring Astraea: Jonson's Masque for the Fall of Somerset," *English Literary History* 61.4 (Winter 1994): 824.

26 Mullaney (2015: 167).

27 Thomas Nashe, *Selected Works*, ed. Stanley Wells (Abingdon: Routledge, 1964), 65.

28 Consider, also, how the early modern imagination considered graveyards to be spaces where the dead could converse with the living. Fame, in the physical form of the funereal monument, promised a form of extended life in these spaces. For more on this notion, see Scott Newstok, *Quoting Death in Early Modern England: The Poetics of Epitaphs Beyond the Tomb* (New York: Palgrave Macmillan, 2009) and Armando Petrucci, *Writing the Dead: Death and Writing Strategies in the Western Tradition* (Palo Alto: Stanford University Press, 1998). Another intriguing point of view is Alastair Fowler's *Time's Purpled Masquers: Stars and the Afterlife in Renaissance English Literature* (Oxford: Clarendon Press, 1996), which examines how deceased writers were stellified within the context of early modern astronomical beliefs. Additional studies of graveyards and their immortalizing function are William E. Engel, *Mapping Mortality: The Persistence of Memory and Melancholy in Early Modern England* (Amherst: University of Massachusetts Press, 1995), Peter

Shylock, *Monuments and Memory in Early Modern England* (London: Ashgate, 2008), and Nigel Llewellyn, *Funeral Monuments in Post-Reformation England* (Cambridge: Cambridge University Press, 2009).

29 A more implicit form of immortality for Shakespeare is his lasting influence on the English language and the writing of subsequent authors. See Marjorie Garber, *Shakespeare's Ghost Writers: Literature as Uncanny Causality* (London: Routledge, 1987), Michael Dobson, *The Making of the National Poet: Shakespeare, Adaption, and Authorship, 1660–1769* (Oxford: Clarendon Press, 1995), and *Canonising Shakespeare: Stationers and the Book Trade, 1640–1740*, ed. Emma Depledge and Peter Kirwan (Cambridge: Cambridge University Press, 2017). Paul Franssen's *Shakespeare's Literary Lives: The Author as Character in Fiction and Film* (Cambridge: Cambridge University Press, 2016) offers yet one more way to think about immortality for authors. The book traces instances in which Shakespeare surfaces as a character in later drama, fiction, and poetry.

30 Kenneth Dover, *Aristophanes: Frogs* (Oxford: Oxford University Press, 1993) *ad* 1058. He also points us to a fragment of the comedian Straton, in which a man complains about his cook's use of neologisms and obscure Homeric vocabulary and bids his cook to speak like a human (ἀνθρωπίνως, fr. 1.46). On this fragment, see Martin Revermann "Paraepic Comedy: Point(s) and Practices," in *Greek Comedy and the Discourse of Genres*, ed. Emmanuela Bakola, Lucia Prauscello, and Mario Telò (New York: Cambridge University Press, 2013), 102–4.

31 On the process of canonizing the classical triumvirate of Aeschylus, Sophocles, and Euripides in the fourth century, see Johanna Hanink, *Lycurgan Athens and the Making of Classical Tragedy* (Cambridge: Cambridge University Press, 2014).

Afterword

1 For one classicist's praise of Zimmerman's play, see Joseph Farrell, "Metamorphoses: A Play by Mary Zimmerman," *AJP* 123 (2002): 623–27.
2 Zimmerman (2002: 5), adapting David R. Slavitt's 1994 translation of Ovid's *Metamorphoses*.
3 On the playful, deceptive syntax and meaning of Ovid's own proem, see Stephen Wheeler, *A Discourse of Wonders: Audience and Performance in Ovid's Metamorphoses* (Philadelphia, University of Pennsylvania Press, 1999), 8–20.
4 Marvin Carlson, *Shattering Hamlet's Mirror: Theatre and Reality* (Ann Arbor: University of Michigan Press, 2016), 124.
5 On the tragic elements of Ovid's poetry, see Daniel Curley, *Tragedy in Ovid: Theater, Metatheater, and the Transformation of a Genre* (Cambridge: Cambridge University Press, 2013).

6 Andrew Feldherr, "Metamorphosis in the *Metamorphoses*," in *The Cambridge Companion to Ovid*, ed. Philip Hardie (Cambridge: Cambridge University Press, 2002), 177.
7 This story by Ovid occupies a notable place in the tradition of discussing the divine as it so closely parallels the story of Sodom and Gomorrah. In that tale, two angels visit a town and are barred from every door until they are taken in by Lot and his wife. After being served a meal and reveal themselves as divine, the angels tell the elderly couple to leave the town and not look back while it is destroyed. We note two interesting parallels in these stories, parallels that are significant for Zimmerman's play. One is the theme of *theoxenia*: gods' testing humans by assessing their openness to welcoming strangers. The other is the destruction by a flood, which contrasts with Zimmerman's treatment of water as a source of inspiration for the theater.
8 Zimmerman (2002: 77).
9 Zimmerman (2002: 77).
10 Zimmerman (2002: 77).
11 Zimmerman (2002: 78).
12 Zimmerman (2002: 79).
13 Zimmerman (2002: 77).
14 Zimmerman (2002: 79).
15 Zimmerman (2002: 81).
16 Julia Reinhard Lupton, "'Out, Out, Brief Candle': Shakespeare and the *Theatrum Mundi* of Hospitality," in *"If Then the World a Theatre Present...": Revisions of the Theatrum Mundi Metaphor in Early Modern England*, ed. Bjorn Quiring (Berlin: De Gruyter, 2015), 39–40. She further observes that "spatial reorganizations, which set the scene of subjective and existential self-stagings, connect the performance of hospitality as a theatre of life to the work of theatre proper, which also defines itself as an open plateau defined by entrances and exits in the presence of others" (40).
17 Zimmerman (2002: 82).
18 Zimmerman (2002: 83).
19 Zimmerman (2002: 83).
20 The original distribution of roles is described in "A Note on the Casting"; see Zimmerman (2002: 85–86).
21 Zimmerman (2002: 7).
22 For those readers interested in the reception of Ovid in the early modern period, there are quite a few excellent studies. See Note 23 in the Introduction for frequently cited volumes. Some additional starting points are *Metamorphosis: The Changing Face of Ovid in Medieval and Early Modern Europe* (Toronto: Center for Reformation and Renaissance Studies, 2007), edited by Alison Keith and Stephen Rupp; A.B. Taylor's edited volume, *Shakespeare's Ovid: 'The Metamorphoses' in the Plays and Poems* (Cambridge: Cambridge University Press, 2000); *Shakespeare's Erotic*

Mythology and Ovidian Renaissance Culture (Farnham: Ashgate, 2013), edited by Agnès Lafont; Lisa S. Starks-Estes' *Transforming Ovid: Violence, Trauma, and Virtus in Shakespeare's Roman Poems and Plays* (Basingstoke: Palgrave-Macmillan, 2014); Liz Oakley-Brown's *Ovid and the Cultural Politics of Translation in Early Modern England* (Farnham: Ashgate, 2006); and Goran Stanivukovic's edited volume, *Ovid and the Renaissance Body* (Toronto: University of Toronto Press, 2001).

23 On the use of Ovid in *As You Like It*, see Yves Peyré, "*Femmina masculo e masculo femmina*: Ovidian Mythical Structures, Leonardo Da Vinci, Michelangelo and *As You Like It*," in *Shakespeare's Erotic Mythology and Ovidian Renaissance Culture*, ed. Agnès Lafont (Farnham: Ashgate, 2013), 173–82, and François Laroque, "Ovidian Transformations and Folk Festivities in *A Midsummer Night's Dream, The Merry Wives of Windsor*, and *As You Like It*," *Cahiers Élisabéthains: A Biannual Journal of English Renaissance Studies* 25 (April 1984): 23–36.

24 On the reception of Ovid's *Ars Amatoria*, or *The Art of Love*, in the Renaissance, see M.L. Stapleton's *Harmful Eloquence: Ovid's* Amores *from Antiquity to Shakespeare* (Ann Arbor: University of Michigan Press, 1996) and "Making a Politic Gentleman: The First *Ars amatoria* in English," in *Ovid and Masculinity in English Renaissance Literature*, ed. John S. Garrison and Goran Stanivukovich (McGill-Queen's University Press, 2020), 202–22.

25 States (1985: 3).

26 Zimmerman (2002: 3).

27 Zimmerman (2002: 3).

Bibliography

Allan, William. 2008. *Euripides: Helen*. Cambridge: Cambridge University Press.
Allen, Don Cameron. 1980. *Mysteriously Meant: The Rediscovery of Pagan Symbolism and Allegorical Interpretation in the Renaissance*. Baltimore: Johns Hopkins University Press.
Aquinas, Thomas. 1964–1981. *Summa Theologica*, vol. 34, edited by Thomas Gilby. New York: McGraw-Hill.
Arrowsmith, William. 1973. "Aristophanes' *Birds*: The Fantasy Politics of Eros," *Arion* 1: 119–67.
Artaud, Antonin. 2013. *The Theatre and Its Double*. New York: Grove Press.
Auerbach, Erich. 2013. *Mimesis: The Representation of Reality in Western Literature*. Princeton: Princeton University Press.
Austin, John L. 1975. *How to Do Things With Words*. Oxford: Oxford University Press.
Bacon, Francis. 1594. *Gesta Grayorum*. London.
Bacon, Francis. 1901. *The Advancement of Learning*, edited by J. Devey. New York: P.F. Collier & Son.
Bacon, Francis. 2008. "Of Masques and Triumphs," in *Francis Bacon, The Major Works*, edited by Brian Vickers, 416–17. Oxford: Oxford University Press.
Bailey, Amanda, and Mario DiGangi. 2017. "Introduction," in *Affect Theory and Early Modern Texts: Politics, Ecologies, and Form*, edited by Amanda Bailey and Mario DiGangi, 1–23. New York: Palgrave Macmillan.
Bailey, Cyril. 1977. *Lucretius: De Rerum Natura*. Oxford: Oxford University Press.
Baker, Anthony. 2019. *Shakespeare, Theology, and the Unstaged God*. New York: Routledge.
Barad, Karen M. 2007. *Meeting the Universe Halfway: Quantum Physics and the Entanglement of Matter and Meaning*. Durham: Duke University Press.
Barish, Jonas A. 1981. *The Antitheatrical Prejudice*. Berkeley: University of California Press.
Barkan, Leonard. 1990. *The Gods Made Flesh: Metamorphosis and the Pursuit of Paganism*. New Haven: Yale University Press.
Barkan, Leonard. 1991. *Transuming Passion: Ganymede and the Erotics of Humanism*. Stanford: Stanford University Press.
Barthes, Roland. 1989. "The Reality Effect," in *The Rustle of Language*, edited by Francois Wahl and translated by Richard Howard, 141–48. Berkeley: University of California Press.
Barthes, Roland. 1993. "The Death of the Author," in *Image-Music-Text*, translated by Stephen Heath, 142–48. London: Fontana.

Bassi, Karen. 2000. "The Somatics of the Past: Helen and the Body of Tragedy," in *Acting on the Past: Historical Performance Across the Disciplines*, edited by M. Franko and A. Richards, 13–34. Hanover: Wesleyan University Press.

Bate, Jonathan. 2019. *How the Classics Made Shakespeare*. Princeton: Princeton University Press.

Beaumont, Francis. 2008. "The Masque of the Inner Temple and Gray's Inn," in *The Dramatic Works in the Beaumont and Fletcher Canon*, vol. I, edited by Fredson Bowers, 112–44. Cambridge: Cambridge University Press.

Beckwith, Sarah. 2011. *Shakespeare and the Grammar of Forgiveness*. Ithaca: Cornell University Press.

Benjamin, Walter. 1982. "The Storyteller: Reflections on the Works of Nikolai Leskov," in *Illuminations: Essays and Reflections*, edited by Hannah Arendt, 83–109. London: Fontana.

Benson, Sean. 2009. *Shakespearean Resurrection: The Art of Almost Raising the Dead*. Pittsburgh: Duquesne University Press.

Bergeron, David. 1995. "The Apollo Mission in *The Winter's Tale*," in *The Winter's Tale: Critical Essays*, edited by Maurice Hunt, 361–82. New York: Routledge.

Bevington, David. 1998. "*The Tempest* and the Jacobean Court Masque," in *The Politics of the Stuart Court Masque*, edited by David Bevington and Peter Holbrook, 218–43. Cambridge: Cambridge University Press.

Bevington, David. 2002. "*Endymion*: Introduction," in *English Renaissance Drama: A Norton Anthology*, edited by David Bevington, Katharine Eisaman Maus, and Eric Rasmussen, 75–79. London: W.W. Norton.

Blasina, Andrea. 2003. *Eschilo in scena: Dramma e spettacolo nell' Orestea*. Stuttgart: Metzler.

Blondell, Ruby. 2016. *Helen of Troy: Beauty, Myth, Devastation*. New York: Oxford University Press.

Booty, John (ed.). 1976. *The Book of Common Prayer, 1559*. Charlottesville: University of Virginia Press.

Bowie, Angus M. 2007. "Religion and Politics in Aeschylus' *Oresteia*," in *Oxford Readings in Classical Studies: Aeschylus*, edited by M. Lloyd, 323–58. Oxford: Oxford University Press.

Branagh, Kenneth, dir. 2006. *As You Like It*. London and New York: BBC Films and HBO Films. DVD.

Bread. 1971. "If." Track 4 on *Manna*. Hollywood: Elektra.

Brown, Peter G. McC. 2002. "Actors and Actor-Managers at Rome in the Time of Plautus and Terence," in *Greek and Roman Actors: Aspects of an Ancient Profession*, edited by Pat Easterling and Edith Hall, 225–37. New York: Cambridge University Press.

Burrow, Colin. 2013. *Shakespeare and Classical Antiquity*. Oxford: Oxford University Press.

Burton, Robert. 1621. *Anatomy of Melancholy*. Oxford.

Butler, Martin. 1999. "Courtly Negotiations," in *Politics of the Stuart Court Masque*, edited by David Bevington and Peter Holbrook, 20–40. Cambridge: Cambridge University Press.
Butler, Martin and David Lindley. 1994. "Restoring Astraea: Jonson's Masque for the Fall of Somerset," *English Literary History* 61.4: 807–27.
Bynum, Caroline Walker. 2005. *Metamorphosis and Identity*. New York: Zone Books.
Cano-Echevarría, Berta, and Mark Hutchings. 2012. "The Spanish Ambassador and Samuel Daniel's *Vision of the Twelve Goddesses*: A New Document," *English Literary Renaissance* 24: 223–57.
Carlson, Marvin. 2003. *The Haunted Stage: The Theater as Memory Machine*. Ann Arbor: University of Michigan Press.
Carlson, Marvin. 2016. *Shattering Hamlet's Mirror: Theatre and Reality*. Ann Arbor: University of Michigan Press.
Cartelli, Thomas. 1991. *Marlowe, Shakespeare, and the Economy of Theatrical Experience*. Philadelphia: University of Pennsylvania Press
Castiglione, Baldassare. 1528. *The Book of the Courtier*. Venice: Aldine Press.
Cavell, Stanley. 1979. *The World Viewed: Reflections on the Ontology of Film*. Cambridge: Harvard University Press.
Chambers, Edmund Kerchever. 1923. *The Elizabethan Stage*, 4 vols. Oxford: Oxford University Press.
Christenson, David M. 2000. *Plautus: Amphitruo*. Cambridge: Cambridge University Press.
Clark, Albert C. 1991. *Cicero: Orationes*. Oxford: Oxford University Press.
Clark, Anna. 2019. "Gods and Roman Comedy," in *The Cambridge Companion to Roman Comedy*, edited by Martin T. Dinter, 217–28. Cambridge: Cambridge University Press.
Csapo, Eric. 2000. "From Aristophanes to Menander? Genre Transformation in Greek Comedy," in *Matrices of Genre: Authors, Canons, and Society*, edited by Mary Depew and Dirk Obbink, 115–34. Cambridge: Harvard University Press.
Csapo, Eric. 2014. *Actors and Icons of the Ancient Theater*. Oxford: Wiley-Blackwell.
Csapo, Eric, and William Slater. 2009. *The Context of Ancient Drama*. Ann Arbor: University of Michigan Press.
Curley, Daniel. 2013. *Tragedy in Ovid: Theater, Metatheater, and the Transformation of a Genre*. Cambridge: Cambridge University Press.
Daniel, Samuel. 1967. *The Vision of the Twelve Goddesses*, edited by Joan Rees, in *A Book of Masques; in honour of Allardyce Nicoll*, edited by T.J.B. Spencer and Stanley Wells, 17–42. London: Cambridge University Press.
Dawson, Anthony B. 2006. "Priamus is Dead: Memorial Repetition in Marlowe and Shakespeare," in *Shakespeare, Memory, and Performance*, edited by Peter Holland, 63–86. Cambridge: Cambridge University Press.
de Grazia, Margreta. 2007. *Hamlet without Hamlet*. Cambridge: Cambridge University Press.

de Grazia, Margreta. 2010. "Anachronism," in *Cultural Reformations: Medieval and Renaissance in Literary History*, edited by Brian Cummings and James Simpson, 13–32. Oxford: Oxford University Press.

Demetriou, Tania, and Tanya Pollard. 2017. "Homer and Greek Tragedy in Early Modern England's Theatres: An Introduction," *CRJ* 9.1: 1–35.

de Montaigne, Michel. 1603. *The Essayes or Morall, Politike and Militarie Discourses of Lord Michaell de Montaigne*, translated by John Florio. London: Edward Blount.

Depledge, Emma, and Peter Kirwan (eds.). 2017. *Canonising Shakespeare: Stationers and the Book Trade, 1640–1740*. Cambridge: Cambridge University Press.

Diels, Hermann, and Walther Kranz. 1952–. *Die Fragmente der Vorsokratiker*. Berlin: Weidmann.

Diggle, James. 1981–1994. *Euripidis Fabulae*, 3 vols. Oxford: Oxford University Press.

Dinshaw, Carolyn. 2012. *How Soon is Now? Medieval Texts, Amateur Readers, and the Queerness of Time*. Durham: Duke University Press.

Dobrov, Gregory W. 2001. *Figures of Play: Greek Drama and Metafictional Poetics*. New York: Oxford University Press.

Dobson, Michael. 1995. *The Making of the National Poet: Shakespeare, Adaption, and Authorship, 1660–1769*. Oxford: Clarendon Press.

Dod, John, and Robert Cleaver. 1610. *A Godly Form of Household Government*. London: R. Field for Thomas Man.

Dover, Kenneth. 1993. *Aristophanes: Frogs*. Oxford: Oxford University Press.

Downing, Eric. 1990. "Apatê, Agôn, and Literary Self-Reflexivity in Euripides' *Helen*," in *Cabinet of the Muses: Essays on Classical and Comparative Literature in Honor of Thomas G. Rosenmeyer*, edited by M. Griffith and Donald J. Mastronarde, 1–16. Atlanta: Scholars Press.

Duncan, Anne. 2006. *Performance and Identity in the Classical World*. New York: Cambridge University Press.

Dunn, Francis M. 1996. *Tragedy's End: Closure and Innovation in Euripidean Drama*. New York: Oxford University Press.

Dupont, Florence. 2001. "The Theatrical Significance of Duplication in Plautus' *Amphitruo*." Abridged translation. In *Oxford Readings in Menander, Plautus, and Terence*, edited by Erich Segal, 176–88. New York: Oxford University Press.

Easterling, Pat E. 1985. "Anachronism in Greek Tragedy," *JHS* 105: 1–10.

Easterling, Pat E. 1993. "Gods on Stage in Greek Tragedy," in *Religio Graeco-Romana: Festschrift für Walter Pötscher*, edited by Joachim Dalfen, Gerhard Petersmann, and Franz Ferdinand Schwarz, 77–86. Horn: F. Berger.

Easterling, Pat E. (ed.). 1997. *The Cambridge Companion to Greek Tragedy*. Cambridge: Cambridge University Press.

Easterling, Pat E., and Edith Hall (eds.). 2002. *Greek and Roman Actors: Aspects of an Ancient Profession*. New York: Cambridge University Press.

Edmunds, Lowell. 2016. *Stealing Helen: The Myth of the Abducted Wife in Comparative Perspective*. Princeton: Princeton University Press.

Elton, William R. 1988. *King Lear and the Gods*. Lexington: University Press of Kentucky.
Engel, William E. 1995. *Mapping Mortality: The Persistence of Memory and Melancholy in Early Modern England*. Amherst: University of Massachusetts Press.
Engle, Lars. 2011. "How is Horatio Just? How Just is Horatio?," *Shakespeare Quarterly* 62.2: 256–62.
Enterline, Lynn. 2000. *The Rhetoric of the Body from Ovid to Shakespeare*. Cambridge: Cambridge University Press.
Enterline, Lynn. 2012. *Shakespeare's Schoolroom: Rhetoric, Discipline, Emotion*. Philadelphia: University of Pennsylvania Press.
Erasmus. 1514. *Luciani Erasmo interprete Dialogi & alia emuncta*. Paris: Ascensius.
Ewbank, Inga-Stina. 2005. "'Striking too short at Greeks': The Transmission of *Agamemnon* to the English Renaissance Stage," in *Agamemnon in Performance: 458 BC to AD 2004*, edited by Fiona Macintosh, Pantelis Michelakis, Edith Hall, and Oliver Taplin, 36–52. Oxford: Oxford University Press.
Fabian, Johannes. 2002. *Time and the Other: How Anthropology Makes Its Object*. New York: Columbia University Press.
Farrell, Joseph. 2002. "Metamorphoses: A Play by Mary Zimmerman," *AJP* 123: 623–27.
Feeney, Denis. 1991. *The Gods in Epic: Poets and Critics of the Classical Tradition*. New York: Oxford University Press.
Feldherr, Andrew. 2002. "Metamorphosis in the *Metamorphoses*," in *The Cambridge Companion to Ovid*, edited by Philip Hardie, 163–179. Cambridge: Cambridge University Press.
Fernie, Ewan (ed.). 2005. *Spiritual Shakespeares*. London: Routledge.
Findlay, Alison, and Vassiliki Markidou. 2017. "Introduction," in *Shakespeare and Greece*, edited by Alison Findlay and Vassiliki Markidou, 1–44. London: Bloomsbury Arden Shakespeare.
Finglass, Patrick J. 2011. *Sophocles: Ajax*. Cambridge: Cambridge University Press.
Foley, Helene. 1980. "The Masque of Dionysus," *TAPA* 110: 107–33.
Fowler, Alastair. 1996. *Time's Purpled Masquers: Stars and the Afterlife in Renaissance English Literature*. Oxford: Clarendon Press.
Franssen, Paul. 2016. *Shakespeare's Literary Lives: The Author as Character in Fiction and Film*. Cambridge: Cambridge University Press.
Freud, Sigmund. 1961. *The Future of an Illusion*, edited by James Strachey. London: W.W. Norton.
Frontisi-Ducroux, Françoise. 2007. "The Invention of the Erinyes," in *Visualizing the Tragic: Drama, Myth, and Ritual in Greek Art and Literature: Essays in Honour of Froma Zeitlin*, edited by Christina S. Kraus, 165–76. Oxford: Oxford University Press.
Garber, Marjorie. 1987. *Shakespeare's Ghost Writers: Literature as Uncanny Causality*. London: Routledge.

Garrison, John S. 2016. "Marlowe's Helen and the Erotics of Cultural Memory," in *Sexuality and Memory in Early Modern England: Literature and the Erotics of Recollection*, edited by John Garrison and Kyle Pivetti, 120–28. London: Routledge.

Garrison, John S. 2018. *Shakespeare and the Afterlife*. Oxford: Oxford University Press.

Garrison, John S., and Goran Stanivukovic (eds.). 2020. *Ovid and Masculinity in English Renaissance Literature*. Montreal: McGill-Queen's University Press.

Giamatti, A. Bartlett. 1968. "Proteus Unbound: Some Versions of the Sea God in the Renaissance," in *The Disciplines of Criticism*, edited by Peter Demetz, Thomas Greene, and Lowry Nelson, Jr., 437–75. New Haven: Yale University Press.

Giles, David. 2000. *Illusions of Immortality: A Psychology of Fame*. New York: Palgrave Macmillan.

Godwin, Laura G. 2009. "'There is nothin' like a Dame': Christopher Marlowe's Helen of Troy at the Royal Shakespeare Company," *Shakespeare Bulletin* 27: 69–79.

Goffman, Erving. 1969. *The Presentation of the Self in Everyday Life*. London: Allen Lane.

Goldberg, Jonathan. 2009. *The Seeds of Things: Theorizing Sexuality and Materiality in Renaissance Representations*. New York: Fordham University Press.

Goldhill, Simon. 1986. *Reading Greek Tragedy*. New York: Cambridge University Press.

Golding, Arthur. 1567. *The xv bookes of P. Ovidius Naso, entytled Metamorphosis, translated oute of Latin into English meeter*. London: William Seres.

Gosson, Stephen. 1582. *Playes Confuted in Five Actions*. London.

Gosson, Stephen. 2012. "Playes Confuted in Five Actions," in *The Broadview Anthology of Sixteenth-Century Poetry and Prose*, edited by Maria Loughlin, Sandra Bell, and Patricia Brace, 449–53. Buffalo: Broadview Press.

Gosson, Stephen. 2012. "The School of Abuse," in *The Broadview Anthology of Sixteenth-Century Poetry and Prose*, edited by Maria Loughlin, Sandra Bell, and Patricia Brace, 446–48. Buffalo: Broadview Press.

Gow, Andrew S. Farrar, and Denys Lionel Page. 1968. *The Greek Anthology: Garland of Philip and Some Contemporary Epigrams*, 2 vols. Cambridge: Cambridge University Press.

Grafton, Anthony, Glenn W. Most, and Salvatore Settis (eds.). 2010. *The Classical Tradition*. Boston: Harvard University Press.

Green, Richard. 2002. "Towards a Reconstruction of Performance Style," in *Greek and Roman Actors: Aspects of an Ancient Profession*, edited by Pat Easterling and Edith Hall, 93–126. Cambridge: Cambridge University Press.

Greenblatt, Stephen. 2001. *Hamlet in Purgatory*. Princeton: Princeton University Press.

Greenblatt, Stephen. 2011. *The Swerve: How the World Became Modern*. New York: W.W. Norton.

Gussow, Mel. 2020. "Ian Holm, Malleable Actor Who Played Lear and Bilbo, Dies at 88," *New York Times*, June 19.

Halliwell, Stephen. 1990. "Human Limits and the Religion of Greek Tragedy," *Literature and Theology* 4: 169–80.

Halliwell, Stephen. 2011. *Between Ecstasy and Truth: Interpretations of Greek Poetics from Homer to Longinus*. Oxford: Oxford University Press.

Hanink, Johanna. 2014. *Lycurgan Athens and the Making of Classical Tragedy*. Cambridge: Cambridge University Press.

Hanses, Mathias. 2014. "*Plautinisches im Ovid*: The *Amphitruo* and the *Metamorphoses*," in *Plautine Trends: Studies in Plautine Comedy and Its Reception*, edited by Ioannis N. Perysinakis and Evangelos Karakasis, 225–58. Berlin: De Gruyter.

Hanson, John A. 1959. "Plautus as a Source Book for Roman Religion," *TAPA* 90: 48–101.

Harris, Jonathan Gil. 2011. *Untimely Matter in the Time of Shakespeare*. Philadelphia: University of Pennsylvania Press.

Hegel, Georg Wilhelm Friedrich. 1962. *Hegel on Tragedy*, edited by Anne Paolucci and Henry Paolucci. New York: Doubleday.

Heiden, Bruce. 1993. "Emotion, Acting, and the Athenian *ethos*," in *Tragedy, Comedy and the Polis: Papers from the Greek Drama Conference, Nottingham, 18–20 July 1990*, edited by Alan H. Sommerstein, Stephen Halliwell, Jeffrey Henderson, and Bernhard Zimmerman, 145–66. Bari: Livante editori.

Henderson, Jeffrey. 2012. "Pursuing Nemesis: Cratinus and Mythological Comedy," in *No Laughing Matter: New Studies in Old Comedy*, edited by C.W. Marshall and G.A. Kovacs, 1–12. London: Bloomsbury.

Heubeck, Alfred, Stephanie West, and J.B. Hainsworth. 1988. *A Commentary on Homer's Odyssey*, vol. I. Oxford: Clarendon Press.

Heywood, Thomas. 1611. *The Golden Age*. London: William Barrenger.

Heywood, Thomas. 1612. *An Apology for Actors*. London: Nicholas Okes.

Heywood, Thomas. 1613. *The Silver Age*. London: Nicholas Okes.

Heywood, Thomas. 1613. *The Brazen Age*. London: Nicholas Okes.

Heywood, Thomas. 1632. *The Iron Age*. London: Nicholas Okes.

Heywood, Thomas. 1633. "The Prologue to the Stage, at the Cocke-pit," in *The Famous Tragedy of the Rich Jew of Malta*, by Christopher Marlowe, A6. London: Nicholas Vavsour.

Heywood, Thomas. 2019. "The Apology for Actors (1612)," in *Reader in Tragedy: An Anthology of Classical Criticism to Contemporary Theory*, edited by Marcus Nevitt and Tanya Pollard, 70–73. London: Bloomsbury.

Hirsch, David A. Hedrich. 1991. "Donne's Atomies and Anatomies: Deconstructed Bodies and the Resurrection of Atomic Theory," *Studies in English Literature* 31.1: 69–94.

Hirschfield, Heather. 2003. *The End of Satisfaction: Drama and Repentance in the Age of Shakespeare*. Ithaca: Cornell University Press.

Hock, Jessie. 2017. "'The Mind is Its Own Place': Lucretian Moral Philosophy in Paradise Lost," in *Milton's Modernities: Poetry, Philosophy, and History from the Seventeenth Century to the Present*, edited by Patrick Fadely and Feisal G. Mohammed, 67–84. Evanston: Northwestern University Press.

Holland, Philemon. 1603. *Plutarch: The Philosophie Commonly Called the Morals*. London: Arnold Hatfield.

Hopgood, Alison P. 2014. *Passionate Playgoing in Early Modern England*. Cambridge: Cambridge University Press.

Hopkins, David. 2010. *Conversing with Antiquity: English Poets and the Classics, from Shakespeare to Pope*. Oxford: Oxford University Press.

Hughes, Alan. 2012. *Performing Greek Comedy*. Cambridge: Cambridge University Press.

Hughes, Bettany. 2007. *Helen of Troy: The Story Behind the Most Beautiful Woman in the World*. New York: Vintage.

Hurston, Zora Neale. 1978. *Their Eyes Were Watching God*. Urbana: University of Illinois Press.

James, Heather. 1997. *Shakespeare's Troy: Drama, Politics, and the Translation of Empire*. Cambridge: Cambridge University Press.

Jones, John H. (ed.). 1994. *The English Faust Book: A Critical Edition Based on the Text of 1592*. Cambridge: Cambridge University Press.

Jonson, Ben. 1616. "The Golden Age Restored," in *The Workes of Benjamin Jonson*, 1010–1015. London: William Stansby.

Jonson, Ben. 1934. "To Edward Allen (Alleyne)," in *The Oxford Book of Seventeenth Century Verse*, edited by H.J.C. Grierson and G. Bollough, 152. Oxford: Clarendon Press.

Jonson, Ben. 1970. "*Hymenaei*, or the Solemnities of Masque and Barriers at a Marriage," in *Ben Jonson: Selected Masques*, edited by Stephen Orgel, 47–79. New Haven: Yale University Press.

Kahil, Lilly. 1988. "Helene," *LIMC* 4.1: 559–61.

Kannicht, Richard. 1969. *Euripides: Helena*, 2 vols. Heidelberg: Winter.

Kannicht, Richard, Stefan Radt, and Bruno Snell. 1971–2007. *Tragicorum Graecorum Fragmenta*, 5 vols. Göttingen: Vandenhoeck & Ruprecht.

Karavas, Orestis. 2005. *Lucien et la tragédie*. Berlin: De Gruyter.

Kassel, Rudolf. 1965. *Aristotle: De Arte Poetica Liber*. Oxford: Oxford University Press.

Kassel, Rudolf, and Colin Austin. 1983–. *Poetae Comici Graeci*, 8 vols. Berlin: De Gruyter.

Kastan, David Scott. 2014. *A Will to Believe: Shakespeare and Religion*. Oxford: Oxford University Press.

Kauer, Robert, and Wallace M. Lindsay. 1992. *P. Terenti Comoediae*. Oxford: Oxford University Press.

Kaytor, Daryl. 2015. "Shakespeare's Gods," *Literature and Theology* 29.1: 3–17.

Keefer, Michael. 2004. "Fairer than the Evening Air: Marlowe's Gnostic Helen of Troy and the Tropes of Belatedness of Historical Mediation," in *Fantasies of Troy: Classical Tales and the Social Imaginary in Medieval and Early Modern Europe*, edited by A. Shepard and S.D. Powell, 39–62. Toronto: Centre for Reformation and Renaissance Studies.

Keilen, Sean, and Nick Moschovakis. 2017. *The Routledge Research Companion to Shakespeare and Classical Literature*. Abingdon: Routledge.

Keith, Alison, and Stephen Rupp (eds.). 2007. *Metamorphosis: The Changing Face of Ovid in Medieval and Early Modern Europe*. Toronto: Centre for Reformation and Renaissance Studies.

Kenward, Claire. 2017. "Sights to Make an Alexander? Reading Homer on the Early Modern Stage," *CRJ* 9.1: 79–102.

Kerrigan, John. 1981. "Hieronimo, Hamlet, and Remembrance," *Essays in Criticism* 31: 105–26.

Kiessling, Nicolas. 1975. "Faustus and the Sin of Demoniality," *Studies in English Literature 1500–1900* 15: 205–11.

Kingsley-Smith, Jane. 2010. *Cupid in Early Modern Literature and Culture*. Cambridge: Cambridge University Press.

Knox, Bernard M.W. 1972. "Aeschylus and the Third Actor," *AJP* 93: 104–24.

Koselleck, Reinhart. 2004. *Futures Past: On the Semantics of Historical Time*. New York: Columbia University Press.

Kovacs, David. 2002. *Euripides: Helen. Phoenician Women. Orestes*. Cambridge: Harvard University Press.

Lada-Richards, Ismene. 2002. "The Subjectivity of Greek Performance," in *Greek and Roman Actors: Aspects of an Ancient Profession*, edited by Pat Easterling and Edith Hall, 395–418. New York: Cambridge University Press.

Lada-Richards, Ismene. 2005. "Greek Tragedy and Western Perceptions of Actors and Acting," in *A Companion to Greek Tragedy*, edited by Justina Gregory, 459–71. Oxford: Blackwell.

Lafont, Agnès (ed.). 2013. *Shakespeare's Erotic Mythology and Ovidian Renaissance Culture*. Farnham: Ashgate.

Laroque, François. 1984. "Ovidian Transformations and Folk Festivities in *A Midsummer Night's Dream, The Merry Wives of Windsor,* and *As You Like It*," *Cahiers Élisabéthains: A Biannual Journal of English Renaissance Studies* 25: 23–36.

Lavagnino, John. 2012. "Year of Shakespeare: *Cymbeline* at the Barbican," *Blogging Shakespeare from the Shakespeare Birthplace Trust* (June 6), https://www.bloggingshakespeare.com/year-of-shakespeare-cymbeline-at-the-barbican.

Lazarus, Micha. 2014. "Greek Literacy in Sixteenth-Century England," *Renaissance Studies* 29: 433–58.

Lebeck, Anne. 1971. *The Oresteia: a Study in Language and Structure*. Washington, DC: Center for Hellenic Studies.

Lefkowitz, Mary. 1989. "'Impiety' and 'Atheism' in Euripides' Dramas," *CQ* 39: 70–82.

Lefkowitz, Mary. 2016. *Euripides and the Gods*. New York: Oxford University Press.

Leo, Friedrich. 1895. *T. Macci Plauti Comoediae*. Berlin: Weidmann.

Lindsay, Wallace M. 1910. *T. Macci Plauti Comoediae*, 2 vols. Oxford: Oxford University Press.

Llewellyn, Nigel. 2009. *Funeral Monuments in Post-Reformation England*. Cambridge: Oxford University Press.
Lloyd-Jones, Hugh, and Nigel G. Wilson. 1990. *Sophoclis Fabulae*. Oxford: Oxford University Press.
Lodge, Thomas. 1579. *Defense of Poetry, Music, and Stage Plays*.
Lopez, Jeremy. 2003. *Theatrical Convention and Audience Response in Early Modern Drama*. Cambridge: Cambridge University Press.
Louth, Andrew. 1981. *Origins of the Christian Mystical Tradition: From Plato to Denys*. Oxford: Oxford University Press.
Loxton, Howard. n.d. "Cymbeline," *British Theatre Guide*, https://www.britishtheatreguide.info/reviews/cymbeline-barbican-theatr-7559.
Lupton, Julia Reinhard. 2015. "'Out, Out, Brief Candle': Shakespeare and the *Theatrum Mundi* of Hospitality," in *"If Then the World a Theatre Present...": Revisions of the Theatrum Mundi Metaphor in Early Modern England*, edited by Bjorn Quiring, 39–60. Berlin: De Gruyter.
Lyly, John. 2002. *Endymion*, in *English Renaissance Drama: A Norton Anthology*, edited by David Bevington, Katharine Eisaman Maus, and Eric Rasmussen, 80–128. London: W.W. Norton.
Lyly, John. 2015. *The Descent of Euphues*, in *Three Elizabethan Romance Stories*, edited by J. Winny. Cambridge: Cambridge University Press.
Lyne, Raphael. 2001. *Ovid's Changing Worlds: English Metamorphoses 1567–1632*. Oxford: Oxford University Press.
MacAloon, John J. 1984. "Introduction: Cultural Performances, Cultural Theory," in *Rite, Drama, Festival, Spectacle: Rehearsals Toward a Theory of Cultural Performance*, edited by John J. MacAloon, 1–18. Philadelphia: Institute of the Study of Human Issues.
Macleod, Matthew D. 1972. *Luciani Opera*. Oxford: Oxford University Press.
Maguire, Laurie. 2009. *Helen of Troy: From Homer to Hollywood*. Hoboken: Wiley-Blackwell.
Maguire, Laurie, and Emma Smith. 2013. *30 Great Myths About Shakespeare*. Oxford: Wiley-Blackwell.
Maisano, Scott. 2013. "Now," in *Early Modern Theatricality*, edited by Henry S. Turner, 368–87. Oxford: Oxford University Press.
Mallin, Eric S. 2007. *Godless Shakespeare*. London: Continuum.
Marlowe, Christopher. 1594. *Dido, Queen of Carthage*. London: Thomas Woodcocke.
Marlowe, Christopher. 2002. "The Tragical History of Doctor Faustus," in *English Renaissance Drama: A Norton Anthology*, edited by D. Bevington, L. Engle, K.E. Maus, and E. Rasmussen, 250–85. New York: W.W. Norton.
Marshall, C.W. 2003. "Casting the Oresteia," *Classical Journal* 98: 257–74.
Martindale, Charles. 2015. "Marlowe," in *The Oxford History of Classical Reception in English*, vol. II, edited by P. Cheney and P. Hardie, 579–98. New York: Oxford University Press.
Martindale, Charles. 2017. "Afterword: Greek Texts and the Early Modern Stage," *CRJ* 9.1: 166–76.

Masten, Jeffery. 2016. *Queer Philologies: Sex, Language, and Affect in Shakespeare's Time*. Philadelphia: University of Pennsylvania Press.

Mastronarde, Donald. 1990. "Actors on High: The Skene Roof, the Crane, and the Gods in Attic Drama," *Classical Antiquity* 9: 247–94.

Mastronarde, Donald J. 2010. *The Art of Euripides*. New York: Cambridge University Press.

Maurice, Lisa. 2019. *Screening Divinity*. Edinburgh: Edinburgh University Press.

McCoy, Richard. 2015. "Awakening Faith in *The Winter's Tale*," in *Shakespeare and Early Modern Religion*, edited by David Loewenstein and Michael Witmore, 214–30. Cambridge: Cambridge University Press.

Mikalson, Jon D. 1992. *Honor Thy Gods: Popular Religion in Greek Tragedy*. Chapel Hill: University of North Carolina Press.

Miles, Sarah. 2011. "Gods and Heroes in Comic Space: A Stretch of the Imagination?," *Dionysus ex Machina* 2: 109–33.

Miola, Robert. 1992. *Shakespeare and Classical Tragedy: The Influence of Seneca*. Oxford: Clarendon Press.

Miola, Robert. 1995. *Shakespeare and Classical Comedy: The Influence of Plautus and Terence*. Oxford: Clarendon Press.

Mueller, Martin. 1997. "Hamlet and the World of Ancient Tragedy," *Arion: A Journal of Humanities and the Classics* 5.1: 22–45.

Mullaney, Steven. 2015. *The Reformation of Emotions in the Age of Shakespeare*. Chicago: University of Chicago Press.

Müller, Heiner. 1980. "The Hamletmachine," *Performing Arts Journal* 4.3: 141–46.

Myhill, Nova, and Jennifer A. Low. 2011. "Introduction: Audience and Audiences," in *Imagining the Audience in Early Modern Drama, 1558–1642*, edited by Nova Myhill and Jennifer A. Low, 1–17. New York: Palgrave Macmillan.

Nashe, Thomas. 1964. *Selected Works*, edited by Stanley Wells. Abingdon: Routledge.

Newstok, Scott. 2009. *Quoting Death in Early Modern England: The Poetics of Epitaphs Beyond the Tomb*. New York: Palgrave Macmillan.

Nussbaum, Martha. 1988. "Applying the Lessons of Ancient Greece," interview with Bill Moyers, *A World of Ideas*, November 16, Moyers on Democracy.

Oakley-Brown, Liz. 2006. *Ovid and the Cultural Politics of Translation in Early Modern England*. Farnham: Ashgate.

Oakley-Brown, Liz. 2019. "The Golden Age Rescored? Ovid's *Metamorphoses* and Thomas Heywood's *The Ages*," in *Ovid and Adaptation in Early Modern English Theatre*, edited by Lisa S. Starks, 221–37. Edinburgh: Edinburgh University Press.

Olson, S. Douglas. 2013. *Ancient Comedy and Reception: Essays in Honor of Jeffrey Henderson*. Boston: De Gruyter.

Ong, Walter. 2012. *Rhetoric, Romance, and Technology: Studies in the Interaction of Expression and Culture*. Ithaca: Cornell University Press.

Orgel, Stephen. 1996. *Impersonations: The Performance of Gender in Shakespeare's England*. Cambridge: Cambridge University Press.

Page, Denys. 1972. *Aeschyli septem quae supersunt tragoedias*. Oxford: Oxford University Press.

Parker, Robert. 2007. *Polytheism and Society at Athens*. Oxford: Oxford University Press.

Peele, George. 1589. *A Farewell, Entitled to the famous and fortunate Generalls of our English forces: Sir John Norris & Syr Frauncis Drake Knights, and all theyr brave and resolute followers. Whereunto is annexed: A tale of Troy*. London: Printed by I.C. and to be sold by William Wright.

Pelliccia, Hayden. 2010. "Unlocking *Aeneid* 6.460: Plautus' *Amphitryon*, Euripides' *Protesilaus* and the Referents of Callimachus' *Coma*," *CJ* 106: 149–219.

Perry, Curtis. 2020. *Shakespeare and Senecan Tragedy*. Cambridge: Cambridge University Press.

Petrucci, Armando. 1998. *Writing the Dead: Death and Writing Strategies in the Western Tradition*. Palo Alto: Stanford University Press.

Peyré, Yves. 2013. "*Femmina masculo e masculo femmina*: Ovidian Mythical Structures, Leonardo Da Vinci, Michelangelo and *As You Like It*," in *Shakespeare's Erotic Mythology and Ovidian Renaissance Culture*, edited by Agnès Lafont, 173–82. Farnham: Ashgate.

Pickard-Cambridge, Arthur. 1998. *The Dramatic Festivals of Athens*, 2nd edition. Oxford: Oxford University Press.

Pippin, Anne N. 1960. "Euripides' *Helen*: A Comedy of Ideas," *CPh* 55: 151–63.

Pitcher, John. 2013. "Samuel Daniel's Masque 'The Vision of the Twelve Goddesses': Texts and Payments," *Medieval and Renaissance Drama in England* 26: 17–42.

Pollard, Tanya. 2017. *Greek Tragic Women on Shakespearean Stages*. Oxford: Oxford University Press.

Pollitt, Jerome. 2001. *The Art of Ancient Greece: Sources and Documents*. Cambridge: Cambridge University Press.

Powell, J.G.F. 2006. *M. Tulli Ciceronis: De re publica, De legibus, Cato maior de senectute, Laelius de Amicitia*. Oxford: Oxford University Press.

Prynne, William. 1633. *Histriomastix: The Player's Scourge, or Actor's Tragedy*. London.

Rabinowitz, Nancy S. 1981. "From Force to Persuasion: Aeschylus' *Oresteia* as Cosmogonic Myth," *Ramus* 10: 159–91.

Revermann, Martin. 2006. *Comic Business: Theatricality, Dramatic Technique, and Performance Contexts of Aristophanic Comedy*. Oxford: Oxford University Press.

Revermann, Martin. 2013. "Paraepic Comedy: Point(s) and Practices," in *Greek Comedy and the Discourse of Genres*, edited by Emmanuela Bakola, Lucia Prauscello, and Mario Telò, 101–28. New York: Cambridge University Press.

Rhodes, Neil. 2011. "Marlowe and the Greeks," *Renaissance Studies* 27: 199–218.

Rissman, Leah. 1983. *Love as War: Homeric Allusion in the Poetry of Sappho*. Königstein: Hain.

Roisman, Hanna (ed.). 2013. *The Encyclopedia of Greek Tragedy*. Hoboken: Wiley-Blackwell.

Rusten, Jeffrey. 2019. "The Phanagoria *Chous*: Comic Art in Miniature in a Luxury Tomb in the Cimmerian Bosporus," in *Ancient Theatre and Performance Culture Around the Black Sea*, edited by David Braund, Edith Hall, and Rosie Wyles, 59–81. Cambridge: Cambridge University Press.

Sartre, Jean-Paul. 2015. "The Work of Art," in *The Imaginary: A Phenomenological Psychology of the Imagination*, edited and translated by Jonathan Webber, 188–94. London: Routledge.

Schechner, Richard. 1985. *Between Theater and Anthropology*. Philadelphia: University of Pennsylvania Press.

Schleiner, Louise. 1990. "Latinized Greek Drama in Shakespeare's Writing of *Hamlet*," *Shakespeare Quarterly* 41.1: 29–48.

Schmidt, Gary A. 2013. *Renaissance Hybrids: Culture and Genre in Early Modern England*. London: Routledge.

Schmitz, Thomas. 2010. "A Sophist's Drama: Lucian and Classical Tragedy," in *Beyond the Fifth Century: Interactions with Greek Tragedy from the Fourth Century BCE to the Middle Ages*, edited by I. Gildenhard and M. Revermann, 289–314. Berlin: De Gruyter.

Schneider, Brian W. 2016. *The Framing Text in Early Modern English Drama: 'Whining' Prologues and Armed Epilogues*. London: Routledge.

Schneider, Rebecca. 2011. *Performing Remains: Art and War in Times of Theatrical Reenactment*. New York: Routledge.

Schopenhauer, Arthur. 2010. *Studies in Pessimism*. Whitefish: Kessinger Publishing.

Schwarz, Kathryn. 2000. *Tough Love: Amazon Encounters in the English Renaissance*. Durham: Duke University Press.

Scully, Stephen. 2015. *Hesiod's* Theogony: *From Near Eastern Creation Myths to* Paradise Lost. New York: Oxford University Press.

Seferis, George. 1995. "Helen," in *George Seferis: Collected Poems*, translated, edited, and introduced by Edmund Keeley and Philip Sherrard. Princeton: Princeton University Press.

Segal, Charles. 1962. "Gorgias and the Psychology of the Logos," *HSCP* 66: 99–155.

Segal, Charles. 1971. "The Two Worlds of Euripides' *Helen*," *TAPA* 102: 553–614.

Segal, Charles. 1997. *Dionysiac Poetics and Euripides'* Bacchae. Princeton: Princeton University Press.

Seznec, Jean. 1953. *The Survival of the Pagan Gods: The Mythological Tradition and Its Place in Renaissance Humanism and Art*, translated by Barbara F. Sessions. New York: Pantheon Books.

Shakespeare, William. 1623. *Mr. William Shakespeare's Comedies, Histories, & Tragedies*. London: Printed by Isaac Jaggard and Edward Blount.

Shakespeare, William. 1632. *Mr. William Shakespeare's Comedies, Histories, & Tragedies*. London: Printed by Thomas Cotes for Robert Allot.

Shakespeare, William. 2016. *The Complete Works: Modern Critical Edition*, edited by Gary Taylor, John Jowett, Terri Bourus, and Gabriel Egan. New York: Oxford University Press.

Shapiro, James. 2015. *The Year of Lear: Shakespeare in 1606*. London: Simon & Schuster.

Sher, Anthony. 2018. *Year of the Mad King: The Lear Diaries*. London: Nick Hern Books.

Shylock, Peter. 2008. *Monuments and Memory in Early Modern England*. London: Ashgate.

Sidney, Philip. 2012. "The Defense for Poesy," in *The Broadview Anthology of Sixteenth-Century Poetry and Prose*, edited by Marie Loughlin, Sandra Bell, and Patricia Brace, 713–39. Buffalo: Broadview Press.

Silk, Michael. 1985. "Heracles and Greek Tragedy," *G&R* 32: 1–22.

Silk, Michael. 2004. "Shakespeare and Greek Tragedy: Strange Relationship," in *Shakespeare and the Classics*, edited by Charles Martindale and Anthony B. Taylor, 241–57. Cambridge: Cambridge University Press.

Singer, Milton (ed.). 1958. *Traditional India: Structure and Change*. Philadelphia: American Folklore Society.

Slaney, Helen. 2016. *The Senecan Aesthetic: A Performance History*. New York: Oxford University Press.

Slater, Niall. 1985. *Plautus in Performance: The Theater of the Mind*. Princeton: Princeton University Press.

Slater, Niall. 1992. "The Idea of the Actor," in *Nothing to do with Dionysos? Athenian Drama in Its Social Context*, edited by John J. Winkler and Froma I. Zeitlin, 385–96. Princeton: Princeton University Press.

Slater, Niall. 2014. "Gods On High, Gods Down Low: Romanizing Epiphany," in *Plautine Trends: Studies in Plautine Comedy and Its Reception*, edited by Ioannis N. Perysinakis and Evangelos Karakasis, 105–26. Berlin: De Gruyter.

Slavitt, David R. 1994. *The Metamorphoses of Ovid*. Baltimore: Johns Hopkins University Press.

Smit, Betine van Zyl. 2016. *A Handbook to the Reception of Greek Drama*. Chichester: Wiley.

Smith, Angus. 2016. "Myth and Legend," in *The Ashgate Research Companion to Popular Culture in Early Modern England*, edited by Andrew Hadfield, Matthew Dimmock, and Abigail Shinn, 103–18. New York: Routledge.

Smith, Zadie. 2018. *Feel Free*. London: Penguin Books.

Sofer, Andrew. 2009. "How to Do Things with Demons: Conjuring Performatives in Doctor Faustus," *Theatre Journal* 61.1: 1–21.

Solmsen, Friedrich. 1934. "ΟΝΟΜΑ and ΠΡΑΓΜΑ in Euripides' *Helen*," *CR* 48: 119–21.

Solmsen, Friedrich, R. Merkelbach, and Martin West. 1990. *Hesiodi Theogonia, Opera et Dies, Scutum, Fragmenta Selecta*. Oxford: Clarendon Press.

Sourvinou-Inwood, Christiane. 1997. "Tragedy and Religion: Constructs and Readings," in *Greek Tragedy and the Historian*, edited by Christopher Pelling, 161–86. Oxford: Oxford University Press.

Sourvinou-Inwood, Christiane. 2003. *Tragedy and Athenian Religion*. Lanham: Lexington Books.

Spenser, Edmund. 1609. *The Faerie Queene*. London: Printed by H.L. for Matthew Lownes.

Spiller, Elizabeth. 2009. "Shakespeare and the Making of Early Modern Science: Resituating Prospero's Art," *South Central Review* 26.1/2: 24–41.

Stanislavski, Constantin. 1989. *An Actor Prepares*, translated by Elizabeth Reynolds Hapgood. New York: Routledge.

Stanislavski, Constantin. 1999. "Types of Actors," in *Stanislavski's Legacy: A Collection of Comments on a Variety of Aspects of an Actor's Art and Life*, translated by Elizabeth Reynolds Hapgood, 13–19. New York: Routledge.

Stanivukovic, Goran (ed.). 2001. *Ovid and the Renaissance Body*. Toronto: University of Toronto Press.

Stapleton, M.L. 2014. *Marlowe's Ovid: The Elegies in the Marlowe Canon*. Farnham: Ashgate.

Starks-Estes, Lisa S. 2014. *Transforming Ovid: Violence, Trauma, and Virtus in Shakespeare's Roman Poems and Plays*. Basingstoke: Palgrave-Macmillan.

Starnes, DeWitt T., and Ernest William Talbert. 1955. *Classical Myth and Legend and Renaissance Dictionaries*. Chapel Hill: University of North Carolina Press.

States, Bert O. 1985. *Great Reckonings in Little Rooms: On the Phenomenology of Theater*. Berkeley: University of California Press.

Steggle, Matthew. 2007. "Aristophanes in Early Modern England," in *Aristophanes in Performance 421 BC–AD 2007: Peace, Birds, and Frogs*, edited by Edith Hall and Amanda Wrigley, 52–65. London: Legenda.

Sullivan, Garrett A. 2005. *Memory and Forgetting in English Renaissance Drama: Shakespeare, Marlowe, Webster*. Cambridge: Cambridge University Press.

Sutherland, Gil. 2016. "'Great Interpreter of Shakespeare' Yukio Ninagawa Dies," *Stratford-Upon-Avon Herald*, May 13, https://www.stratford-herald.com/52307-great-interpreter-shakespeare-yukio-ninagawa-dies.html.

Taplin, Oliver. 2003. *Greek Tragedy in Action*. London: Routledge.

Taylor, Anthony B. (ed.). 2000. *Shakespeare's Ovid: 'The Metamorphoses' in the Plays and Poems*. Cambridge: Cambridge University Press.

Thomas, Keith. 1971. *Religion and the Decline of Magic: Studies in Popular Beliefs in Sixteenth- and Seventeenth-Century England*. London: Penguin.

Thomas, Keith. 2009. *The Ends of Life: Roads to Fulfilment in Early Modern England*. Oxford: Oxford University Press.

Torrance, Isabelle. 2013. *Metapoetry in Euripides*. New York: Oxford University Press.

Turner, Denys. 1998. *The Darkness of God: Negativity in Christian Mysticism*. Cambridge: Cambridge University Press.

Turner, Victor. 1957. *Schism and Continuity in an African Society. A Study of Ndembu Village Life*. Manchester: University of Manchester Press.
Turner, Victor. 1990. "1980 Address." Quoted in *Means of Performance: Intercultural Studies of Theatre and Ritual*, edited by Richard Schechner and Willa Appel, 1. Cambridge: Cambridge University Press.
Ussing, Johan Louis. 1875. *T. Maccii Plauti Comoediae*, 5 vols. Oxford: Oxford University Press.
van Dijkhuizen, Jan Frans. 2007. *Devil Theatre: Demonic Possession and Exorcism in English Renaissance Drama, 1558–1642*. Cambridge: D.S. Brewer.
Vaughan, Virginia Mason. 2019. *Shakespeare and the Gods*. London: Bloomsbury Arden Shakespeare.
Wagner, Matthew D. 2012. *Shakespeare, Theatre, and Time*. New York: Routledge.
Walton, J. Michael. 2006. "Benson, Mushri, and the First English 'Oresteia,'" *Arion: A Journal of Humanities and the Classics* 14.2: 49–68.
Walton, Kendall L. 1990. *Mimesis as Make-believe: On the Foundations of the Representational Arts*. Cambridge: Harvard University Press.
Wells, Stanley. 2007. *Is It True What They Say About Shakespeare?* Ebrington: Long Barn Books.
West, Martin. 1998–2000. *HomeriIlias*, 2 vols. Berlin: De Gruyter.
West, Martin. 2017. *Homerus: Odyssea*. Berlin: De Gruyter.
West, William N. 2010. "Replaying Early Modern Performances," in *New Directions in Renaissance Drama and Performance Studies*, edited by Sarah Werner, 30–50. Basingstoke: Palgrave Macmillan.
Wheeler, Stephen. 1999. *A Discourse of Wonders: Audience and Performance in Ovid's Metamorphoses*. Philadelphia: University of Pennsylvania Press.
Whitman, Jon. 2003. *Interpretation and Allegory: Antiquity to the Modern Period*. Boston: Brill Academic.
Whitmarsh, Tim. 2015. *Battling the Gods: Atheism in the Ancient World*. New York: Knopf Doubleday.
Whitney, Geoffrey. 1586. *Choice of Emblems*. Leiden: Francis Ralphelengius.
Whittington, Leah. 2016. *Renaissance Suppliants: Poetry, Antiquity, Reconciliation*. Oxford: Oxford University Press.
Wiles, David. 2014. *Theatre and Time*. New York: Palgrave.
Williams, Raymond. 1975. *The Country and the City*. Oxford: Oxford University Press.
Wilson, Nigel G. 2007. *Aristophanis Fabulae*, 2 vols. Oxford: Oxford University Press.
Wilson, Robert. 1594. *The Cobbler's Prophesy*. London: John Danter.
Wind, Edgar. 1967. *Pagan Mysteries in the Renaissance*. New York: Penguin.
Winkler, John. 1990. "Double Consciousness in Sappho's Lyrics," in *The Constraints of Desire: The Anthropology of Sex and Gender in Ancient Greece*, 162–87. New York: Routledge.
Winnington-Ingram, Reginald P. 1948. "Clytemnestra and the Vote of Athena," *Journal of Hellenic Studies* 68: 130–47.

Worman, Nancy. 1997. "The Body as Argument: Helen in Four Greek Texts," *CA* 16: 151–203.
Worman, Nancy. 2001. "This Voice Which is Not One: Helen's Verbal Guises in Homeric Epic," in *Making Silence Speak: Women's Voices in Greek Literature and Society*, edited by A. Lardinois and L. McClure, 19–37. Princeton: Princeton University Press.
Worthen, William B. 2014. *Shakespeare Performance Studies*. Cambridge: Cambridge University Press.
Wright, Matthew. 2005. *Euripides' Escape-Tragedies: A Study of Helen, Andromeda and Iphigenia Among the Taurians*. New York: Oxford University Press.
Yates, Frances. 1964. *Giordano Bruno and the Hermetic Tradition*. Chicago: University of Chicago Press.
Yates, Frances. 1966. *The Art of Memory*. London: Routledge.
Zeitlin, Froma I. 1981. "Travesties of Gender and Genre in Aristophanes' *Thesmophoriazousae*," *Critical Inquiry* 8: 301–27.
Zeitlin, Froma I. 1992. "Playing the Other: Theater, Theatricality, and the Feminine in Greek Drama," in *Nothing to Do with Dionysos? Athenian Drama in Its Social Context*, edited by John Winkler and Froma I. Zeitlin, 63–96. Princeton: Princeton University Press.
Zimmerman, Mary. 2002. *Metamorphoses*. Evanston: Northwestern University Press.

Index

Achilles 3, 22–23, 62
actor 1–4, 7–9, 12–13, 20–23, 25–28,
    35–40, 42, 47–48, 57–64, 67, 69–76,
    80–89, 94–95, 96–97, 99–100,
    102–3, 108–9, 112–15, 121, 124–26,
    129–30, 140, 142–45, 147, 152 n.25,
    158 n.4, 163–64 n.1, 169 n.15,
    171–72 n.19
Aelian
    Historical Miscellany 47, 55
Aeschylus 5, 16, 19, 34, 87, 99, 114, 136–38,
    169 n.15, 171 n.7, 173 n.31
    Agamemnon 37, 95–100, 102, 122
    Eumenides 43–44, 96, 98, 102–3
    Libation Bearers 95–96, 100–2
Agamemnon 95, 98–101, 122, 169 n.13
Alcaeus 87
    Ganymede 87
Alcmene 77–78, 81
Alexander of Troy, *see* Paris
Ameipsias
    Kottabos-Players 123
Aphrodite 21–22, 24, 32, 38, 50–51, 55, 94,
    131, 160 n.21
Apollo 3, 24, 32, 37, 59, 83, 93, 96–102, 107,
    118, 131, 155 n.8
apotheosis 20, 69–70, 72, 77, 117, 123, 136,
    138
Aristophanes 10–11, 40, 87, 99, 150 n.16,
    167 n.38
    Birds 29–30
    Frogs 10–11, 81–82, 136–38, 171 n.7
    Peace 40
Aristotle
    Poetics 19, 119–20
Artemis 21, 32, 44, 131, 152 n.32, 165 n.13,
    166 n.24
Athena 3, 22–23, 37, 43–44, 50, 77, 96–97,
    99, 102–3, 132–34, 165 n.13
Athenaeus 123
audience 1–4, 8–10, 12–13, 20, 23, 25–26,
    28, 34–35, 38–39, 48–49, 52–54,
    57–59, 60–62, 71–72, 81–86, 102–3,
    100–14, 129, 132, 136, 142–44, 147,
    155 n.12, 158 n.4

Bacon, Francis 70, 76, 111, 155 n.12,
    162 n.48
Barkan, Leonard 4, 74
Barthes, Roland 113, 117, 170 n.34
Baucis and Philemon 140–47
Beaumont, Francis
    *The Masque of the Inner Temple and
    Gray's Inn* 69, 74–79, 133–34
Butler, Martin 70, 133

Carlson, Marvin 60, 64, 126, 140
celebrity 67, 70, 125–30, 134–36, 172 n.19
Ceres 25–26, 28, 94, 152 n.32, 165 n.13
Cicero 125
    De Amicitia 110–11, 136
    De Inventione 47
    De Oratore 125
class status 16, 70, 72–74, 79–80, 89–90,
    114, 120, 128, 130, 133–34
costume 21–22, 60–61, 67, 70, 79–80, 88,
    99, 167 n.30
Cratinus 87, 160 n.21, 167 n.38
Cupid 32–34, 75–76, 135, 142

Daniel, Samuel
    The Vision of the Twelve Goddesses 69,
    71–74
deus ex machina 19–20, 31, 39–40, 43–45,
    48–49, 154 n.1
Diana, *see* Artemis
didaskalos 23–24, 93, 96, 136–37
Dionysus 10, 21–22, 38, 57, 81, 93, 123,
    137–38, 166 n.30
disguise 3, 40, 53, 62, 81–82, 87, 140–46

Easterling, Pat 10, 23, 48, 93
epiphany 2, 9, 48–49, 51, 55–57, 102–3,
    117

Erasmus 65
Eupolis 122
Euripides 5, 10, 19, 21, 64–65, 78, 93, 99,
    117–18, 136–38, 154 n.4, 160 n.19,
    161 n.41, 166 n.27, 167 n.40,
    171 n.7, 173 n.31
  Bacchae 10, 21–22, 57, 93, 96
  Bellerophon 39–40
  Electra 143
  Helen 20, 47–48, 52–57, 63–64
  Heracles 37–38
  Hippolytus 21–22, 44
  Ion 43–44
  Medea 39
  Orestes 87, 168 n.5

fame, *see* celebrity

Ganymede 38, 40, 42
ghosts 1, 16, 55–56, 60, 64, 89–90, 102, 104,
    106–9, 126, 170 n.36
Gorgias
  Encomium of Helen 50, 159 n.13,
    160 n.28
Gosson, Stephen 35, 42, 62

Halliwell, Stephen 35, 119, 159 n.7
Helen (of Troy) 47–66, 129
Hera 25–26, 28, 37, 54, 56, 63–64, 71,
    76–77, 90, 128, 131, 165 n.13
Heracles 30–31, 37–38, 48, 77–78, 81, 86,
    126–27, 152 n.32, 170 n.27
Hercules, *see* Heracles
Hermes 24, 54, 65–66, 69, 75–76, 78–85,
    87, 94, 108, 128, 131, 140–44,
    167 n.36
Herodotus 63, 160 n.19
Hesiod 35–36, 38
  Theogony 29, 82, 96
  Works and Days 131
heterochrony 35, 102–3, 106
Heywood, Thomas 69, 172 n.22
  The Apology for Actors 34
  The Golden Age 131–32
Homer 3, 35–36, 38, 48, 50, 52, 63, 131–32,
    159 n.11
  Iliad 3, 49, 62–63, 83, 118
  Odyssey 3, 49–50, 54, 94
Horace 43

hospitality (*or xenia*) 140–46, 174 n.7
Hymen 40–43

immortality 11, 43–45, 62, 68, 77–78,
    117–18, 121–22, 124–38, 142, 144,
    166 n.24, 171–172 n.19, 173 n.29

Jonson, Ben 5–6, 43, 125, 136
  The Golden Age Restored 132–34
Juno, *see* Hera
Jupiter (or Jove), *see* Zeus

Lada-Richards, Ismene 2, 155 n.5
Lefkowitz, Mary 10, 37, 153 n.48
Lucian
  Dialogues of the Dead 47, 64–66
  The Fisherman 81
Lucretius 67–68, 164 n.3
Lyly, John 5, 59, 155 n.8, 161 n.41, 166 n.24

Marlowe, Christopher 5, 64–65, 69,
    154 n.54, 158 n.3
  Dido, Queen of Carthage 38–39, 94
  Doctor Faustus 35, 47–49, 58–65, 69,
    124, 129, 158 n.3, 161 n.33,
    161 n.37, 162 n.49, 163 n.65
mask 2, 10, 35, 54, 58–59, 66, 69, 87–89,
    99–100, 103, 108, 114, 124–26, 135,
    145, 161 n.41
masques 25–28, 34, 43, 69–77, 86, 89, 111,
    132–34, 165 n.10, 166 n.26
mechane 19, 39–40
Medea 39–40
Menelaus 49–51, 55–58, 62, 63
Mercury, *see* Hermes
metamorphosis 4, 53–54, 60, 70, 72–74,
    78–83, 87–89, 109–10, 126, 139–45
Milphio 82
Milton, John 157 n.36
mimesis 9, 38–39, 48–50, 52–54, 57, 62, 65,
    97–98, 113, 143
Minerva, *see* Athena
mise-en-abyme 23, 25–27, 31

Odysseus 3–4, 22–23, 31, 49
Orestes 95–103, 107, 111, 143
Ovid 6–7, 15, 75, 146
  Metamorphoses 59, 67–68, 74, 76–78,
    139–45

Paris 32, 52, 54, 60, 62–64
Peele, George
    The Arraignment of Paris 32
    "The Tale of Troy" 64
Philemon, *see* Baucis and Philemon
Plato 12, 36, 58
    Cratylus 67
Plautus
    Amphitruo 69–70, 78–89
    Curculio 123–24
    Poenulus 82
playgoer 2, 8, 12, 23, 26, 34–35, 38–39, 49, 52, 57, 60–61, 64, 66, 136, 145, 147
Plutarch 33–34
prologue 20–23, 52–54, 78–80, 82–83, 85–86, 97–99, 102–3
prophecy 1, 22, 24, 31, 90–91, 93–94, 96, 98, 101–2, 124
Proteus 33–34, 69
Pylades 95–97, 101, 107, 110–11, 113

royalty 24–26, 69, 71–75, 79, 90, 119–20, 166 n.24, 171 n.7

Sannyrion
    Danaë 87
Sappho
    fr. 16 50
    fr. 147 43
Schechner, Richard 7
Seneca 6
Shakespeare, William 5–6, 8, 12, 25, 28, 113–14, 125, 134–36
    A Midsummer Night's Dream 68
    Antony and Cleopatra 16, 126–29
    As You Like It 25, 40–43, 145–46
    Cymbeline 1–2, 40, 44, 70, 89–91
    First Folio 5
    Hamlet 7, 16, 22, 73–74, 94–95, 99, 104–15, 121–22, 124, 140
    King Lear 16, 118–21

Much Ado About Nothing 145
Pericles 44–45
Second Folio 136
The Tempest 25–28, 94–95, 142
Timon of Athens 32–34
The Winter's Tale 24, 59–60, 76, 102
Silk, Michael 6, 48
Slater, Niall 84, 152 n.25, 167 n.36
Sophocles 5–6, 19, 30
    Ajax 20, 22–23
    Antigone 16, 30, 36, 122
    Oedipus at Colonus 20
    Oedipus the King 20, 93
    Philoctetes 31
Sourvinou-Inwood, Christiane 10
Spectator, *see* audience, playgoer
Spenser, Edmund 68–69, 133–34
Stanislavski, Constantin 83, 163 n.1
States, Bert O. 2, 58, 60, 126, 147

Taplin, Oliver 7
Terence
    Phormio 82
Turner, Victor 19, 152 n.28

Venus, *see* Aphrodite

Wilson, Robert
    The Cobbler's Prophesy 24, 94

Xenophanes 35–36, 38

Yates, Frances 12, 126

Zeitlin, Froma I. 49, 52, 159 n.13, 161 n.31, 172 n.20
Zeus 1–2, 13, 16, 26, 30–31, 37–38, 40, 42, 53, 69–70, 74–78, 80–91, 94, 96–99, 102–3, 108, 128, 131, 140–46, 149 n.4, 160 n.21, 167 n.26 169 n.16

www.ingramcontent.com/pod-product-compliance
Lightning Source LLC
Chambersburg PA
CBHW061830300426
44115CB00013B/2325